Marídée

the Memoirs of
María Haydée Corbalán

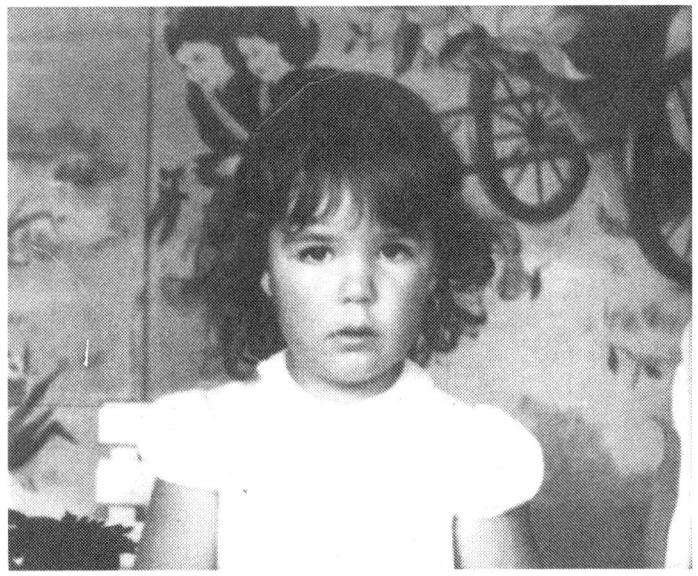

Story by
María Corbalán

With Samantha Martin and Michael Peschka

Plain View Press
P. O. 42255
Austin, TX 78704

plainviewpress.net
sb@plainviewpress.net
1-512-441-2452

Copyright 2007, María Corbalán. All rights reserved.
ISBN: 978-1-891386-97-8
Library of Congress Number: 2007940309

Cover and book design by Melissa Gables. Back cover photo by Mary K. Bruton.

Cover photo, María age 3, Argentina.

To life, that has given me so much!

Maridée

Argentina: Alejandra, Abuela Haydée, Margarita, Monoyo, my mother, and my father Alejandro

My 'gaucho' father on his horse

Introduction

I started this book fifteen years ago. At the time, I was married to a great husband, I was starting my own business, and I was heading into a new phase of my life after having lived, literally, on the edge. I was turning my life around and leaving a huge chunk of my past behind me.

Originally, I never intended this book to be for anyone else's eyes but my own. What I *really* wanted to do was to document for myself all the memories I had of my crazy life up to that point. I wanted so much to remember my friends, both those still living and those who passed from this world way too soon. I miss them like crazy, even today, and recounting all of these stories has been like therapy. I find myself asking out loud: Did I really do that? Did I really say that? Yep, that was me! That was María.

And now, as the work on this book is coming to a close, I'm an even more distant version of the person that you will soon meet.

As I thought about writing this introduction, I worried about how you, whoever you are, would receive the actions described in these pages. Would you understand me? Would you see me clearly? And most importantly... would you know that I have changed?

It seems to me that life is about making a whole lot of choices. And no matter what, you've got to live with the person you create. It's like when you go to a restaurant. Food is one thing that we *all* have in common, right? We all eat. We don't always make the right choices about food. We decide to eat what makes us feel good at the time. Personally, I know that when I go to a restaurant when I'm very hungry and I eat a lot, I feel very guilty.

And guilty is what I feel about a lot of things that I have done in my life. But even today, there are times when I look at the menu and still decide, "Oh well — a little of that is not going to kill me. I'm going to go ahead and eat it. I know it's bad for me, but who cares?"

So perhaps food is not the best analogy for my relationship with my past, because I made a lot of choices that were very bad for me, and I definitely should have cared. I lived a life full of drugs and booze — a *lot* of drugs and booze. It may be very hard for you to read about what I did and not judge me too harshly. But believe me, it's hard to pull my pants down in front of everybody and bare myself! That's definitely what writing this book feels like.

Essentially, this book is about all the things that I have done: the things that I'm not proud of, as well as the way I've grown and changed. Today, at 47, I consider myself to be very happy, living a nice, quiet existence. I'm proud of all of myself, and I like who I am. More than anything, I love being able to put a smile on somebody's face. I can truly say that from my youth until today, I've put a lot of miles in between. The road was long, and believe me, the lessons I learned weren't soft! I learned the hardest way, perhaps by choice. I did some things that are unbelievable to me when I look back on them today, while other things can still give me a good belly laugh.

It really amazes me how I could have been such an unconscious, selfish little bitch—not realizing the danger I was putting myself through, and the consequences and the pain I caused others. But life is a lot like making a cake: it's only as good as its ingredients. You start off with too much freedom and no guidance, add a a bunch of drugs and liters of alcohol, abundant cupfuls of the wrong friends, and put a crazy little girl in the middle. Boy, that's a great recipe for disaster.

And that's exactly what I did.

Nobody likes mistakes, but I don't know anybody who hasn't made them! I can honestly say that it feels like it took me forever to learn my lessons. But the first step in turning my life around was recognizing how I was hurting others and myself. The next step was apologizing to anybody and everybody that I hurt along the way. That was a very high mountain to climb. I have been very stubborn—another mistake. I'm trying to show with actions—not just with empty words—my desire to be humble, honest, generous, and grateful.

The most important life lesson I ever learned is that wisdom is the result of making wise decisions. If I had paid attention to good advice along my life's journey, I know my mistakes would have hurt a lot fewer people. I'm not trying to justify my acts because of my youth, but the bad choices I made were attempts to deflect real pain and fear. Putting off responsibility until tomorrow was so much easier than grabbing the bull by the horns and stopping the madness. But alcohol and drugs were always so near to me. They were here today. I didn't realize how dearly I would pay for "today" when "tomorrow" finally came.

Procrastination and change are not very good buddies.

Was my character good when nobody was watching? Absolutely not! My conscience and I needed to do a lot of work. Over and over, I resolved to count my blessings and shut the door on all the negativity. I resolved to become appreciative and thankful. I really planned to do that "someday" — just not *that* day. *That* day, I always had something else to do. (And "Today" and "Procrastination" were out partying last night!)

I really needed to repent from the bottom of my heart. I knew I was doing wrong and I needed to take account in order to make the decision to change. By changing, I began to open myself to others, to be able to accept hardship and criticism, to grow.

With every wrong decision I made, the results were obviously destructive and expensive. I didn't know how hard it was going to be to peel off the guilt I caused myself. But when the hard work finally began, I can tell you the rewards are immense. Lately, blue days are the ones that I welcome the most, because after they pass, my hope is that the lessons I've learned will stay.

So if you are a perfect person, this is not a book for you. This book is about my imperfect, beautiful life. I hope you enjoy the journey!

~ María

Bell bottom days - traveling at 17

... 1 ...

CUERNAVACA, MEXICO

Every couple of hours the Mexican jail guard strolls over to my cell and stares at me with a mixture of hatred and lust in his eyes. He is fat and sweaty, and his tan uniform is stained a dark brown underneath his arms. Perspiration beads up around his neck and drips down the front of his partially unbuttoned shirt, plastering his matted chest hair to his damp skin. Even though I am weak and exhausted, when he comes near me my body is still able to find the strength to recoil from the stink of him.

It seems like I got here a million years ago, but it's only been two days — two long days filled with brutal interrogations and beatings, and endless hours chained to the wall of this cell. I'm so drenched from the heat of this place that I'm sure I must look like someone threw me into a swimming pool.

My stomach lurches as the fat guard's eyes draw down to my chest. I am wearing shorts and a skimpy tank top with no bra. Despite the pain in my wrists from my shackles and my aching bruised face and body, the only thing I can think about right now is how much I wish I wasn't wearing something that leaves absolutely nothing to his imagination.

I feel him as he studies my breasts, my stomach, my thighs. His eyes burn into my skin, and he runs his tongue suggestively around his lips, flicking it at me. I am so disgusted that I can't help myself.

"Does this make you feel like a man – chaining a girl up like a piñata?" I spit out the words before I fully consider the consequences.

His eyes glaze over and his face turns to stone, and I am sure he's going to hit me again. Hard. But instead he starts to un-cuff me, and as my arms fall limply to my sides, I realize that he is freeing me so he can do something even worse.

"Oh my God, this monster is going to rape me." My body starts to tremble uncontrollably.

My knees buckle, but the guard pins my arms so tightly that they start to tingle from the lack of circulation to my hands. I struggle to free myself from his grasp, but the days of hunger and abuse have sapped my strength. He drags me down the rank corridor to a small room that is apparently the direct source of the stench that fills this whole section of the building.

He hoists me over the lip of a large wooden barrel full of both liquid and solid human waste. This barrel is the repository of the buckets of urine and feces removed from each cell.

He forces my head into it several times, all the way to my shoulders. I gasp for air after each dunking, spitting out small mouthfuls of the sickening contents of the barrel, which I am unable to avoid taking in. My legs flail involuntarily, but I'm not strong enough to fight him off. His grip is vice-like on my arms, and as the guard forces my head beneath the surface of the putrid liquid one last time, I lose consciousness....

•••

A Mexican prison is Hell. Men and women are held in the same area, not separated like in American prisons. And anything you've ever heard of or read or seen about torture — let me tell you, it's absolutely true! I know. I lived through it.

The beatings are unexpected and brutal. My biggest fear was the anticipation of what was in store for me when it was finally my turn.

My captors, the Mexican *Federales*, held the power to decide my fate. They were not governed by rules of humanity; they were free to do whatever they wanted to do to any of us. They were sadistic motherfuckers, monsters who got their money through corruption and cruelty. What's even worse is that they actually relished their task.

Ultimately, they were extortionists and common criminals. The 'blood money' that they got from prisoners as a requirement for our freedom became the very bread that they in turn would feed to their families. But let me tell you, if I were a member of one of their families, I wouldn't want even an ounce of that bread—not even a single *tortilla*.

The year was 1976, I happened to be sitting in a van outside a little Mexican church. Someone, not me, nor any of my friends, had placed a bomb in the church. We had pot in the van.

According to Mexican police, guilty or not, tourist or resident—somebody's got to get fingered. And, oh, how convenient my friends and I were to them.

... 2 ...

In my life, there's always somebody leaving.

My name is María Haydée Corbalán, but to my family I was always Maridée, pronounced 'Mah-ri-deh' in Spanish — a derivation of the combination of my first two names. In 1962, I was not quite two years old. My family consisted of my father, Alejandro, my mother, Margot, my older siblings Alejandra, Margarita, Monoyo, and myself. We lived in Argentina in a small town called Lincoln, on the outskirts of Buenos Aires. We had quite a good, upper-class life. My father was a *gaucho* with a generous chunk of land. My mother was a housewife.

That good life came to an end one particular evening as we drove to a neighbor's house for dinner. It was a day that changed my life forever.

...

I have a framed black and white photograph of a little girl that is set prominently on the fireplace mantel in my living room. It is a picture of me taken on the day my father died.

When I think of that day, I look at that little girl's eyes and I see the sadness, the confusion, and the loss that she had no way of understanding. And I just want to hug her. I want to sweep her up and away and take care of her so that she never has to know the pain that awaits her. Honestly, I still don't understand to this day why I had to lose my father before I ever got to know him — why, forever after, I would always seem to be searching for him.

I also have an old weathered sepia-toned photograph of my father sitting atop a huge horse. I wish I could remember the horse's name. In the photo my father is dressed in the typical gaucho outfit: white shirt, baggy pants, leather boots, and the classic gaucho hat. And—his wonderful silk scarf with polka dots, which is the only thing of his that I have in my possession, my only proof that he existed.

Earlier that day, my family drove to a neighbor's house for dinner. Alejandra, my oldest sister, was eleven years old. She and nine-year-old Margarita and six-year-old Monoyo begged our parents to let us ride in the back of the truck. We loved to feel the wind on our faces, and to have the opportunity to cut up a bit, to laugh and tease each other slightly out of view of the adults.

Margarita usually looked out for me more than my other two siblings did, and I remember leaning against her while she hung onto the side of the truck with one hand and cradled me with the other. I remember giggling to the point of toddler hysteria each time the truck would hit a bump or a dip in the road, and my head would knock against my sister's. My siblings would stand me up and let go of me so they could watch as I tried to steady myself while the truck bobbed along the dirt road.

Suddenly, the truck began to swerve, finally lurching a few times before stopping abruptly, tossing us all around. I looked at my father in confusion, not sure what was happening. He was slumped over the steering wheel and appeared to be sleeping. His hat was on the floorboard and his head rested on the door of the truck. Not understanding what was happening or why, I looked to my siblings, searching for some sort of explanation. It was clear that they had no answers. My mother grabbed my father's wrist and held her hand to his throat.

Margot and Alejandro Corbalán on their wedding day, 1943

··· 3 ···

The entire earth stopped for a few precious moments as my mother reached for my father, tilted his head back, and slowly smoothed his hair from his forehead.

We all sat frozen, watching her fingertips trace his pale lifeless face. Finally, she slid out of the truck and told us, without a trace of emotion, to get out and walk back home. There was nothing exceptional about her words, but her expression told us something was very wrong.

I was only two, but I remember the walk home with utter clarity. None of my siblings spoke as we marched home together, staring down at the road, wondering what had just happened. And what was to become of us. Everything just felt odd. Different.

And I remember turning the corner to our street and seeing that the stained glass windows of our house were a dark orange, which meant it was past dinner and just about time for bed. I asked Alejandra if this meant that I had to go to bed without eating. She shook her head and scooped me up in her arms. I could feel her chest thumping against mine and, as I held tightly to her, I remember being mesmerized by the song playing in her heart.

Many hours later, I woke up to the muffled sound of sobs. Margarita was crying. She sounded like if she cried hard enough, she would be able to produce enough tears to wash all this away.

"Your father is in a beautiful place now. And he'll watch over you forever," my mother's voice sounded soft and very far away. I rolled over in my crib and stared out the window, looking for my father. If Papá was watching – my toddler mind was so literal —why didn't he come in?

In the morning, I was handed a bucket of toys and asked to play quietly. It was raining, and I watched the tiny bubbles forming on the sidewalk outside my window. I wondered if my father was outside in the rain.

I learned later that it was my father's second heart attack. And he was only thirty-eight years old.

My mother had said he was in a better place. I remember thinking that since Tatina, my nursemaid (who was my love, my angel, my savior, and mine, all mine) said the same thing, it must be true. Two adults in agreement equal the seal of authenticity to a child.

Tatina was the first of a long series of maids who raised me. We would begin our day on the porch, waving goodbye to my family each morning as they scurried off to their other worlds. For the next several months an indescribable terror would suddenly overwhelm me when I watched everyone go. After all, my father left once, and he never returned. Tatina was the only one who gave me true solace; she was the one who took care of me day after day, filling me up with kisses. I spent more time with her than with my own family, and I still miss her today.

I wish I still had a Tatina in my life to comfort me.

I soon gave myself a surrogate father figure in Andrés Badano, the neighbor next door who was the kindest man that ever lived. I suppose his incredible likeness to Santa Claus had a lot to do with the excitement I felt in being able to spend time with him. Even in his thirties, he had beautiful white hair, and to me he was an ooooooold man! He had a flabby belly that I loved to bounce on when he tickled me, and I remember that his hands weren't soft, but I didn't care. He had the strongest arms, but nobody ever held me with that much tenderness, and in my secret little world he became my dad.

Badano was my best friend, and he would always pass fresh eggs to me through the bushes bright and early when the chickens were at their egg-laying peak. After a while he started to take me to work with him out in his cab for the entire day. There we were: the diaper-clad kid and Santa, the cab driver, circling the tiny town for hours and munching on fresh roasted peanuts out of a newspaper cone. It was an adventure every day. Badano and Tatina were ingrained in my heart already, and forever will be. They are my best childhood memories. I was devastated when, the following year, we moved away from the ranch and away from Badano.

An aside. When I took a trip to Argentina at the age of forty-six, I went back to that little town desperately hoping to find Badano there. When Toto, his wife, opened the door and I told her who I was, she started to cry—I nearly gave her a heart attack! We hugged each other for the longest time. But I was devastated to learn that he had died at age eighty-four, just the year before. Toto and I got some very beautiful fresh flowers from their own yard and went to visit him at the cemetery. I cried so hard that I gave myself hiccups. But I know that he knows that I came back.

A year after my father died, my mother was diagnosed with breast cancer. This was a long time ago and her breast removal surgery was radical, nothing like the procedures available now. My mother was one of the lucky ones since the cancer was localized, but her scars were gruesome.

While she recovered, we children stayed on a magnificent ranch with some of my father's distant relatives. I can recall grand furnishings and runway-length dining tables that were elegantly dressed for each meal. There were maids in starched uniforms. The actual daily activities of the place escape me now. I don't recall any major traumas living there, so I'm sure we did normal kid stuff while wondering where our mother was.

My fourth birthday came and went before she returned again. She eventually did recover well and was able to defeat the disease completely. My mother is a remarkably strong woman. She had begun a kind of transformation that started after we lost our *papá*, and by this time she had grown almost stoic. We were too young to understand that she must have been through hell. Somehow we seemed to know that she was pained in a way we couldn't fully comprehend, and from more than the scars of her surgery.

Understandably, my mother needed some support, both with her health and because she had been widowed with four small children. In March of 1964, we all went to live with her mother, Abuela Haydée, in Buenos Aires. Abuela Haydée welcomed our little tribe into her tiny efficiency apartment.

The six of us settled in as best we could. Of course we had a maid—so that made seven. Let me save you the trouble of asking yourself if we really needed a maid for such a cramped situation—absolutely! Besides, Celina had been with the family for years. She was a little bonier than Tatina, so every time she gave me a kiss her cheek made an indentation in my face.

Until my mother was able to adjust to the new life that had been thrown at her, we would remain with Abuela Haydée. She bought a bigger place for us when I was six. At that time I was thrust into the Basque educational system: berets, white knee socks, plaid mini-skirt, blue necktie and white gloves. My school looked like a museum with mountains of granite and marble, perfectly chiseled and smoothed to form the floors and walls.

My mother sometimes held three jobs to keep us in that lifestyle. Her main occupation was as the principal of my school. As you can imagine, this had its ups and downs.

In the summer of 1969, upon returning home from a long visit to my aunt's house, I discovered my mother had gotten cozy with some guy named Juan De Angeli. Even though my siblings and I barely knew him, we all prayed that he would marry Mamá and rescue us.

And he did marry her, when I was nine years old. After the wedding, we moved into the biggest house I had ever seen. The corridors were thirty meters long...and *not* for children to run in. I must have missed the memo because the rules caught me completely by surprise. Everything was so different. The napkins didn't have holes, and instead of plates that were divided into sections, we ate off of china and silver.

That stuff I got used to easily enough...but the guy! His expression was as cold and stony as the walls of my school, and no kid would even think of approaching him. I felt as if I had lost my home and was now sentenced to be a perpetual visitor in some stranger's house.

• • •

My 'life lessons' began on Father's Day when I was ten years old.

The other girls in my class were eagerly designing hand-made cards to take home to their precious fathers, and they spoke of these men with pride and love. They were eager to shower their fathers with affection on this special day. No one understood that I felt the same way about my father, but no card I made would ever reach him. Didn't they realize how fortunate they were? I considered making a card for Juan, but the mental image of his furrowed brow told me not to even try.

It was common knowledge that I didn't have a father.

Since he was never spoken of in my house, I had little to hang on to, and I was no longer certain which of my fading memories of him were real anyway.

All of my teachers were aware of my situation. I was content, mostly, to sit and observe the events of this day like some intrusive spectator, uninvited and unnoticed. I preferred to be on the sidelines. One girl—Eugenia—talked to her doll as if it were her father. "Do you like the card I have made for you, *papá*? Yes, I made it for my beautiful *papá* to remember me the whole day and always."

Always? I had no always, no tomorrow, no here and now, and as the days progressed infinitely on, I had less and less of the past.

Tears stung my face as though her words had brought with them a physical blow.

My teacher, seeing my reaction to this innocent reverie and not knowing how to console me, said, "Come now, Maridée. I cannot get this bench to the other classroom by myself. Would you come for a moment and help me? You are always so helpful. And so pretty...."

I wanted to run, to scream, to wail from the agony tearing me up inside. But I stood, swallowed my tears, and mechanically carried the bench without a word. I didn't understand her innocent motivation to rescue me. All I could think was, "How could she do that to me? I know I don't belong here, but surely I must have more significance than just someone to carry a bench." After all, she used to call me "naríz de enchufe," which means "little nose plug," because my nose was so small and cute. I know it probably doesn't sound sweet to you, but I liked it.

It was not as if all the adults in my life shuffled me around. It was all much more subtle. As far as anyone thought, or noticed, Maridée was doing "just fine." How could they have known of all the hours I had stood in front of my mother's looking glass and practiced saying my *"papás"*? I tried it this way and that way, with different inflections and different tones of voice, but always realizing the futility of it all.

I would let the last *"papá"* trail off into a sob.

But no one saw this, because my thick skin was starting to form. I was becoming the ultimate contradiction: a young girl who yearned for emotion and affection, who would then recoil into a shell like a sand crab at the first sign of tenderness. Children are wise.

Soon after our arrival in our stepfather's mausoleum, my three siblings got married and took off, and I was left by myself.

I can remember being terrified to sleep alone; I had always slept with them close by. I was very unsure of where I stood with my mother and stepfather. It seemed clear that an intruder had taken my mother away from me, and there were very few crumbs of concern left over from that relationship to be tossed my way.

At the same time, something amazing was beginning to happen to me. I began to get appreciative looks from other people, especially boys, and my "teeny-bopper" social situations ventured towards dating. I wasn't completely sure what was so admirable about my perky tits and tiny little butt, but suddenly I had more admirers than I could handle — although I sure did try!

And with my newfound attention came temptations that all teens confront eventually: drugs, booze, and sex.

··· 4 ···
BUENOS AIRES

For most of my life up to this point I had pretty much raised myself. Life at home was lonely; the house was always empty. Sure, there were maids around, but their responsibilities were limited to making sure I didn't hurt myself. They weren't there to tell me what to do, nor to keep me company. It shouldn't come as a surprise that by the time I became a teenager, I was beginning to have a problem with authority figures.

It was around this time that the military factions in Argentina had taken over the government, and over the next few months began a process of "social reordering" in which some thirty thousand people turned up missing and presumed dead.

Anyway, one of these thirty thousand missing people was Alejandra's sister-in-law. Fearing they were to be targeted next, Alejandra and her husband grabbed their three children and fled to Mexico to live in exile. I wanted to be an understanding sister, and I knew that this was a safer decision for them, but in a way I was a little resentful. I couldn't help but feel abandoned yet again.

Shortly after Alejandra's departure, and just as my hormones were revving into high gear, my mother entered into what was for her a very dark world: menopause. My budding sexuality, combined with my experimentation with drugs, set off a firestorm between us. My mother and I drifted even further apart.

At fourteen, I lost my virginity to my first boyfriend, Gerardo. He was nineteen. By the time I was fifteen, I was refusing to settle for anything less that what I wanted in life. This included what I wanted from my mother. She had her own ideas for me as well. She dictated orders like I was one of her pupils – and boy, did she like to yell! Affection was the last thing that came from her.

I was gun powder waiting for a match. She was a supernova heading in my direction.

I was beginning to think for myself, so with very little guidance in my life, I concluded that I was the master of my own destiny, and I alone could choose the paths my life should take. At the time, I felt that the most important need I should fulfill was to take care of the emptiness I felt inside. Therefore, goal number one was: not to be lonely.

The situation at home was growing worse by the minute. Throughout my childhood my mother was rarely around, but *now* she suddenly wanted to know where I was going and whom I was with at all times. 'Where was all this motherly concern when I was a child?' I wondered bitterly. When she began trying to limit my preferred activities, I would just leave home for a couple of days, a week, two weeks, whatever.

But I soon spun out of control. I was filling all the gaps that remained in my life with booze and drugs. After disappearing for three days I would come home drunk and stoned, which of course caused huge fights between my mother and me, and this in turn caused fights between my mother and stepfather. I always overheard them talking about me from behind closed doors. I thrived on the drama, and the truth was that I wanted to get away from them. Making my own decisions made me feel like an adult, and I loved it. "Anyway," I thought, "I can live my own life. I'm not hurting anyone else, right?" Wrong!

One day I went to her with a proposition. I said, "I'm thinking about going to Mexico to stay with Alejandra, but I need money for the ticket."

"Oh really?" she said. "And what makes you think I'll agree to even consider this? And what makes you think Alejandra will?"

"I have already spoken with Alejandra." I was lying. "If you let me go, I'll be out of your hair. Then you and your husband can waltz off into the sunset without a care in the world."

She looked at me, stunned. I could see that my last point had moved her in some way, and I assumed it was an appealing notion. She looked away for a moment, thoughtful, and I thought I saw her eyes begin to tear up. Then she said what I had not expected. "All right. You can go to Mexico."

I was actually about to hug the woman when she added, "But first I want you to go somewhere with me."

"Where?" My elation was abruptly postponed.

"I want you to go and just talk with someone. A man I know."

• • •

"A man? Do you mean a shrink? Why should I go and talk to a shrink? My only problem is you, and going to Mexico will solve that issue!"

"If you want to go to Mexico…." She didn't have to finish the thought.

"Oh, all right. But just once, just one time, and then I'm out of here."

"Sure, Maridée, just one hour. One visit." She turned around and went to her room.

I felt victorious! Images of myself lying on a beach in Mexico flooded my mind. I could see myself playing in the surf, meeting all kinds of gorgeous guys, getting high, laughing under the full moon. In Mexico I would be free, and I could almost taste it!

But first I had to spend one afternoon with my mother, one hour with a fucking shrink poking around in my head. "No problem," I told myself. "What's the big deal about staring at a bunch of ink blots, talking about the death of my father and how it did or didn't affect me, about my asshole stepfather."

I was smart; I could breeze through an hour of that psychobabble. And then I would be gone on the next plane. It had been a promise. More than that, I thought, even my mother would be better off, happier not having me around. The sound of lively Mariachi music took over my thoughts and obscured any doubts I might have had.

The next day my mother and I climbed into a taxi and headed for the doctor's clinic. We were silent, the two of us, for most of the ride. Then my mother turned to me, her eyes compassionate and sad.

"Now Maridée, please be open with the doctor, be honest with him. Tell him whatever is troubling you."

"Why don't you tell me what you want me to say? I'm sure this is costing you quite a bit, and I don't want you to be disappointed when this fucking witch doctor tells you there's nothing wrong with me. What have you already told him? That way we can get our stories straight."

"Why do you have to behave like this all the time, Maridée? Why do you have to be so negative all the time? So obtuse?"

"Obtuse"? Where did that come from? This was not my mother speaking—she had been possessed! This struck me as so odd I laughed out loud. Obtuse? What a joke!

"I'm glad to see you are taking this so seriously, Maridée," she said sarcastically. "Why did I even expect otherwise?"

"What *did* you expect, Mamá? For me to jump up and down and say, 'Oh, look! At last my mother is paying attention to me! That makes everything better! What can I do now for her?' Really, you are too much!"

We arrived at the clinic, which looked like it had once been a beautiful mansion: three stories tall with park-like grounds. It was painted all white, and except for the bars on all the windows it didn't seem like a place that housed mentally disturbed patients. 'Odd, though, for a doctor's office,' I thought. 'Oh well, whatever...'

A nurse, who appeared to be expecting us, or at least expecting someone, greeted us at the front door. We entered the reception area and I was distracted by the antiseptic smell of the place and by my surroundings—surprisingly sterile compared to the exterior of the building. I thought little of it when my mother called the nurse by name as we were ushered in. With my peripheral vision I barely noticed when my mother handed the nurse a small plastic bag. I was starting to feel a little uncomfortable in this room, in this situation.

The nurse was saying something to me, and my attention returned to her in mid-sentence. "...Show you to the doctor's office now."

"What? Oh, yes," I said. I looked at my mother. Was she going to go with me? All of a sudden I wasn't so sure about this whole scenario. My mother was still standing there, watching me. As our eyes met, she smiled weakly and nodded that I should follow the nurse. No, apparently she wasn't going with me. The nurse gently took my arm and began to lead me to a door in the far wall.

She pushed it open, revealing a long corridor. I looked back at my mother, who was still standing there. The fact that she wasn't taking a seat and wasn't looking for a magazine to help her pass the hour didn't set off any alarms, really, but only added to the growing, nameless sense of foreboding I had begun to feel.

• • •

I tried to picture myself on a beach, dancing in the moonlight, and I told myself just to concentrate on the plane, on Mexico, on Alejandra's kind face. I would be there before I knew it....

We were a few feet into the corridor when I heard the door shut behind us. It sounded solid, heavy, and there was a small electronic sound, like a click, that made the hairs on the back of my neck stand up. I was feeling oddly confused, my head was swimming with the Pine-Sol smell of the place and the totally alien quality of what was happening. It felt like I was watching myself in a movie, and I could almost hear the audience saying, "No, don't do it, don't go in there!" Ridiculous, I told myself.

The nurse was talking again, but she sounded kind of far away. I tried to focus. "No, the trip was fine," I answered the presumed question. The nurse looked at me and smiled questioningly.

"Excuse me?" she asked.

"The road here was...the...didn't you just ask...?"

"Here's the doctor's office." The nurse's voice sounded very different than just a moment ago. A surge of panic, of adrenaline, seized me and rushed through me, and I wondered what the hell was going on in my mind. What a time for a flashback! She opened the door and, still holding onto my arm, she directed me into the doctor's office.

A man behind the desk stood up to greet us. The nurse led me to a chair on the near side of the big desk. My heart was pounding in my chest, and I scanned the room quickly. There were framed diplomas on the wall behind the desk, which displayed a blotter pad, some notebooks, a name plate, a small cardboard cylinder with pens, pencils, paperclips, that type of thing. On the far wall were a couple of paintings—done by patients, I assumed. Or maybe the doctor had children.... I looked closer at the artwork—definitely done by patients! Either that, or his children were pretty fucked up.

Then the nurse spoke. "Doctor Grana, this is Maridée Corbalán." As she did so, I turned my attention to the doctor, barely noticing that the nurse then put a plastic bag down on his desk. Where had I seen that before? No time to think about that now. I had to zero in on the doctor...what was he saying?

"Won't you take a seat?" he asked, as he gestured toward the chair.

"Cool," I said, trying to sound nonchalant. I plopped down into the chair and pulled my feet up underneath me, sitting hippie-style. I didn't want him to think he could intimidate me in any way, or that I considered this session anything to be overly concerned about. I already knew how I felt about authority figures.

"Now, I'd like us to talk about whatever you want to. How about starting with how you are feeling right now, and we'll try to work backwards," he said.

"Right now? At this very moment?" I shot back impatiently, but without hostility. With more effort than I expected, I tried to set aside my uneasiness and my growing fear. I couldn't let him see it. I needed to stay alert!

As the doctor was responding, my eyes again scanned his desktop. The plastic bag ... with something in it. It looked like some kind of material, some fabric. It reminded me of a pair of panties I had at home.

It *was* my underwear!

Before Doctor Grana could realize what was happening, I grabbed the bag from his desk. The movement startled him and he recoiled in his chair. I opened the bag and discovered that it also contained socks and my toothbrush from home!

"What the hell?" I shouted.

"Calm down, Maridée, calm down. Your mother just brought along a few things she thought you might need during your stay here...." The doctor was trying to regain his composure and to take control of the situation. "It's nothing to get overly anxious about...."

He started to go on, but I cut him off.

"What do you mean, my *stay* here? I'm not staying here; I'm going to Mexico! I don't belong here—there's nothing wrong with me! My mother is outside waiting to take me...."

But as soon as the words passed my lips, I remembered her standing—not sitting—watching me being taken away by the nurse. I looked again at the plastic bag. She had brought this! I knew she was no longer in the reception room.

The word "obtuse" echoed in my mind and I realized I had been set up by my own mother! All the tiny clues that should have been giant red flags warning me to run had been there all along, and I had been so stupid!

As I began scanning the room again, this time for a way out, the nurse burst into the room followed by a large man dressed in white. I may be a lot of things, but I am not a hysterical nutcase. I know when I'm beat, and rather than give everyone the show they were expecting, I calmed myself down with an iciness that impressed even me. I had already, in an instant, mentally played out every possible scenario, and I had chosen the one that offered me the best advantage considering my circumstances. I opted for maturity and reason.

"What's the next step, Doctor Grana?" I asked.

He was obviously impressed by my response—surprised even—but still wary. Straightening his glasses, he took a breath. "I imagine you'll want some time to reflect on this change of plans for your immediate future. If you'll follow Nurse Zamora, she'll show you to your room where you can collect yourself, freshen up a bit if you like, and then we'll arrange a tour of the facilities to help you get your bearings. We can resume our interview later on this afternoon. Will you...do you mind going with the nurse?"

I looked him calmly in the eyes, took a deep breath, and replied, "What choice does a rational person have? Of course I'll follow the nurse."

As we walked the corridors and climbed the stairs to the dormitories, I kept my expression blank, emotionless. But inside I was both plotting my route to freedom and, at the same time, executing my mother and stepfather in every painful way I could think of *(maturity only goes so far at fifteen years old)*.

My room was plain, like what I imagined a jail cell to be, although years later I would certainly become intimately acquainted with true jail cells, and would have found this room quite cozy by comparison. I had a roommate, Gabriela—'Gabi' for short—who seemed completely normal one minute: lucid, rational, almost pleasant, but in mid-thought she could fall into a mystifying chasm of total incoherence. At these times I didn't know what the hell she was talking about. The next minute she was as sane as you or…well, anyway….

The following days and nights became a blur of medicated nothingness. Four pills, four times a day. I was afraid to sleep at night because there were, of course, no locks on the dormitory doors, except for the ones that led to freedom and the outside world.

And there were some truly disturbed individuals walking the halls, many of whom would be really dangerous people if not for their meds. Who knew if they were at adequate levels to keep their violent or depraved tendencies in check? There was one old lady I really avoided. She had taken some sort of sharp instrument and cut her legs from the knee down in concentric rings which circled her entire leg like a spiral-cut ham, about a half-inch apart and all the way down to her ankles.

I had brief daily sessions with Doctor Grana in which I mostly sat and drooled on myself while his voice was a babbling brook of soft monologue in the background. There was not, however, any noticeable "foreground" for contrast. But most of the day was filled with "meditation," medication, art therapy—the artwork on the doctor's office wall was done by patients—naps, meals, and lying around on the lawn like a boneless chicken.

I was so drugged that I didn't really know who I was, much less where I was or why I was there. In ten days I put on ten or eleven pounds, and felt more like a spineless buffalo as I crushed the soft green grass below me and drooled. Was I in Mexico yet?

I have been asked whether I was scared in the mental hospital. The answer is definitely *yes*. But you don't understand how completely "out of it" you are. You don't know what is going on *at all*. It's later, when and *if* you get out, that the true terror of your situation hits you.

Afterwards, as the fog begins to lift and clear, the feelings and images of panic, of helplessness, of truly insane people and situations hit hard. It's like sleepwalking through a field of rattlesnakes, then waking up and imagining what *could* have just happened. In some ways it's worse than actually being bitten by the snake, because you realize how completely defenseless you were, and the terrifying possibilities that crowd your mind are worse than any reality.

As the days passed I did become somewhat more acclimated to my new state of "zombie-hood," and, through the fog, I could begin to reason on a very basic, very primitive level. I knew I had to do something, and I wanted to ask Doctor Grana for permission to call my mother. I had no idea, of course, that my mom had paid him off to keep me there while she tried to save her marriage, and because of all the medication I could hardly talk anyway.

But finally, after ten days, I managed to tell him, "Look, I don't belong here, I am scared of these people, and I want to talk to my mother." So he let me call her from his office.

I guess Mother felt a little guilty, or maybe the drugged tone of my voice scared her, but she came. We waited for her in the doctor's office. Upon her arrival, her face was all the mirror I needed. I was fat and ugly and puffy, and my eyes were all glassy—and all this in only ten days.

I looked at her and I said, "Why did you do this to me? Look at me, mamá." I wanted to ask her if she was happy, if her little plan for me had worked to her satisfaction, but I couldn't have enunciated half of these thoughts if I had wanted to.

She checked me out right then and took me home in the taxi. But unfortunately, it didn't end there.

Life at home wasn't much different, except that I was out of the nuthouse, but not at all free. I was kept on a strict schedule, tailored by Dr. Grana: I had to wake up at eight o'clock, eat breakfast, I could go out in the yard for ten minutes, I could read three pages of an approved book, I could make no phone calls or see any friends at all, and I could only go out with my mother to shop for about thirty minutes at a time. They continued with the medications, the same four pills, four times a day. They were turning me into a nut, whether I was one to begin with or not!

After a month of this routine I became more and more depressed, wanting to sleep all day long. Eventually I had an idea of how to help myself. My least favorite medication was a clear liquid. One day when my mother was somewhere else, I found the bottle and emptied it out and I replaced it with water, so she would see me drink that and think I was still getting fucked up on it. I became very good at putting the pills in my mouth in my mother's presence and spitting them out later. After I started to sort of get my balance again, I picked up the phone and called Alejandra. I told her that somebody had to help me here because I wasn't going to make it if this kept up. Alejandra must have called back later and talked to Mamá, because only then did she agree to let me go to Mexico.

On the plane out I promised myself that I would never go back to Argentina and that I would never go back to my mother. The whole experience was severe enough to make me never want to see my family again for as long as I lived.

Going to Mexico now held none of the expectation I had imagined just two months previously. This was a flight to freedom now, just as it had been for my sister and her family after the death of her sister-in-law.

I was going there to save my life, and I would do whatever I had to in order to survive on my own.

... 5 ...
MEXICO CITY

Although the plane touched down in Mexico City without incident, my pulse was racing. I was sixteen years old now and, for the first time, I was totally free. Free from the confines of my mother. Free of house arrest. And free from the political brutality of Argentina.

My travel visa was for six months, and my mother warned me that I must return to Argentina by the end of those six months, or else. I would have said anything to get out of there, so I swore an oath that I would adhere to her condition. *(Yeah, right!)*

But nothing is ever how you expect it to be. When I arrived at my sister and brother-in-law's house, Alejandra and her husband were not getting along well. Not at all! In fact, it was almost all-out war between the two of them. They were both busy professionals who worked all the time and they had three small children. I'm sure that my presence in their house had little to do with their fighting, but I soon felt myself going crazy from all the yelling.

After a couple of months, I started to think about moving out on my own to try and find some kind of serenity. The problem was how to achieve that. After all, I was only sixteen, so what could I do to get some income?

I started with the only thing that I had, which was a newspaper. I searched the classified ads and found the perfect job: "French-speaking receptionist/ personal secretary wanted in a small financial office." I didn't speak a word of French and had only the vaguest idea what secretaries actually did, but what I lacked in qualifications I made up in enthusiasm. I dressed up as professionally as I could (I thought professional meant tight, short, and low-cut), and headed down to the address listed in the ad.

The office was in a very beautiful section of Mexico City. I was so impressed with how clean and grand everything looked that I was determined to work in this part of town. I found the address and entered the building. It turned out to be such a small company that I was to interview with the owner himself!

His name was Adolfo Millán, a wealthy Mexican in his fifties. It was clear to me from the moment that I laid eyes on him that he was an impeccable man. I could tell right away that he wore the finest suits from France. Even his silk necktie seemed carefully chosen in order to complement his eyes and silvering hair.

All through the interview he never took the opportunity to hear even a word of the French that I had no idea how to speak, because he never took his eyes off my boobs! As I casually mentioned to him that I spoke several languages fluently (I was so full of it), I couldn't help but realize that as this information rolled off of my full, pouty lips, it went directly into his right ear and fell, unheard, out of his left.

The entire interview felt like lying to a principal at school; after all I was a teenager and to me he was an old man. A good-looking one…but still old! I was scared that he would find out that the only French that I knew was from little kindergarten songs!

I always thought that money was power, and so I figured since he had a lot of it, I was intimidated. But little did I know that because I had a certain little something between my legs, I was actually the one who had the power over him! The interview was a success, and he asked me to start work the following day.

I raced home to tell Alejandra my exciting news. She was a sociologist and earned the impressive salary of twelve thousand pesos per month, which was a very comfortable living in Mexico at that time. She was so happy and proud of me for snagging a job so quickly that she offered to help supplement my little salary in the beginning so I could find an efficiency apartment somewhere.

"What are you going to be earning, Maridée?" she asked sweetly. The smile fled her rapidly flushing face when I told her that I was to start at eleven thousand pesos! "A year?" The math didn't add up in her head.

"No. Per month," I tossed out nonchalantly. Her mouth fell open. But deep down I knew she was secretly happy for me, and that night the two of us went out to celebrate my new career.

Now I needed to determine where I was going to live, so soon afterwards I set out on my search for the perfect place. Someone, I can't remember who, told me in passing about these great cabins for rent, and I was excited to go check them out. When I arrived at the address I had been given I almost turned around immediately. First of all, it was in the worst part of Mexico City, scary even during the day—not to mention the smell of the nearby greasy *taquerías*. But I decided it couldn't hurt to check them out anyway, especially since I had already come all this way.

I entered through a massive wooden door and found myself immersed in a corridor of exotic greenery that sprouted out of copper pots, and low stone walls adorned with sterling silver candleholders that lit the way at night. At the far end of the corridor was an altar overflowing with statues of saints, also illuminated with candles, and a small courtyard flanked by tidy little cottages. It was an exquisite sight!

I found the landlady's apartment and nervously asked her if there were any available. I was in luck! I almost jumped out of my skin with happiness when she told me there was one cabin available, and it was furnished!

I fell in love with my little cabin the moment I stepped inside. The floors and ceiling were made of hardwood, there was a tiny dining table that folded out from the wall, and it was furnished with beautiful antiques carved with floral designs. We went back to her apartment to finalize the rent, which at the time was equivalent to about fifty American dollars per month. Such a deal! It was even better than finding the right man!

To top it off, she had two maids who took care of all the cabins. She explained to me that she rarely left her place, which for me was truly fantastic—no more watchful eyes looming over my every move. Her own apartment was also full of antique furniture, but included a piano, many shelves full of books, and fantastic artifacts and other ancient treasures. She shared with me that she had been an archeologist before retiring, and this love of world antiquities was evident in the tasteful decoration of her immaculate home. Her house smelled wonderful, like incense! It felt like I was inside a church from all the frankincense and myrrh.

In my own little cabin, warm, beautiful things surrounded me. It gave me—finally!—a real sense of security and peace. The only drawback was that the one and only telephone was attached to a pole in the courtyard, so I had to go outside to talk. Luckily I found a little umbrella that I kept by my door so that on rainy days when the phone would ring I wouldn't get completely soaked. That was the idea, anyway, even though it only protected my head in most cases.

Meanwhile, as I began my new job, I was pleased to find that Adolfo was wonderful to work for, and so kind to me. My duties included answering his telephone, making coffee, flirting with him, and making periodic calls to France to check on investments and other financial undertakings. I was able to accomplish all these tasks with ease—except for the last one, which, because I didn't speak French, I just decided to blow off. Despite our age difference, as I watched him talk and move, I was quickly becoming deeply enamored of Adolfo, who to me was just the most fascinating man in the world.

Wishing to appear properly virginal, I waited to have sex with him until a full day and a half after I began my job, when he invited me to his home for lunch. I was dessert, of course. Adolfo impressed me so much. He had a chauffeur for his big American car. And such a mansion! It was really beautiful. At least what I saw of it was.

Things were great for a little while. I would reshuffle all the papers on my desk and write myself new memos so it would look like I had actually accomplished something. Meanwhile, Adolfo would chase me around my desk, so to speak.

I remember one day, I arrived at the office early as usual, as I had to try and cover up for the fact that I hadn't done shit the day before. But on that day I could not find my key to the office door!

I was tugging and pushing, trying all the windows, but nothing was working. The place was locked up tight and I was completely afraid of getting busted by my boss. In desperation, I looked around and suddenly spotted a rock. I picked it up quickly and held it, staring at one of the windows to the office. I was trying to concoct a believable story about a break-in—which of course would also involve stolen files! Although international espionage was an appealing story, I wasn't sure I could sell it to Adolfo.

Just then this kid walked by. I say he was a kid, but he was probably only a couple of years older than me, maybe eighteen or nineteen. He saw me with the rock in my hand and quickly figured out what I was about to do. "Locked out?" he asked casually.

"Yeah, I lost my fucking key," I responded.

"Want some help?" I eyed him suspiciously for a moment. Then I decided that maybe he could pass for an international saboteur, and I figured it couldn't hurt to include him in my plot. I handed him the rock.

"Go for it," I said. He tossed the rock aside and pulled out a huge key ring.

"Damn!" I said. "That's a lot of keys!"

"Masters," he told me.

"Uh, whatever," I said, not really sure what he meant by that. He walked to the front door, eyed the lock, selected a key, put it in and just like that, opened the fucking door! This guy was a pro!

"Hey, how did you do that?" I was amazed.

"Experience," he answered. I thanked him profusely and introduced myself. He said his name was Memo, and that he was on his way to the restaurant next door.

"No shit? You go there a lot?" I asked.

"I'm a friend of Manolo, the owner," he replied.

"Really! I've never seen you there. I go almost every day for lunch."

"Not usually up that early." It appeared talking wasn't his strong suit.

"Well, thanks again, maybe I'll see you around," I said, and flashed him a smile.

"Maybe," he said as he headed off.

Memo was very handsome, with his curly brown hair, little sweet eyes, and a warm smile. He and I eventually ran into each other again and in fact, we came to be pretty good friends. Actually, once I got to know him I found out that he actually spoke a lot—almost like a normal person! Turns out he was some kind of cop or security guard, which of course explained his miraculous ability to open my office door.

I raced into the office, shuffled my papers around, turned on the coffee pot and proceeded with my daily routine of transforming the appearance of the office from hardly operating to operating hard.

I remained madly in love with my boss as long as I worked for him—almost two months! I couldn't believe that it took that long for him to discover that I had never called France once, never spoken with an associate, never seen to any aspect of his quickly crumbling business! He let me go very sweetly, I thought, and I knew then that he loved me, too.

··· 6 ···

The night I went out with my sister to celebrate my new job with Adolfo, we happened to meet a guy from Argentina named Juan. He was a nice guy, very intelligent, very good-looking—dark hair and the most beautiful blue eyes! We liked him. And, the fact that he was thirty-six years old made him pretty appealing to me. Something about older men made me feel spoiled!

We had another thing in common, too: his brother had just joined the ranks of the hundreds of people who were disappearing every day in Argentina. Juan had recently broken up with his girlfriend, and was understandably depressed about the entire situation. So, over the next two months we stayed in touch, and as we did we were growing closer, and I guess you could say, we were starting to date.

When he lost his place, I invited him to move into my little cabin. He was a professor at the university in Mexico City, so he seemed to be somewhat stable, but as the days passed his depression grew stronger and began to take bizarre turns.

He really wanted children; possibly he felt he needed to create a family in light of having lost his brother, I don't know. I was so young then, and I told him, "Okay, well, maybe one day."

But the "okay" turned out to be "not okay" real soon.

When I found myself pregnant, I panicked. I found myself starting to wonder what the hell I was doing with this guy. Having just lost my source of income, I was not exactly prepared for the responsibility of a child. I worried and I wavered, going back and forth about whether I could do the "mom" thing. I guess because of the relationship I had with my own mother, not to mention my young age , I realized this was something that I didn't want to do.

I had an abortion. I can only hope that my baby in Heaven understands what a hell his life would have been if he had been born. I hope he forgives me for my decision.

The Mexican restaurant next door to my former office was called *Torremolinos*. Now that I was once again jobless, I decided to stop by and visit all the employees who had become my friends. But perhaps I also had an ulterior motive. I sat at the bar across from the owner of the place.

"It's a little late in the day for a lunch break, isn't it?" Manolo asked me.

"I only wish it were a lunch break," I replied sadly.

"What's up with the sad face, *pebeta*?" (*Pebeta* is a term of endearment.)

"Adolfo let me go," I moaned.

"Oooh, that's too bad." He sounded concerned. "What are you going to do now?" I told him I had no idea, but that I had to come up with something pretty quick. He asked if I knew how to wait tables, and I asked him how hard could it be?

Working at *Torremolinos* was a blast. I was one of only two women working there, and the other, Eloisa, was practically a fossil and looked like an old man. But my male customers were precious! Almost every night I went home with bouquets of roses that they would buy for me from the little kids on the street! Even Adolfo continued to come in, and he always left me a huge tip. My income wasn't eleven thousand pesos per month anymore, but it was plenty to get by on, and as I said, working there was a lot of fun. I would work until two in the morning – and being a teenager, I rarely went straight home from work.

Back at the cabin, Juan was writing a book and still teaching. But his depression continued to worsen and I was becoming more and more concerned about his mental state. Because I was so young, I just wasn't up to dealing with it. It was much more fun to party with my friends from work, with the customers, and with the bikers.

What made things worse was that Juan and I had both heard from friends in Argentina that the situation with the *militares* had gotten so bad that people who thought they were after them had begun to carry cyanide pills under their pinkie nail. The police would stop you on the street or come to your home saying your name was on a list of people to be questioned, and if you went with them you were never seen again.

As it was becoming known, all they would do before killing you was to interrogate you to get the names of all your friends and associates, so many of them chose death by suicide over the torture and the horror of death at the hands of these monsters. It was like the Nazis all over again, which is not too surprising as so many of them fled to South America after the war. I'm not implying that there were Nazis involved in this situation – the *militares* were locals – but it seems that a government which would allow known or suspected war criminals to enter their country and take up residence is probably not too far off politically and idealistically from the government which had created and fostered these other beasts.

As I have said, Juan was an intelligent man—a professor—and perhaps it was this high level of education and understanding of what was actually happening that led him into such a terrible mental state. At thirty-six, he was also twice my age, more politically aware, more personally involved. He eventually deteriorated to such a level that he was no longer capable of continuing to teach at the university, so he would just sit in the tiny cabin and stare out the window. He had no income so I was paying the rent, and the strain was becoming intolerable. I was starting to fear that if I allowed this to go on much longer his depression would drag me to the murky bottom of insanity with him. But I had already seen enough of that for a lifetime.

My motorcylce god! Dean and his dog Nicolás

... 7 ...

One night at the restaurant, a guy came in and, once again, my life took an unpredictable turn. He looked like a Greek god. His mother was Cuban, his father Mexican, but he was born in New York City. He wore tight jeans that showcased his perfect ass, and his eyes were the most beautiful dark blue I had ever seen. You could balance a cigarette in the curl of his eyelashes, they were so long!

His name was Dean.

Dean had been traveling around Mexico in a van with his three Alaskan Malamutes named Nicolás, Tarkus and Nieves. He had an aggressive "in control" attitude that appealed to the fatherless girl I was. He knew what he wanted and he went for it. Here was someone, I thought, who knew how to live life! He exuded freedom and excitement. Faster than a speeding locomotive, I fell for this superman. From the moment he stepped off his bike and entered the restaurant, it seemed that he had been sent by the heavens to be mine alone, and instantly I wanted to spend the rest of my life with him. Little did I know how sadly prophetic that desire would be.

It was only a few days later that I told Juan he was too much for me to deal with; he needed to get on with his life and to move out. "But I don't have anyplace to go, Maridée," he complained. I looked around my little cabin that had once felt so safe and secure, but had now become a suffocating tomb. I looked at Juan, beautiful but quickly on the road to becoming totally deranged, and then I thought of Dean.

Moving out wasn't too difficult.

I didn't want to hurt Juan more than I had to, so I left my place to him, but that still wasn't enough. He wasn't too happy about me exchanging my beautiful cabin for a van, and exchanging him for Dean. But the fact that he was going nuts brought back terrible memories and scared me shitless. And what do I do when I'm scared? I run.

I moved into Dean's van that night after work. Not long after that Dean was ready to continue his tour of Mexico. I was more and more in awe of this dashing adventurer, more and more in love with him every minute. His stories fascinated me and even scared me a little, but I knew that I, too, was ready for a change—for some excitement—and I was dying to throw caution to the wind and to live life large and recklessly.

There was definitely an air of danger in Dean, but it was thrilling. Also, my visa was nearing its expiration and there was no way I was going to return to Argentina. I needed to disappear into the interior of Mexico. There was no law, no force of nature, no threat to my body or mind that could make me go back to my country. I would do anything, say anything…endure almost anything to avoid that fate. Dean seemed like the perfect ticket to obscurity. I gave my immediate notice to Manolo. Of course, there was nothing they could do to stop me from leaving, but we had all grown pretty close by now and they were sad and disappointed to see me go.

I'm not entirely convinced that Dean and I were as much "liberated" from our problems, as we were just two confused kids that got together but still remained very much alone. It really was the same craving of the unknown that had gotten me evicted from Argentina: tons of spare time with nothing to achieve or to contribute in any way. Because Dean was so different from anyone I'd ever met, however, I didn't realize that I was throwing myself into another losing situation.

Along with Dean came a new identity for me; he was the first to call me "María" instead of "Maridée." Since he had already gained so much control over me, it felt like he'd done me some kind of favor. I thought I was becoming more of an adult, and it seemed that the use of my given name gave me a new personality, someone I could make and mold into a new image. "Maridée" belonged to the past.

I thought I was so in touch with my emotions. Yeah, right! What I was in touch with was a bottle of whiskey in one hand and a bottle of downers in the other. And at my feet was all the marijuana I could ever want. I smoked joints like they were cigarettes—any mother's worst nightmare!

After a while, though, my honeymoon with Dean started to wear off. Romance turned to tedious days of trying to survive. If we weren't fighting or free-basing, it was only because one of us was too exhausted to continue the ritual. It was a cycle of uppers to get you going, booze to slow the shakes, and downers to bring you in for a landing. Wherever we happened to be when Dean couldn't or didn't want to drive any more became our home for the night.

•••

One hazy morning, we were rudely awakened by five *Federales* demanding to search our van. They had been following us for several days and we were kind of expecting them to pull this type of thing. The search of our van would surely bring enough trouble to be a colossal pain in the ass. Being the mavericks that we were, we told the *Federales* they were lousy cocksuckers and zoomed off!

We had a close call in one of the busiest intersections of Mexico City. Bobbing and weaving through the crowded, narrow streets, we nearly hit a flock of Catholic schoolgirls, a blurry mass of plaid uniforms that seemed to stretch for miles. Dean slammed on the brakes and the van spun around like a ballet dancer before we rolled the van over three full turns.

I ended up pinned between my door and the gravel that had become one with my shoulder. Miraculously, once I heard the sirens on the approaching cop cars, I made a partial recovery and Dean and I disappeared into the tiny back streets. Dean was a mess. He had busted open his forehead as he sailed through the windshield. My arm was visibly broken, not to mention possessing much less skin than it had just a few seconds before, but I would live. The dogs had not been hurt, simply growled at the onlookers before climbing back into the toppled van to protect their shattered domain.

We tried unsuccessfully to flag down a ride. In fact, people mostly sped up as they passed us. Eventually, at a red light, we came across a taxi driven by an elderly oriental man. We threw ourselves into the back of his car. He took one look at his bloody invaders and went into hysterics.

"No kill, no kill!" he pleaded.

"Man, take a chill pill," Dean told him.

The man still did not move, gazing at us with terrified eyes.

I yelled at him, "You're a taxi driver, right? So drive!"

He lurched the taxi into the flow of traffic and managed to get us to the hospital.

•••

Dean and I were given a series of shots to deaden the pain as we were stitched up. The nurses, who were amazed by our unusually high tolerance for medication, flocked around my charismatic superman and listened adoringly to his stupid jokes about our unfortunate accident. I didn't much care. I was immersed in my concern for the dogs and the van we had left at the scene.

Out in the hall, we took a moment to assess our new looks. Dean's head and chest were wrapped in gauze; I had a hefty cast running from my left wrist to my shoulder. He looked at me and said, "It does something for you, María. It's that 'wounded look' that men find so irresistibly sexy. Shit, I think we ought to break the other one!"

I wasn't amused. "We have to go back, Dean. My passport is in the van—everything's in the van!".

He just smiled. "Hey, am I twisted?"

"Twisted sounds so unfriendly," I replied sarcastically, thinking that "completely fucked up" was a better description.

"I prefer to be addressed as *mentally untidy*," he laughed.

We had a taxi drive us to the crash. There were cops crawling all over the place. They had the dogs tied up while they were scrutinizing every inch of the van, looking for clues as to who we were. Finally one of the cops jumped out with my passport in his hand. There wasn't much I could do, so we decided to face the music.

To our amazement they didn't arrest us. We were dropped off at the house of Dean's friend Andrés. The next day, we got the van back from the towing yard. Dean made it worth the attendant's time to look the other way as we drove out. There was not one piece of glass left except for the rear windows.

It was truly disgusting—the bugs that normally squish and splat against the windshield now sailed on through, exploding on contact with either our faces or the back of the van. It wasn't pretty.

Dean promised to make it up to me by taking me on a romantic getaway to Acapulco for the weekend. It was only a six-hour drive, so I figured with my mouth clenched and sunglasses on I would probably survive.

• • •

There are checkpoints in Mexico, as most people know, and of course we came upon one. I was asleep in the back of the van when I felt Dean toss a bulging bag of pot at me, shouting for me to hide it. I immediately stuffed it down my pants. As you can imagine, our open-air hippie van was flagged down for a closer inspection. I stepped out and saw all these gun-yielding monkeys eyeing me with hard-dick expressions and I thought, that's it—we're busted! At the very least, we knew we were in for harassment from these bastards. They get bored standing out there in the sun and they tend to go a little *loco*. They're not exactly brain surgeons to begin with.

An inspection of our bodies as well as the van was ordered. I sucked my stomach in and held my breath while all those hands rubbed up and down. Fortunately they never found the bag. We knew the law in Mexico says that if the police find a certain number of marijuana seeds on you, they can bust you!

Now it was time to search the van and the stupid cops told Dean to move the van to the side of the road. Dean climbed back into the driver's seat and didn't think twice before he mumbled to me to jump back in the van. I did so and somehow we pulled it off: we crouched down and Dean stomped on the gas and we tore out of there. I felt pain all over as I anticipated machine guns showering us with bullets, but the only noise was Dean's psychotic laugh.

"You really got off on that, didn't you?" I asked, shaking my head in disbelief.

"It got us both off a cold bench in a stinking jail cell, didn't it?" he retorted proudly.

We made it to Acapulco and I tried without success to relax on the sandy beach. We rented a little *palapa* made of bamboo and palm fronds. The walls were apparently made of driftwood or orange crate material. I knew that the road we had come in on was the only way out as well.

"Lighten up, María," Dean urged. "You're no fun lately. Why can't you just quit stressing about every little thing?"

He poured coconut-scented oil across his ripped chest. But this time Dean's sex appeal wasn't enough to distract me from the situation—I was really afraid.

"Dean, don't you care how we'll get back? You think they'll just move out of your way with a smile? You know as well as I do that they're going to blow our heads off!" I began to get pissed off.

"Did they shoot at us before? No. We're small fries, María. They don't waste their time on people with a few seeds in their car—they go for the big dogs, the ones dealing heroin and cocaine, maybe we should do that.

Here it came…Dean was getting into his preaching mode. I hated when he was condescending, although I always tolerated it, it would have been dangerous to comment on it at all.

I knew that doctors had determined that Dean was manic-depressive. But he hadn't been locked away in a pill-pushing wonderland as I had been; his mom put him in a high security place with locks and straps and doctors lining up outside your door to listen to every word you utter. That should have been a clue to me, but I understood all about scheming mothers. He was supposed to take medication but he didn't because he didn't like it. His illness rolled like the tide, sometimes destroying anything in its way. Often I got in the way and was swept off my feet – not, however, by romance. Every time he experienced one of these dismal periods in his life, he would change emotional gears without warning.

"Are you crazy? Is the thrill-seeker inside of you taking over again?"

With one swift movement, Dean pushed me against the unstable wall, then picked me up by the throat. *(They always do that by the throat! I don't know why and I doubt if they do either).* He stuck his face in mine and smiled blissfully as I coughed and gagged and held my throat in pain.

Then he put me down, patted me on the ass and walked the short distance to our hotel room to lie on the bed. That was another thing I noticed: Dean's bursts of violence are more often than not followed by bursts of tranquility.

Later, lying in bed next to each other, he spoke softly to me. "I was kidding, María! Do I shoot heroin?"

"No," I admitted, but hesitantly.

"Then why would I want to get mixed up with that shit? A person would have to be crazy to get mixed up with heroin!"

I am embarrassed to say that at that time I saw the logic in his statement. Even more embarrassing is the fact that I believed his sincerity.

Our life continued in this chaotic pattern for several more weeks. We continued to argue, which would lead to a beating, which would lead to sex, which seemed at last to calm him down for a while. Finally I felt like I needed a vacation from our vacation, a vacation from the bruising, some time to think and to heal. I loved Dean, but it hurt to be with him.

This time we decided to get out of the big city and go to a small, quiet place with our friends Claudia, Andrés and Flowers. I thought that maybe if a bunch of us went, Dean wouldn't get so moody. At least—not so violent. For whatever reason this type of behavior attracted me with perverse fascination. Each day brought some kind of trouble with Dean. It's hard to recall every situation, but two incidents stick in my mind like they just happened yesterday. In fact, years of therapy have not been able to erase them.

We found ourselves—on my birthday! —in the tiny picturesque city of Cuernavaca. The weekend began like any other in our bizarre way of life: mushrooms and downers by the fistful. When the mushrooms really started to kick in, the guys decided they needed some whiskey. Given that Cuernavaca was such a small town, the liquor store was easy to find, even with everything mushrooming before our eyes.

Since the little mishap in Mexico City, we were still without a windshield, so I offered to stay in the van with the dogs while the others went to purchase the liquor. As I was sitting in the passenger seat of the van, I noticed a beautiful little church across the street. I was thinking how fine it was with its smooth stone arches and stately pillars that wiggled like worms.

It was a lovely building and it struck a chord in the back of my mind, reminding me of the church I attended as a child in Argentina. I started to laugh hysterically at that point, less from the memory than from the mushrooms. Then I became aware of something moving towards me like a formation of giant ants. As they marched nearer I stopped laughing. There were fifty or so machine-gun-toting *Federales* swarming the building. I shook my head and rubbed my eyes, but they continued to pour out of nowhere. I spotted what I immediately decided was the leader of the group, the "queen." He was dark, tall and utterly vicious-looking! He was shouting something that I couldn't quite make out, but as he headed my way I found myself not wanting to hear. In fact, I didn't want to be anywhere near here, but it was too late!

That's when I noticed the revolting way his face was pulsing in perfect rhythm with his stride. Ah…the magic of mushrooms! I had always assumed that I wouldn't have to be sober to take on a small army of cops; that job was delegated to the dogs. My job was to act as an ornament and general plaything for Dean, and although I had a long list of complaints about how he did his job protecting me from trouble, at least until now he had done it.

The security of the ferocious furry protection I was counting on was gone with the windshield. All three dogs showed themselves out through our gaping, wrap-around exit. Fucking mutts! This one skinny cop pulled me from the van, broken arm and all, and was prodding the end of his gun into my stomach with one hand while covering my face with his other.

Then a three-hundred-pound inbred cop stepped in and was shouting at me through a shower of spit. Given the choice, I would have much rather had the gun back in my stomach than this guy flinging his fucking slobber around. I cupped my hand over my ear casually as though there was too much background noise for me to hear him. This move was to buy me some time while I searched frantically for brain cells not yet affected by the hallucinogens, if any, to move to the front line. My plan was to remain calm and delicately provide the officer with some reasoning that his tiny brain could handle, if only my tiny brain could come up with it! Surely I could convince him that this was all one of those crazy misunderstandings.

But he was already addressing me, and here I was in another dimension, where there was time to gather one's thoughts and make a studied decision after lengthy reflection. 'Damn, why do we have to play in your dimension?' I thought.

He bent down closer and screamed, "I'm going to ask you one more time, *cabrona*, which one of you put the bomb inside the church?"

"What bomb?" I asked, convinced that I must really be tripping now. If ever you find yourself in Cuernavaca and someone asks you this question, be certain that my response was not acceptable! I was probably seconds away from being a little too dead when I heard Dean telling them to leave me alone.

As good as his intentions were, things only got worse. The tightest handcuffs in the world (sadly, I do have near-global handcuff experience) had become one with my wrists as they were twisted behind my back, arm cast and all.

They grabbed Dean and tossed us both back in the van. The vicious-looking cop jumped in and took over the driver's seat and another guy wearing a suit sat facing Dean and me. We sat on the floor Indian-style as we had done a thousand times before, but this time no one was passing a bong around. An automatic prayer began swelling in my head, picking up speed and volume every time it bounced off the inside of my throbbing skull: 'I know that I really, really fucked up this time, bless me Jesus! Please, please, please just let me live through this fucking nightmare and I'll never do anything wrong ever again, oh, God, bless me Jesus!"

But I must have said it wrong, because when I opened my eyes the cops were still there. I was so scared that I *almost* wanted my mother.

My heart was pounding in my chest as the hefty cop walked past the van. Moments later I was almost happy to be joined by Flowers, Claudia, and Andrés as they were all thrown into the van beside me. Apparently my friends had not had a chance to get away, even though they were walking far behind Dean when the cops swarmed him.

A fourth cop had been called in to assist with the "terrorists" who had just been brought to the scene, and he bumped into one of the back speakers as he jumped into the van. For a few excruciating seconds, the speaker cover bounced back and forth like a metronome. With each flop of the cover, the number of charges against us increased and decreased before my blurry eyes. Finally, to my dismay, our generous cache of marijuana spilled out from its hiding place in the speaker.

I was holding onto the insane notion that maybe this cop would understand that we were just some harmless free spirits and tactfully put the speaker back together without a word. Since I had never been busted before, I thought it was at least possible that if I explained it wasn't pot, the nice officers would apologize and take off. Failing that, maybe I could tell them I had no idea things had gotten so out of hand, or that this experience had been a wakeup call for me and yes, I had seen the light, the error of my ways. Things didn't seem to be going down that way, though, and I was left with an irrational mantra of "what ifs" racing through my brain at lightning speed: What if they fill me up with holes? What if they keep us in prison forever? What if they pull out my toenails? 'What if they show me their toenails? I'd never survive *that*!' (I know it's not a laughing matter, but don't forget I was high and hallucinating, and some pretty strange shit does go through your mind...).

They seemed angry enough to kill us all, bless me Jesus!

I tried to keep up with all the accusations the cops were flinging at us but I couldn't possibly take them all in. The way they fed off of our fear made it hard to speculate how far they would take their game, although it was clear that the root of their sadistic pleasure was control.

The van finally stopped and the first thing to hit me as I was pushed out was the rancid smell in the air. It was just like the *callejones* and *taquerías* behind my first apartment in Mexico City. I would never have considered grease and urine to be nostalgic odors, but the memories of the security I had felt in my beautiful little cabin on the courtyard only added to the remorse I felt at this moment.

Handcuffed, we were driven to what the cops told us was our final destination. The jailhouse would be our home for the foreseeable future, they had said. "¿*Te gusta?*' one of the cops asked as we were removed from the van, "Do you like it?" He picked his ear with his pinky nail.

"I want to call my sister!" I told the fat one.

"But of course," he sneered, "Just as soon as you admit to putting the bomb in our cathedral. After that you can call the Pope for all I care, and for all the good it will do you."

They kept insisting on the bomb thing and I didn't know if I was in the wrong place at the wrong time, or if this was one of those situations where false charges are invented for the amusement—or the benefit—of the officers making an arrest.

"I don't know anything about a bomb! Look at me, I could be your girlfriend, your daughter," I pleaded.

"You're a whore," he spat out.

··· 8 ···

I was separated from Dean and the others immediately. We were led to separate sections of the ancient stone building and I was chained to the cell wall, still wearing the cast on my arm from having flipped the van. Judging from the screams and groans of the other inmates, I figured that if being chained to the wall was all I had to endure then I was lucky. I still maintained some thread of optimism. Or was it naiveté?

There was another older guard in my section of the jail. He had one long clump of slimy hair he insisted on wrapping around his head like a living turban. He would come over and scratch his crotch while he told me of the many unfortunate young girls that he'd seen come and go from this hellhole. Apparently, he had had a brother whose murder remained unsolved, so every person who came to be imprisoned in this jail was, to him, a suspect in that crime. He wanted all of us to pay for his grief.

After twenty-four hours in prison, we were no closer to even imagining an end to this insanity. We were never allowed a phone call. We were never told of any formal charges. We never saw another person besides the brutish guards who walked the stinking corridor and taunted and tortured us. Over the next couple of days they played games with me and tried to make me think that Dean or one of the others were spilling their guts about the bomb. Being separated and denied food or water, not to mention facing the specter of death, we had no idea what the truth was or whether the others were succumbing to the torture and making up stories just to get out of here, dead or alive.

The only food I got was what was given to me by the other prisoners, who only had for themselves what relatives or friends on the outside would toss through the bars or over the barred, open-air rooftop. After some desperate begging on my part, the guy next to me started throwing pieces of bread over the stone wall that separated our two cells. His generosity was the only thing that kept me alive and allowed me to realize that people can retain their humanity, even in the direst of situations.

The guards had no interest in treating us humanely. It certainly didn't bother them to see us go hungry day after day. When it rained, we would be rained upon. When the Mexican sun baked the region, my skin would burn and blister and the iron manacles would sear my wrists.

I was visited by an unfamiliar police officer about a week later. He wore a starched uniform and his nose wrinkled up from the stink of our cells. I took him to be a senior officer, like a captain or something. "How long have you been chained up like this?" he asked, and I thought I caught a glimmer of compassion in his tone.

"Too long," I choked out through dry sobs.

"Would you like to tell me about it?" he asked softly. I tried to compose myself enough to communicate the terror and the agony I was enduring, the hopelessness I felt, the injustice of my incarceration and the inhumanity of the guards, but my throat was parched, my lips cracked, and my mind couldn't focus for more than a second on any one thought.

All I could do was sob silently. The possibility of even a kind word from this man gave me hope, and that hope caused me to sob even more deeply, more desperately. If this man wouldn't listen to me, wouldn't help me, I knew I would die.

He called to the fat guard, who I had come to call 'Dunker," to open the cell and unchain me. Dunker snapped to and waddled over with greater speed than I had yet seen him exercise. He retrieved his key ring and opened the padlocks. I collapsed onto the dirt floor. The senior officer had Dunker bring me a tiny sip of fresh water, and after a moment I was ready to speak. I looked into this man's eyes, searching for truth, for hope, for anything human, and I thought I made a connection.

"My name is Captain Aguilar," he told me. His voice was soft, almost a whisper, "I want you to tell me how you are doing and how you have come to be here. Can you do that?"

"My name is María Corbalán. I am a citizen of Argentina. My sister lives in Mexico City. Can I call her, please? Can I call the Argentinean Embassy?"

"They have already been contacted. You know that you are in violation of your visa, don't you? And the charges against you are very serious in nature."

I didn't know if any of what he said was true. The way I felt, I could easily become one of the "disappeared" ones like my sister's in-laws in Argentina. I thought of Juan in Mexico City and what this would do to him, what it would do to my sisters and yes, even my mother, if I never made it out of here alive.

"You know that you must tell me if you have any knowledge of the bomb at the cathedral—it is the only way I can help you," he spoke sincerely and with growing compassion.

"But I do not know anything about any bomb!" I cried. "I was only sitting in the van with my dogs! We came here for a vacation! I have done nothing wrong! My mother had sent me a check for my birthday—it was in my pocket—and the officers took it, they stole it! It was all I have! Besides that there is nothing I can tell you, Sir! So please, please help me!"

Captain Aguilar stood up and called to the guard. His whole demeanor changed before my eyes and I saw that his soft compassion had been nothing more than a tool he deftly wielded for interrogation purposes. "Return this girl to her chains! She is not willing to cooperate!"

"No! No, please! I am going to die on that wall! If I knew anything, anything at all, I would tell you! Don't you believe me?"

Aguilar turned sharply outside my cell and glared at me, but he said nothing. He marched off down the corridor while the fat guard chuckled as he turned the key in the cell door.

The next day I was unchained and for the first time I was allowed to walk around the small courtyard. I could see Dean behind the bars of his cell across the dirt yard, and he smiled and waved. Any smile from Dean signaled elation when we were out in the real world, so if he smiled here, in this place, he must know or at least suspect something. I was almost afraid to consider what it might be.

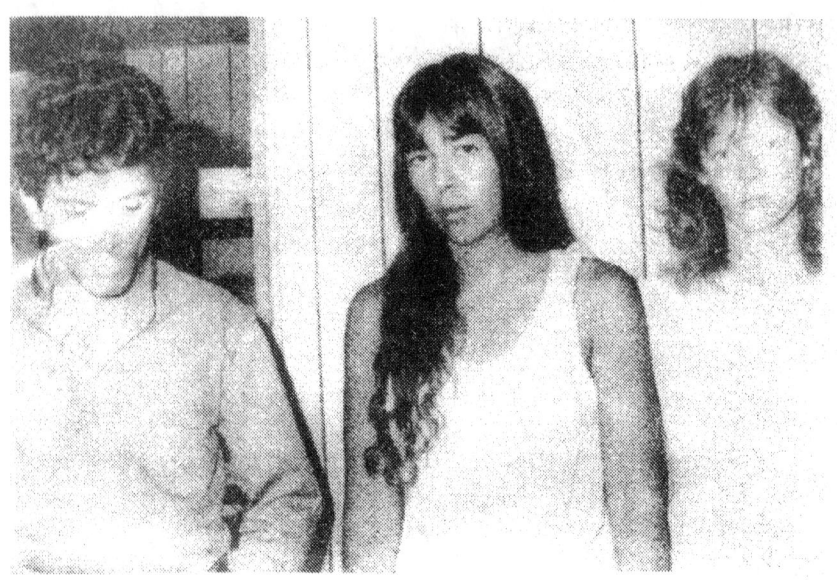

My first experience with publicity left something to be desired. 1986.

··· 9 ···

The next day Aguilar had all five of us removed from our cells and herded into a van. Dean and I were not allowed to touch each other. We couldn't kiss, but his eyes conveyed everything that I, too, was feeling at just being able to be together again. It seemed like a gift from God to see his beautiful face, to feel his warmth next to me on the cold floor of the van. I thought of how much we had shared together in these past short months, about the passion between the two of us, the love we had made, and yes, even those beatings which were his distorted expression of affection.

We were both dirty, we stank like skunks, but I didn't notice this at all. It was in his eyes, on his lips and within his very soul that this message was made obvious to me: he needed me. We needed each other.

I was afraid to hope that we were about to be released, but I fought to keep my spirits up anyway. The only thing I knew for sure was where I didn't want to be, although it was beginning to seem more and more that my destiny was set, immutable, and the rest of my life might be lived in a six-foot-square cell. I prayed that the misunderstanding about the bomb would be cleared up, and I swore that I would make many changes in my life if it were. If Dean and I were to continue, he would have to settle down—I couldn't allow myself to be put in this kind of situation ever again. The part that really tore at my heart was that I knew I would still be with him no matter what he did. He was all I had.

My inner terror gained momentum once more, not knowing where we were being taken. It was easy to see my friends were mentally broken down. We were all becoming introverted after being together for only a thirty-minute van ride.

We pulled into a long driveway that led to a beautiful three story red brick mansion with a gorgeous azalea garden out front. It obviously belonged to someone important, and although the estate was breathtaking, I knew from the experience of the mental clinic in Argentina not to get my hopes up. After all, this was obviously not where we were being taken to be released. It's ironic that when I was in the beautiful mansion that was the mental facility in Argentina, all I wanted was to get to Mexico, and now that I was in Mexico I was basically in the same situation, facing another beautiful mansion, another place to suffer.

They led us out of the van and we took a few seconds to enjoy the sight and the fresh air. We were not taken in through the front door of the estate, nor even around to a side entry, but were shoved down a narrow flight of steps into a dark basement room. They left us there, locked in absolute darkness for several hours. Finally, one at a time, we were taken upstairs, where our nightmare continued. The surrounding estate might have been magazine perfect, but we were merely in another cell facing a new hell.

At last my turn came, and I was dragged upstairs to the kitchen where there was a metal desk and a metal chair set on top of a plastic sheet. You would not believe the fear and panic this image caused. "Why is there plastic on the floor under the chair?" I asked, terrified of the answer. But none was offered.

I was made to sit on the chair facing several men—including Captain Aguilar—who were seated on the other side of the desk. I felt like throwing up, and my mind raced with images of torture, picturing my own blood collecting in pools in the waves and contours of the plastic drop cloth. I was afraid to walk on the plastic for fear that I would hear the crunch of someone's extracted tooth as it broke beneath my feet, or feel the slime of someone else's bodily fluids which had not been completely rinsed away from the victim before me.

All these thoughts exploded into my head, but honestly they never, to my knowledge anyway, occurred in real life. The bloody torture *implied* by the plastic drop cloth was all that was necessary to make me shake convulsively, tears filling my eyes, my lower lip quivering in fear. One by one the men across the desk would ask me questions about the day of our arrest, about our intentions, about the bomb found in the church. They did eventually slap and push me as it became obvious that I would not answer them to their satisfaction; I would admit only to being a tourist, not a terrorist.

For three days and nights this horror continued, but at least, down in the inky darkness of the basement, I was free to hold and to be held by Dean, to rest my head on his beating chest and to imagine that we were once again on the beach, looking up at the stars.

Dean wanted to make love to me, but I was shy with Claudia, Andrés and Flowers in the room with us, and I quietly spurned his advances. Dean was much more accustomed to this type of confinement than I was; he was much bolder with his sexual advances and unconcerned about what anybody thought, and he couldn't understand why I was refusing him. On one occasion he grew furious with me and slipped off his belt in one swift motion. I knew what was about to take place.

It wasn't enough that I had to endure the interrogations in the kitchen above: now I was going to have to take it from Dean. Again. I closed my eyes and tried to prepare myself for the first blow from his belt. It came with great force and a cracking sound like a whip. I didn't cry out, but I did cry.

On the third day of interrogation, I spoke with Aguilar directly. "Captain Aguilar," I began, "Isn't it obvious to you that we don't know anything about any bomb? If we happen to die in your custody, which believe me is not an impossibility, you will not get the answers you are seeking, and you'll have to answer to the American and Argentinean governments."

He shrugged as if to say he could care less about what other governments might think. It was clear the man was a megalomaniac who considered himself to be his own government, his own boss, and acted accordingly and with apparent immunity, at least up until now. I could see that tactic wasn't going to get me anywhere.

So I said, "Look, you obviously like nice things. This is a beautiful home. I could feel very comfortable here because it reminds me of the home I grew up in—on a smaller scale, of course. Dean grew up much better off than I did. Our families are quite rich, you see. So if you'll just let Dean call his parents and let me call my sister in Mexico City, we can easily make some sort of arrangement that will secure your belief in our innocence."

I studied his reaction to these words very carefully. He was stone-faced, as I expected. He did not say anything immediately, but I was sure that I had seen a spark in his eyes for the briefest moment.

I was returned to the basement, where I told Dean what had transpired in the kitchen above us, and how I felt sure Aguilar was considering the offer I had made to him. Dean was quiet for a second and I assumed he was taking in this hopeful news, but because of the dark I couldn't see his face.

Then he grabbed me in the dark and shook me. "Why the hell did you have to do that?" He slapped me hard. "They're not going to let us buy ourselves out of this fucking hell-hole! Now they're gonna kill us for sure! What were you thinking, *tonta!*"

He really rattled my confidence, and I began to doubt myself for a minute. I tore myself away from him and retreated to a corner of the damp basement, where I sat alone and finally cried myself to sleep.

The next morning, Dean and I were hauled up to the kitchen, this time together. There was a telephone on the desk, and Captain Aguilar was alone this time. I knew right away what this meant: my offer had been accepted. Dean was suspicious, however, and I could see the paranoia in his eyes.

But we sat down and I looked up at Aguilar. "How much is this going to cost us?" I asked matter-of-factly and with as much sincerity as I could muster. He quoted me a figure, and I picked up the phone. The whole time he kept his hand on his holstered gun. I dialed the number for Alejandra, who—thank God!—picked up immediately.

"Maridée?" She sounded more worried than I had ever heard her.

"Yes, it's me, Alejandra." I wasn't sure what she knew, what she had heard about my absence.

"Where have you been? Are you all right?" The sound of her voice made me break down on the spot. I had trouble choking out my words through my tears.

"Alejandra…I'm in trouble…" There was a pause on the other end of the line.

"What kind of trouble, Maridée? What do you need? Where are you?"

"I've been in jail, and it's been…. Look, Dean and I need eight thousand dollars to get out."

"Dean? Oh, God, Mother is going to have a heart attack for sure this time." The thought of my mother's inevitable reaction caused my throat to tighten up.

"Do you *have* to call her?" I pleaded. I knew the answer before she spoke, and I began to steel myself for what I knew was coming, what I had feared all along.

• • •

"Maridée, I don't have that kind of money, and your visa is up anyway. Mother has been calling ten times a day wanting to hear from you, demanding that you come back immediately. She's threatening all kinds of actions."

What else could I do? I told her to go ahead and get the money however she could, even if she had to call our mother. The situation was life or death.

Next, it was Dean's turn. He called his mother and she agreed to wire five thousand immediately. Minutes later, Alejandra called. The remainder of the eight thousand was also being wired directly to Aguilar's account.

Dean still didn't believe we were going to be released. He was sure they would take the money and then kill us anyway. He asked Aguilar if we could be allowed to take a shower before being returned to Mexico City to face our deportation, and he hesitantly agreed.

Once in the bathroom, with guards outside the door, Dean climbed out the window and hoisted himself up the brick wall of the bathroom, clinging to the tiny edge that stuck out beyond the mortar. He must have looked like a spider, clinging with just his fingertips and toes. He somehow managed to squirm through the tiny window opening high in the wall, and he fell two stories to the hard ground below. There were more guards waiting for him there, having somehow been alerted or maybe just in case he tried to escape, I don't know.

They caught him as he fell, and they took out brass knuckles and beat him to a pulp. He was deposited back down into the basement where the rest of us waited. I was furious that he would risk his life like that, that he would risk *our* freedom on such a reckless stunt, and most of all, that he was obviously prepared to leave me there all alone, possibly to die.

Still, I reasoned that he was not on his medication and that can be a scary thing.

We waited in the dark of our basement prison for a word from above, for mercy from God and our parents, for freedom from manacles and chains, and for the light of a new day.

Margarita, Jorge (her husband), me, Alejandra and Chito (their wedding day), Monoyo and his date

··· 10 ···

The minute the money had been paid, Dean and I were immediately sent our own ways. Dean was driven to the Texas border because he was an American citizen. I don't remember the details, but somehow the dogs Nicolás, Tarkus and Nieves were returned to Dean unharmed. I boarded a flight to Buenos Aires, to my mother…and to hell.

As relieved as I was to be out of jail and away from the torture and abuse of both Dean and Aguilar, the second-to-the-last place on earth I wanted to be was in Argentina. Remember, I had vowed never to return and had truly endured the worst life had to offer in order to stay away. But return I did.

My mother met me at the airport and I'm sure she had been planning a few choice words for me. A year and a half is a long time in which to prepare a biting sermon, but she was so shocked when she saw me, she was speechless. I wasn't just thin, I was nearly emaciated, and the last time she had seen me I was still overweight from my stay at Doctor Grana's clinic. Life on the road followed by a few weeks in a Mexican jail are a sure-fire way to shed pounds, although I can't say that I'd recommend it.

Once we were on the way home, she finally looked over at me. She stared for quite some time, and I could sense the flood of emotions passing through her: anger at my disobedience, compassion for what I had been through, denial of any responsibility on her part, but mostly, disappointment at not being able to go through with the sermon she had had circulating in her head for over a year.

Finally her features relaxed, and I assumed she figured she would only have to postpone that sermon for a day or two and not chuck it altogether.

"Well, it's good to see you again, Maridée." I was about to lie and say it was good to see her again, too, but she turned away and looked out the window of the taxi. We rode the rest of the way home in silence, and after a few moments I fell asleep.

When we arrived at the house, I carried my little bag containing the few articles of clothing I owned and headed off to my bedroom, but my mother stopped me. "Oh, Maridée, I forgot to tell you—your brother has moved back home and has taken over your old room. You'll have to sleep in the guest room for now…" Her voice just trailed off like a car running out of gas.

I passed my stepfather in the foyer but neither one of us said a word to each other.

I went into the guest room and locked the door behind me, wishing to lock out my mother, my past and my thoughts all in one simple motion. I dropped my little bag on the floor at the foot of the bed, and undressed. The guest bath was spacious and warm. I filled the tub, adding a little scented bath oil. The water was steaming and I slid into the perfumed liquid. I closed my eyes and tried to clear my mind of everything. Off I floated....

When I woke up I was in bed, and there was someone tapping softly on the bedroom door. "Maridée, you have a telephone call!" my mother sang out softly, "Are you awake? It's Dean, calling from America. Do you want to take it?"

I rolled over and picked up the phone next to the bed. "What the fuck, dude?" I was barely awake and my voice was scratchy.

"That's my María!" Dean sounded too awake. I considered hanging up on him and going back to sleep, but he went on, "Man, is Texas a drag, María, I hope you never have to go there. I called my mom the minute I crossed the border and got a ticket to L.A. You wouldn't believe the weather here—it's great! The sun is shining and the beaches rock! There's only one thing missing, Babe, and that's you. Why don't you come up for a while?"

My eyes rolled back in my head, and I said, "Dean, you're impossible. Look, I'm just waking up — can you call me later?"

"Just waking up? It's four in the afternoon!" I could hear traffic in the background; it sounded like rush hour.

"What day is it?"

"It's fucking Tuesday, where have you been?"

"Tuesday? God, I must have been tired!" Two days had passed already! "Dean, can you call me later? I've got to get up."

We said brief goodbyes and I hung up. I was still having a hard time waking up, but I got out of bed and threw on some clothes. I found my mother in the dining room, sitting at a table and just leafing through some magazine. She looked up at me over her reading glasses.

"You must have been exhausted, Maridée. I was about to call the po...." She stopped in mid-sentence, realizing that she had just said about the worst thing she could have possibly come up with in this situation.

"I didn't mean...I'm.... Well, would you like some lunch? Or breakfast, I suppose? I could make you some eggs, if you like...."

"Eggs would be fine." That old depression was coming over me again, I could feel it. This big house with so many lonely, ugly memories, the sound of my mother's voice, everything I saw or heard made me want to just tune it all out, to run away, to get high or do whatever it took to feel free of it all.

I followed my mother to the kitchen and sat at the little table as she started to pull out all the pots and pans, food from the fridge, and what seemed like a million utensils. "Please don't make this a huge production, mamá, just fry a fucking egg and get it over with, won't you?"

"I just wanted to make you a nice, healthy.... Oh, all right, Maridée. Have it your way." She started to put everything away in silence, obviously defeated.

She fried one egg and tossed it on a plate. Handing it to me, she sat down across the table and watched me eat. "So how is Dean, Maridée? Where was he calling from—Texas was it?"

"California. Los Angeles." I said between bites.

"Oh, Los Angeles, where they make the movies! And how is he? You know he's been calling day and night, but I wanted to let you sleep. He seems like a nice boy, Maridée. We've been talking quite a lot."

"Yeah, right." If she only knew....

"Well, he *has* told me about his fine family—they seem very respectable and quite wealthy on top of that!"

"He wants me to come to Los Angeles." I said it without any emotion at all.

There was a moment of silence, and when I had finished the egg, she took the plate and set it in the sink for the maid to wash later. Then she turned to me, her eyes narrowed, and out came the finger, wagging in my face like a dog's tail.

"There is no way, after all that has happened, after all *we* have been through, that I am ever letting you out of this country again unless you are married, or, God forbid, you turn twenty-one first. That decision is final! But if Dean wants to come here to do the proper thing and marry you, that's another thing."

I got up from the table and was about to go back to my room when I suddenly found myself in the twilight zone.

"Anyway, I was thinking about getting you an apartment, Maridée. What would you think of that?" She could change lanes faster than a stock car driver! Talk about obtuse.... "Something near here, of course, in the neighborhood. It wouldn't be big, and you'd have to get a job and take over the rent as soon as possible—I'm not rich, you know. But you're a grown woman now and I'm sure you want your privacy...."

I took two seconds to consider my options: there weren't many at this point. I knew I was going to be out of the house and out of the fucking country as soon as possible, one way or the other. An apartment would take care of Part One of my plan for the moment, and that would give me more time to work on Part Two. I agreed.

A couple of hours later Dean called again. "What's shakin', Babe?" He was definitely in the Californian mode.

"Well, for starters, my mother just offered to get me my own apartment. There must be something going on that she's not telling me. It's not like her, considering all that's just happened."

Dean didn't have to ponder this one at all and he quickly shot back, "It's a trap, María, she's afraid you'll disappear again. This is her way of trying to keep her clutches on you."

"So what? I can still take off anytime I want to. In fact, it'll be easier than having to sneak out of her house in the middle of the night."

"Good point, but listen, why don't you just forego the apartment and meet me here in L.A.?" He sounded sincere, but he also sounded stoned.

One part of me wanted to be free from Dean and his violent, psychotic and totally irrational outbursts. In fact, if I never saw him again I would be quite content. The jail experience had put an end to any hold he had over me emotionally, and for once I felt free to go on with my life, except for one thing: my mother.

I searched my mind for options. If I go with Dean, it'll be the same thing all over again. Dean was a walking time bomb, and with him came the terrible rages and beatings. If I stayed here, my mother would drive me insane and I would have to kill her. I hated everything about Argentina and my mother for what I had gone through — being abandoned and ignored all my childhood, the terror of the mental hospital, the criticisms, the control. My fear of Dean was real, but I could handle it. My hatred for everything and everyone at home was so deeply rooted in my psyche, that it was insurmountable for me at the time.

"Dean, let me think about it, let me clear my head for a couple of days, will you? Why don't you call back on Thursday?" I knew that I was just buying time, putting off the inevitable, and I didn't even want to bring up my mother's crazy suggestion that we get married. Dean was crazy enough to go for the idea, and that was the last thing I wanted in my life.

"Whatever you say, but you know we're not done yet—we'll never be done. You're my girl, María."

"I know, Dean." We hung up and I sat on the edge of the bed, trying to think.

That night my sleep was interrupted with terrible nightmares. I dreamt that Dean and I were in jail, chained to the wall. He was angry with me for something I had said, and he was threatening to beat me, to torture me, and then to kill me. The scary thing was, Dean was naked and dead and his skin was a waxy pale bluish white. I was wearing a wedding dress. All I could do was watch as Dean furiously tried to break out of the chains so he could attack me. I could see that every time he pulled against the chains, a little of the mortar would crumble away and the chains were becoming looser and looser. I was in a wild panic, knowing that at any moment the mortar would give, Dean would be free, and I would be beaten to death. Outside the cell, Aguilar was pacing back and forth, laughing madly at my hysteria, only it wasn't really Aguilar, it was my mother. I awoke screaming, my bed was soaked with sweat.

In the morning I stumbled into the dining room for breakfast. I could hear my mother talking on the phone in the kitchen. She sounded very excited about something, very happy, laughing and cooing like a baby. Who the hell could she be talking to? I strained my ears to try to pick up some of the conversation. When I heard her say, "I don't think she's awake yet," I knew instantly who it was.

She stuck her head through the doorway and saw me sitting at the table. "Oh, wait a minute, Dean, she is awake after all. Let me pass the phone to her."

It made sense. My two biggest nightmares had joined forces against me. I felt completely overpowered, helpless to the point of desperation. She handed me the phone and I held it for a moment, looking for some way to use it to kill myself. No sharp edges. Bludgeoning myself wouldn't work— I'd pass out before I would die. It wouldn't fit in my mouth for a quick strangulation, either. Lacking any other ideas, I spoke to it. It sounded like Dean.

"Good morning, Sleepy-head!"

"What do you want, Dean?"

"I want my fiancée to speak to her husband-to-be with a little more enthusiasm, Babe!"

Now she had done it! My mother still stood in the doorway, watching me. I shot her a death glance and her smile slid of her face. She turned and exited into the kitchen.

"What did that *bruja* say to you, Dean?" I was fuming!

"What's with the attitude, María? Having a hard time waking up in the morning?"

"What makes you think I would ever marry you, you bastard?"

"Because it's the only way for you to get out from under your mother's fucking control, that's why, my love. And besides, you're crazy about me! You're my girl, remember?"

Once again, I was trapped. He was right, and I knew it. I shut my eyes and prayed to God, to the blessed Virgin, and to Jesus in Heaven. As I opened my eyes, I saw that my prayers had been ignored, yet again. I was alive, still in my mother's house, and still on the phone with...my future husband.

Yes, Dean knew how to make me melt....

Living in Los Angeles with Dean

··· 11 ···

At first my mother insisted on having the wedding in Buenos Aires, but Dean wanted Los Angeles—and I wanted out! So they compromised, and decided to hold it in Mexico City. The thought of committing a sacrilege—I mean "consecrating a sacrament"—in Mexico just seemed too perfect! Why not enter the bond of holy matrimony in the same country that had bound us to a jail cell wall and dunked my head in a barrel of shit-water?

There were just too many correlations between the events fate had thrust on us before and what we were about to enter into willingly now. The problem was, marriage seemed to be the only way I could get out of the frying pan in Argentina, and I just had to hope for the ability to walk on fire once we got to Mexico. In other words, step two in my plan was promoted to step one—get the hell out of Argentina, then deal with the situation at hand.

My mother arrived in Mexico City. I was with her, of course, but she was the one who "arrived"; I was only there like the rest of her baggage—to serve its purpose and stay out of the way. I knew the part by heart, but this time it actually served my plan as well.

We met Dean in the lobby bar of the very fancy hotel where he was supposedly staying. He was sober enough to impress my mother, and she gushed charm all over the hotel. The two of them made quite a picture together. After visiting for a couple of hours my mother announced that we were all exhausted from the trip and needed to go on to our rooms. We needed to be up early to prepare for the ceremony!

I followed my mother dutifully up to the room we had reserved, and Dean stayed in the bar. When the bar finally closed, he went off to his room — a park bench across from the hotel. He was low on cash and had decided to spend the money his mother had given him for travel expenses on partying.

Needless to say, he was up with the sun and waiting for us again in the bar the next morning. "Have you been here all night?" my mother asked jokingly. Dean and I looked at each other.

"Well, Dean," my mother went on without missing a beat, "I hope you slept as well as I did. Aren't the beds comfortable here? I'm starving! Shall we get a bite to eat?" She headed off to the hotel restaurant. Dean and I followed a few yards behind her. As usual, my mother talked nonstop. She always expresses what she sees with her eyes through her mouth. So having a quiet moment around her is close to impossible.

When she was pretty much out of hearing range, I whispered to Dean. "You don't really want to go through with this, do you?"

"Not on your life!"

We both smiled and picked up the pace to catch up with Mother. At times like this, I really almost liked Dean. Too bad these moments were so rare....

We all enjoyed a peaceful and relatively pleasant breakfast. As the plates were being cleared by a young Mexican girl around my age, my mother signaled to me to look at her by tilting her head toward her, opening her eyes big and puckering her lips, an expression very common to her when she wanted to put somebody down. Noticing my mother's glance, the girl smiled at us.

"¡Buenos días! ¿Como estás?" my mother was forced to say.

Then my mother whispered just loud enough for the girl to hear, "Look at that girl! Aren't you glad, Maridée, that you are marrying so well? At least you'll never have to serve food and clear away the plates of strangers like this poor thing!"

I almost dropped dead of embarrassment. I looked at the girl and saw her kind but weary expression. I saw how she tried to carry herself with dignity but was having a hard time believing it herself, her eyes always downcast and servile. For a moment I lost myself in thought as I studied her.

And then Dean spoke.

"Margot, María and I have decided not to marry, after all," he explained without a trace of regret. Forgetting all about the bus girl, I was thrown into high gear, ready for the attack, the retreat, and the search and rescue of the battle that was about to begin. My eyes darted about the room, searching for snipers hidden behind plants or columns, hit-men or mercenary psychiatrists hired by my mother for just such an assault—there were none. Strangely, my mother had just picked up the check and was scrutinizing it.

"What's that, Dean?" she asked distractedly. She hadn't been paying attention! A false start! She had won this first volley.

"I said, 'María and I have decided not to marry after all.' I'm sorry you have come all this way, and have had such high expectations, just to be disappointed," Dean was full of self-confidence, but spoke kindly. I slowly backed my chair away from the table, ready to make a run for it if things got as ugly as I expected.

Like a chameleon, Mom turned white to match her roots. It was a direct hit, a tying point for our side. She clutched at her heart in her very best Sarah Bernhardt performance to date, her eyes widened like saucers of blood, her lips snapped open and shut almost noiselessly. Then just as dramatically, the blood drained from her eyes, her cheeks apparently absorbing every drop, turning a deep scarlet. Her eyes narrowed and began to dart between the two of us, back and forth, loaded weapons aiming first at me, then Dean, unsure which one of us to assassinate first.

"What are you telling me?" she screeched, and everyone in the dining room just about ducked for cover! I was too terrified to speak. I looked at Dean, imploring him to sacrifice himself as the first casualty on our side. This was a crucial moment; it was up to Dean to rescue me if he wanted me to follow him to California. If he failed in his mission, I would be dead. I think he knew that, because he held up a defensive hand towards my mother and started to try to explain, but my mother launched herself out of her chair and tore out of the restaurant like a cruise missile. It appeared that we had won the battle!

We left without paying, of course, and headed to Dean's room—the park bench—where we sat for a moment in silence, just happy to be alive. And *free*!

After we caught our breath, Dean began to tell me about Los Angeles...*all* about Los Angeles! I heard about the many beaches populated with surfers, muscle men, and drug dealers...about the nightlife in Hollywood, the thousands of bars, and the drugs...about the millions of movie stars, the expensive cars, and the drugs...about the hustlers, the whores, and the drugs.... My mouth was watering! He told me how he imagined our life there, how carefree and fucked-up we would be, and how we would finally be happy together in this amazing paradise.

My mind was reeling with his perfectly painted descriptions, and I was buying into it. He was turning on the old charm, which was what first snared me in Mexico City, a thousand years and a million beatings ago. If he truly felt this way about it, maybe there was a chance....

Across the wide boulevard we saw my mother throw herself into a taxi. A hotel porter quickly deposited her luggage in the trunk of the vehicle. As it pulled away from the curb, our eyes met through the dirty glass of the window. It was like watching a stranger on her way to some other destination, involved in some other life, and I thought no more about it. I was so drugged with hopes for the future, with dreams of a happy life in California, with fantasies about this "new Dean."

I could already smell the Pacific breeze, and feel it lifting my hair. The past floated away like a piece of beach trash drawn out with the tide.

··· 12 ···

Two days later we were in the tiny cottage in Los Angeles that Dean had rented from a Mexican lady named Clotilde. Our cottage was in the back yard of the nice big house she shared with her daughter Cristal, and the four of us became fast friends.

Los Angeles was every bit as beautiful as Dean had described, perhaps even more so. I had never seen anything like Redondo Beach and we spent a great deal of time there just bumming around, playing in the surf and tanning on the warm sand. And I loved to people watch.

The first few weeks were as wonderful as Dean had promised, and I was thrilled. Every day was a festival of alcohol and pot, and we indulged like there was no tomorrow. We would walk along the beach until we collapsed from either exhaustion or the massive volume of whiskey. Dean's mom had agreed to reinstate his allowance, and he stretched it like a rubber band so that he wouldn't have to go get a job, God forbid. So usually we didn't eat much, and saved all of our money to *par-taaay*.

Then the newness of being reunited began to wear off. Dean and I weren't really communicating—we were barely functioning at all—and his patience began to wear thin. What do you know, history *does* repeat itself! Little disagreements began to crop up here and there, then full-fledged arguments about who drank whose whiskey, or who smoked more than their share of the pot, or simply, "Why are you looking at me that way?"

When the fists came out of retirement I knew I had better do something to secure an escape route. I was totally dependent on Dean because of the money and because I didn't speak a word of English. This time I began working on both Part One and Part Two of my solution at the same time. I forced myself to learn ten new words of English every day, and I started to look for a job. The first day I learned *please*, *Marlboro* and *pussy*. It wasn't a flying start, but it was something!

I found a job as a bus girl in a very nice restaurant. On my first day of work, the image of the bus girl at the hotel in Mexico City came back to me, along with my mother's words about marrying well and never having to clear the dirty plates of strangers. I wondered if her comments had been a prophecy or a curse. More than likely it was nothing more than the way fate likes to operate. When my visa expired after thirty days in L.A., I became one more wetback in the States.

It wasn't too bad, though, and I had already been a waitress at *Torremolinos* in Mexico City. My real problem was the language barrier. The only upside to this was that when I would show up for work with a black eye or a bruised face, I never had to explain how I had gotten them because of my limited English.

I remember one customer, a rather good-looking man, asked me for Sweet and Low. I misunderstood him and thought he was trying to pick me up, to flatter me. I smiled brightly, thanked him, and grabbed his money off the table! He was pretty amused, though, and refused to take the money back once I understood what he had meant. I was so embarrassed! When he left the restaurant, he smiled at me and gave me a torn corner of his bill on which he had written his name and phone number. His name was Roger. I smiled and cast my eyes to my feet, but I took his number and stuffed it in my pocket.

A few nights after the Sweet and Low episode, Dean and I really got into it, and I fled the house bruised and beaten for the last time. I was furious and frightened, terrified to be alone in this Paradise Lost. I cried relentlessly, sobbing as I headed for the beach, not knowing what to do next or where to turn. I only knew that I could never go back to that bastard.

I was nearing the beach and I reached into my pocket to grab a smoke when I felt the little torn corner of the bill from the restaurant that the nice man had given me. At first I was going to throw it away and I headed for the trash can in front of the convenience store I was just passing. I held it in my hand, all crumpled up, and watched as my hand hovered over the hole. It wouldn't let go of the paper.

I knew that it would be wrong...it would be crazy to call this stranger at a time like this! He didn't know me from Adam, so why would he be willing to help me? But this piece of paper represented my last hope. And so what if he did hang up on me?? At least I would have tried!

I walked the few steps over to the pay phone on the outside of the store. I cried as I fumbled for change in my pocket. I could feel my face swelling up from the beating, and I had to brush away tears as I deposited the coins into the phone. I was sobbing so hard that I could barely see the number that Roger had written. Oh, please be there, my unfamiliar savior! Dear God, please let him be there, please send me some help! Maybe I don't deserve it, but I really need it.

I dialed the number and let it ring, each buzz counting scores of tears chasing down my cheeks. I was about to hang up when Roger answered the phone. "Hello?" his voice, so pleasant and carefree. I was afraid to dirty it with my pathetic intrusion.

"Hello?" he said again. Would he be my savior?

I was afraid, but I answered him in my broken English, *"Is Roger? Is María...from restorante. Give number me...in restorante?"* I was frustrated and embarrassed. Why wouldn't the words come to me? He would never be able to understand.

"María! It's great to hear from you! How are you?"

All I could do was shake. "Please...help...me..."

It was all I could get out. The call was to a number outside the area code I was calling from, and a voice interrupted my plea for help with a demand to insert another quarter. I finally found one just in time to prevent a disconnection, and there was Roger's voice again. "Where are you, María? What's happened?"

I looked up at the street sign. I was at the corner of Thornton and something else, I don't remember now. My English was so bad that he couldn't understand what I was saying, and I was crying so hard I don't think I would have been any more understandable in Spanish. I just stood there for a few minutes, the phone pressed against my swelling face, crying. There was no one on foot anywhere near me—nobody walks anywhere in Los Angeles—and again the recorded voice asked for more money! I tried the coin return and, by a miraculous act of God, there was a quarter there. I put it in, and it worked.

I was starting to spell out the names of the cross streets where I was standing before the line was disconnected for good. I wasn't really sure if Roger had understood. I really didn't believe he would come and rescue me anyhow. Why should he? I sat on the sidewalk and just cried, my head in my hands, my knees tucked up under my chin.

I stayed that way for over an hour, each passing minute an eternity in which I prayed for help, prayed for Roger to appear, and then convinced myself that I would die here on this corner.

At last I heard a car cruising by at a very slow speed. Just as it passed me, I saw out of the corner of my tear-filled eyes a brilliant red glow—the brake lights of a car stopping. Roger jumped out of the car and ran over to me. "María? Are you María?" He was out of breath; he must have been driving all over the place, running up to every Hispanic-looking teenager he saw, asking if they were María!

I looked up at him, stunned with disbelief. "Roger?" I burst into tears again. My prayers had, for once, been answered. The look on his face when he saw my swollen features, the scrapes and cuts, my stringy hair, displayed such deep concern and compassion that I felt he was not a mortal man but a beautiful angel, so full of grace. He helped me up off the sidewalk and led me slowly towards his cream-colored BMW. I was dirty and tear-stained and afraid to stand too close to him, but he put his arm around me and pulled me close as he walked me to the passenger side of his car.

We drove in silence for an hour. At the time I didn't know where we were, what he understood of my situation, what he wanted from me, or where we were going – we just drove. When we arrived at his apartment he parked the car and ran around to open my door, just like in the movies. He extended his hand to me and I accepted his help. He led me by the hand to the front door of his apartment.

He was behaving like a true gentleman, but I was still unsure of his intentions. The chance that he was simply a nice person wasn't exactly high on the list of possible motives. He showed me around the apartment, which was large, clean and beautifully decorated with expensive things. He was speaking in English and the sound of it was very kind, but for all I knew he was telling me that this would be about the time he usually murders and eats his dates!

He pointed me to the bedroom and gestured that I should sleep in his bed. I meekly shook my head no and pointed to the sofa. To my surprise he nodded and went to bring some sheets and a pillow, then went to work making up a place for me to sleep. I slept very little, but I did so completely unmolested and when I awoke the next morning Roger was already in the kitchen preparing breakfast for us.

• • •

That day several of Roger's friends stopped by to visit and I'm sure they were pretty shocked to see who he had sleeping on his sofa. I weighed about a hundred pounds, my face was all bruised and swollen, and my hair was long and stringy. I couldn't say much more than "please" and "Marlboro." The third word in my repertoire I just didn't bring up! I didn't want to show off or to give anyone ideas. But Roger never acted embarrassed by my presence and never seemed to apologize to his friends.

Several days passed. In the evenings we would sit together on his balcony with a cocktail and we would talk. We never really understood what the other one was saying until much later in the night—the more our brains became lubricated, the better we were able to understand each other, or at least that's how it seemed.

Roger was one of those people who document significant strides in their lives with rolls of glossy film stored lovingly in bulging albums. That was how I got a good feel for who he was. As corny as it sounds, language really was secondary.

One day I indicated — I don't remember how — that I wanted to invite a girlfriend over for dinner. He let me know that I was welcome to do that. Lilli was a hooker and she looked the part, but Roger treated her like she was visiting royalty. Now that's what I call class! What a pair: a homeless girl and a bimbo in yuppieland!

The next day Roger began introducing me to the ladies in his apartment building, apparently in an attempt to upgrade my associates. I may have led a rather bohemian life the prior few years, but you'll remember I grew up eating off of silver plates and being served by maids, so I was certainly able to mix with, if not completely out-class, his Valley Girl friends, and I know it must have surprised the hell out of him to discover that I may have been friends with Lilli, but I was not cut from the same cloth.

You see, that's a common misconception Americans tend to share: that simply because we don't speak English, we are poverty-stricken, ignorant and socially inferior laborers. And it's funny: when you go to a country where you don't speak the language, people think you're deaf! For some reason they yell at you *("Do-nde es-tah the bathroom?")* Has that ever happened to you when you've traveled? Many people would say that's the price you pay when you move to another country, but it just seems wrong, since the world belongs to all of us.

Anyway, Christmas was approaching and since I had so impressively shifted from associating with hookers to socialites, Roger invited me to share Christmas with his family. Still, because of the language thing I was hesitant. "Oh, look Mother," I could hear him in my mind, "I brought a bus girl home from the restaurant—can I keep her?" I had seen pictures of his grand family estate and it only conjured uncomfortable memories of my own past, so I declined his sweet offer.

Well, Christmas passed and, stupid kid that I was, I was starting to miss Dean. I called Clotilde to check on him and she told me Dean had been arrested. Again. Drinking and driving, this time. At any given time Dean had a list of pending offenses, so if he ever got pulled over for something lame, it meant a couple of days behind bars. It was a last resort to send Dean on an errand because you knew he'd most likely be gone for a week or so. This time I was smart enough not to bail him out.

I begged Roger to take me to get my things. I only had the clothes I was wearing the night he picked me up from the street corner, and I had been trying to wear Roger's clothes, which really didn't work too well. I couldn't find my key, so Roger reluctantly broke in to one of the back windows, crawled through the opening and found the closet where my things were. Poor Roger, the ultimate yuppie, climbing through the window of some little bungalow to steal some girl's clothes! How I must have terrorized him!

I kept watch just in case by some miracle Dean got out of jail early and came home. But our mission was successful and we made it back to Roger's apartment without a problem. Still, I couldn't stop thinking about Dean. A few days later I just decided that, as absolutely perfect as Roger had been, I was bored. I left one day and went back to Dean, and I never saw Roger again. I don't know what I was thinking. I wish I could see Roger again to thank him for all his help and to apologize for leaving the way I did.

I suppose we all have regrets in our life. My handling of Roger is one of mine. I so want to make it right with him somehow. I hope one day I can hug him and tell him that I can speak English now, and that I'm not that dumb anymore. The saddest thing is that I never knew Roger's last name, otherwise I'd be trying to find him, first and foremost, like I said, because he was a beautiful human being, and second—what an idiot I was! What a "catch" I lost!

Dean and I took each other back, but he never apologized for the way he had beaten me. Maybe he didn't remember—sometimes I think God gives us blackouts so that we can go on living with ourselves the next day. But we fell back into honeymoon mode for a few weeks, which eventually drifted once again into drunken brawls.

Not much later I was out of the house again. By this time my sister Alejandra was fed up with my choice of friends and boyfriends and she refused to help me. So once again I called my mother and begged for a ticket home. I told her I had learned my lesson, I was no longer a kid, and if she wouldn't help me I would go back to Dean and let him kill me. She thought about the two choices a little too long for my comfort, but she finally relented.

I went to a cop I'd met several times while filing various domestic abuse charges against Dean, which were always dropped the next day. He agreed to take me by the house and then to the airport. Dean was blown away when we walked in. He tried all that macho testosterone shit about "if I can't have you nobody can." He actually tried to bar us from entering. "You can't come in – you don't have a warrant," he boasted.

"Don't need one," the officer replied casually. "I've been invited in by María here." This infuriated Dean—nobody told Dean he was wrong!

"You can't do this to me, María!" he yelled, practically spitting.

"I have a cop at my side, he has a gun at his side and you have to *step* aside, *novio*," I said in a tone that let him know I was determined to keep this departure civil yet controlled. His face turned red and he stepped towards me a little too threateningly. The cop delivered a warning in Dean's own language: with his hands wrapped tightly around Dean's throat.

I got my things and we left. Dean chased the patrol car for almost four blocks, screaming for me not to leave him, to give him another chance, that he would die without me. I had heard it all before.

"Go ahead, Dean," I thought as I took my seat on the plane, my memory going over and over the incident. "You might as well plan on dying without me, because you're not going to be dying with me!"

Skinny Maria, too many nights of partying.

··· 13 ···

It had been a very long, very humbling flight back to Buenos Aires. I reluctantly left the plane with the other passengers after having been denied my request that the jet let off all the other travelers, then taxi further down the lot and let me out near the far fence.

Fortunately my sister Margarita was there with my mother to pick me up. I walked up to them, tired and more than a little intoxicated from twenty-something hours of scotch snorkeling.

"Well, here you are," said Mother as she turned and headed for the airport exit. Margarita and I caught up with her and we headed for the car lot. Margarita was asking about the flight, trying to make small talk to fill the chasm of silence. "Don't talk to her, Margarita. She's drunk and she won't remember a word of what you say five minutes from now. Let's just go home."

Well, welcome home, Maridée!

In the taxi on the way home, I forced enough courage to say something. "I guess I have the guest room again..."

Without turning her head my mother answered, "Certainly not, my doctor has warned me of fatal coronary arrest if you return to my house." Margarita quietly explained to me that I had a place waiting for me: the same one I might have had the last time I was in Argentina. I was being dropped off there. I was actually somewhat relieved! Margarita smiled at me and I knew she had some kind of secret in store.

We were nearing the beautiful historic district where my mother lived and I was wondering what had happened to the little place where I was supposed to be dumped off. Had the driver forgotten, or taken a wrong turn? Just as I was thinking this, the taxi pulled into the drive of a beautiful old home, three stories tall and unsurpassably enchanting! It was so romantic in its architecture that you could almost hear the whispers of elegant Colonial ghosts within the walls.

The taxi stopped before the elaborate carved stone entryway and the driver got out and opened the trunk to retrieve my little bag.

"Give her the key, Margarita." My mother never even turned around.

"Your room is off the right corridor, all the way at the end, the last door on the left. I offer classes here during the day, but at night you have the run of the house. There are to be no parties, no drugs, and no liquor bottles lying around anywhere—there are small children here from morning till early afternoon. You will find employment as soon as possible. You will adhere to these simple rules or you will be out on the street. You are not my daughter; you are a tenant. Is that understood?"

I had known that things would be uncomfortable, but I hadn't expected this. I couldn't have hurt Mother that badly, could I? Margarita had handed me the key, but she was afraid to look me in the eye, and she kept her gaze in her lap. I got out of the taxi and picked up my bag. I heard my mother tell the driver to go on, and slowly, painfully slowly, they drove out of sight.

"She really knows how to deflate a person's homecoming," I said out loud as I headed for the front door.

Inside the house was spectacular, full of exquisite antiques, chandeliers, and the magnificent hardwood floors on each story were laid with regal red carpets. "She always did have taste," I whispered to myself after entering the main salon.

I made my way to my bedroom, which had been recently cleaned and prepared with fresh bed linens. The bathroom was similar to the one in the guest room at home and was also set up with bath oils and salts, new luxurious towels and a silver champagne bucket—without the champagne, of course.

The following day I wandered about the old house and found a sewing machine in one of the rooms. In a closet I found some great fabric. I had been in Los Angeles long enough to observe the current fashions, especially those of Roger's female friends in the apartment complex, and I had really wanted a particular kind of short pant they were all wearing. So I decided to make myself a pair.

A few days later when Margarita came over to take me out for lunch, I wore my new pants. Not only did Margarita fall in love with them and ask me to make her a pair, so did just about every girl we passed. People started asking me where I had gotten them. I told them I had just returned from Los Angeles and that all the movie stars were wearing this type of pants.

I started taking orders for them, so many that I had to hire a seamstress to make them. The icy gulf between my mother and me slowly began to melt just a tiny bit, as she saw my industriousness and success with the pants endeavor. I'm sure it also helped that I kept the house impeccably clean and there were no reports of wild drugs and alcohol orgies. Within six months I had made enough profit to take a 'vacation'—with no return ticket!

I booked a train tour of South America for two weeks. My mother even arranged for a travel visa with my promise to return immediately after. She even packed me a care basket! She took me to the train station and, as I was boarding the train, she shouted out, "You will be back, won't you?" I smiled and waved. I felt very guilty doing this, but it was the only way I could bail out of Argentina, still being a minor.

The trip through Bolivia, Peru, Ecuador and the other countries of my continent was wonderfully relaxing and unbelievably beautiful! I had time to think and to reflect on all I had been through the past couple of years. I felt like I was finally getting my shit together. Now I had had a taste of earning a good income, being more independent, and I loved it. It felt so good, and this trip was turning out to be a great reward — except that in my "rotten-tomato" head I had ulterior motives.

I met three guys on the train and we started hanging out together. They were really nice and were also on vacation. We rode the train all over, through mountains and jungles, cities and tiny villages. We met a couple more backpackers and invited them to join us. The six of us had a great time, laughing and crying and telling the stories of our lives. We decided to head towards Colombia and all that country had to offer partiers like us. All along the way we met other people, they joined us, and by the time we reached Colombia we were a pack of about thirty kids all traveling together and raising hell. By now I had been behaving nicely for way too many months and I needed to be out there partying like there was no tomorrow, so I found the way and the company.

Before I knew it, almost four weeks had passed and I was beginning to run out of money. I still had a few hundred in travelers' checks, but I knew that it was only a matter of a very short time before that would be gone. At the next big train station I got off and, working up a false sense of hysteria and a few tears, I found a pay phone and called the number on my travelers' checks. "Hello? Help me, please, they're gone—they're just all gone! I was asleep on the train and when I woke up they were all gone!"

"Miss?" said a voice on the other end, "Slow down, please. What's gone? Try to calm down and speak clearly!"

"All my travelers' checks—they've been stolen! All my clothes, my travel visa, everything in my backpack—it's all gone!"

So I doubled my spending money and felt a great sense of relief. Now I had the freedom to really do something. I got through the next two months that way (I wish I knew then what I know now about karma!). Then I started to wonder what to do next. April was already here and soon winter would be starting in South America. So I bought an airplane ticket to Mexico City.

At the airport, I called my mother.

"Maridée? Where are you now? Are you in trouble again?"

"No, mamá, everything's great! I've been having the best time, I've met some really cool people — no problems."

"I don't understand…then why are you calling?" Her voice sounded tight, confused.

"I'm calling to wish you a happy birthday, mamá."

There was a pause on the other end.

"That's…I can't believe you remembered. Thank you, Maridée," she said softly.

"Of course, mamá." I fidgeted with the telephone cord, wrapping it nervously around my fingers and releasing it again.

Then she finally said it. "You promised to return home in two weeks."

Home. I was wondering if I would ever know what home meant. All my life that word had filled me with a sense of boredom and frustration, of longing and defiance. But most of all, I guess it was a word that caused pain. Home. Where was mine? My home was merely the road, whether really or metaphorically. Home was something yet to come; a sense of peace, of comfort within myself, somewhere in the future.

"I know, mamá, I lied to you," I confessed.

She sighed as she resigned herself. "Will you at least stay in touch? Will you call me once in a while and let me know you are all right? A mother worries...."

"I'll call you soon," I said. Another lie.

She sounded sad as she hung up, unable to carry the conversation farther. She had learned through tears and torment that I was my own person and would not bend to her wishes, or to the wishes of any other person.

And deep inside, I'm sure she questioned whether it might have been better not to carry three jobs as we were growing up; maybe it would have been better to have had less, but to have had each other. What is that American saying? "You can't go home again." You really can't correct the mistakes of the past or return to an earlier time to make up for an error in judgment. You just have to learn to live with the consequences of your actions, painful as they may be.

Needless to say, it was many years before I would return to Argentina.

Days at "el quince". Me and Flaca

··· 14 ···

I was nineteen years old and back in Mexico. Was it really less than three years ago that I had first come here to stay with Alejandra? So much had happened since then: working for Adolfo, then at *Torremolinos*, meeting Dean, Acapulco, Cuernavaca, jail and deportation, Mexico City and the marriage that didn't happen, Los Angeles and Dean, Los Angeles and Roger, back to Buenos Aires and then a tour of all South America. And now, once again, Mexico.

Oh, and Juan, too! I forgot Juan....

When I lived here before, I'd met a bunch of people who lived in a compound of little cabins on a mountainside outside of Mexico City. We used to call it *El Quince* because it was located at kilometer 15 (*quince*) along the highway out of the city. It was known as a place to score reefer.

I jumped in the first taxi outside the airport and headed for *El Quince*. Minutes later I was paying the driver and hauling my backpack up the trail to the cabins. Arriving there I found a couple of people I knew from before, and they greeted me with cheers and enthusiasm.

One of the people most excited to see me was a girl of seventeen, who was only fifteen when we first stumbled across each other at *El Quince*. She was of Mexican and Hungarian descent, with caramel-colored hair and European features. Like me, her family had been very wealthy. When I knew her before, her family was living in one of the grandest mansions in all Mexico, and also owned numerous vacation homes in various parts of the country.

Since I last saw her, though, her father had died and her mother had gambled away the entire fortune: the houses, the artworks, the jewelry...everything was gone. This girl was now homeless, but, contrary to what anyone would have thought, she was happier than ever; homelessness actually agreed with her! She had always been thin, and she still was. Her name was Desiree, but I always called her Flaca, which means "skinny" in Spanish.

I adored her from the moment I met her. She was very street-smart but also very well educated, as well as bilingual in English and Spanish. Her intuition and curiosity about life intrigued me. She fascinated me by always challenging me and making me think—and she seemed to truly care about me and what was going on in my mixed-up head! She was cute, she was gay...and she ended up being my lover.

I had never even considered a relationship with another woman before, especially a physical one. I loved men, I loved being around men, I loved the attention men paid me, I really loved the sex, and really—there was not a gay bone in my body. But Flaca was interested in me. I was flattered, of course, even though I really wasn't that way. Still, I was fascinated with her as a person and as a friend. What a mind she had! Being in Flaca's company was like nothing else.

One night, at one of the cabins, we were smoking pot, drinking whiskey and talking. I was telling her all about Dean and how miserably he had treated me. Recalling my experiences in jail and in California, I was in tears. Flaca leaned over and kissed me.

I don't know what happened next, it was as if a flame consumed me. My mind went numb and, without even realizing what was happening, I kissed her back. It felt—not like what I had imagined—but surprisingly natural at the moment. I kissed her again.

Before I knew it we had pretty much become a couple. We started crashing at various cabins in the mountains. We dropped some heavy drugs for a while but then the whole scene got old. After one girl we were crashing with pawned all my stuff—and then told us we got robbed—we saw no reason to stick around. Of course, we stayed long enough to give *her* stuff away. "We got robbed again!" we told her.

We decided that we needed a change of scenery.

Flaca and I knew a guy named Beto, who always had career opportunities available. We got in touch with him and he offered us a cushy position in New York City, so we said, "What the hell?"

Beto arranged for our airfare and the hotel in New York. Our job was simply to baby-sit about a dozen suitcases for four months. We were accompanied by Flaca's brother, Alex, and an old friend, Yuri. All we did was sit around and get stoned while Beto came and went. One by one the suitcases started disappearing, the pot inside along with them.

Just as the next-to-last suitcase had been emptied and was taken away, we were tipped off from the hotel maid (whom Alex was having a fling with) that someone in the room next to ours died mysteriously. She said there was a police investigation.

That night there was a knock on our door. We all jumped. Everyone hesitated, but Yuri assumed responsibility and got up to open the door.

Two plain-clothes cops pushed their way inside. I remember that Flaca was sitting on the bed, and she grabbed the covers and pulled them around her for some kind of imagined protection.

But I was sitting on a Samsonite full of reefer!

"Can we help you?" Yuri asked.

Both cops scanned our room with their eyes. One of them said, "There's been a murder next door. Do you know anything about it?"

As we each proclaimed our innocence, I could feel my ass starting to burn from the heat of my attention on that fucking suitcase. I felt sure they knew. "Please, please, please, don't ask to look inside!" I pleaded in my head, while trying my best to look naïve and innocent. They asked us if we had seen anything suspicious, or if we had noticed anybody coming or going from the guy's room, things like that. One of them stayed by the door while the other made a quick sweep into the bathroom and back out again.

Then I realized that the cop by the door stopped his gaze and held it right on me…right on my boobs, I should say. I thought, "All right, fuck it, I'm just gonna have to work it and keep his eyes off my ass!' So I smiled, twirled my hair, touched my lips with my fingers, batted my eyes…all the things that girly girls do (and I usually don't!). It seemed to work.

"All clean," one cop said to the other. Then he added to us, "If you remember anything, give us a call."

They left. Thank God.

We all breathed a sigh of relief after that one, considering that only a few weeks before we had had at least twelve suitcases in the room filled with drugs! What timing….

We decided it was time to get out of town! Beto took the last suitcase, paid us our babysitting fee, thanked us, and the four of us took off for Miami.

··· 15 ···

We arrived at a five-star hotel on the beach, money practically pouring out of our pockets. We took full advantage of room service, the pool, the sauna, the whole nine yards. We were living large and treated ourselves like kings. We did nothing in moderation.

One day Alex returned to the room after an extended absence. "Where the hell have you been?" Yuri asked, "We thought you got busted!"

"Calm down, man. Everything's fine! In fact, I've been out analyzing the action in Miami. It's a cool scene, and I've come up with a plan. Check this out: why don't we grab a bulk order of Quaaludes and sell them on the beach, five bucks a pop? We'd make a killing!"

Flaca looked at me with an expression that said, "If we do this, they're not all for your own consumption, María."

I waved her expression away like she didn't know what she was talking about. The idea of a Quaalude—or ten! —sounded delicious at the moment. As we all agreed to the idea, Alex collected the necessary money from each of us and took off for the Miami underworld. He was back with the stash in forty-five minutes.

We headed off to the beach presumably to start pushing, but first we each took two Quaaludes. We had all agreed to meet back in two hours, and we wandered the Miami beaches most of the day. But as we had become more and more laid back, we had a hell of a time meeting up with each other. It was late afternoon by the time we finally came together at our last round-up point. I was bouncing and floating in the most remarkable way, I remember. Flaca was quite serene herself.

Yuri and Alex seemed to collect friends as easily as seashells along the beaches. I had made a friend or two myself, but one guy wanted to get me alone and pass some quality time in the luxury of an industrial trash bin. I don't always require dinner and a movie, but that was definitely pushing the limits! So I was able to escape his clutches, and Flaca rescued me before anything happened.

That night in the hotel room, we sat around and shared the stories of our various adventures from that afternoon. We had collected quite a bundle of cash, and at one point Flaca mentioned a desire to see Las Vegas. Alex had been married to the daughter of a magazine tycoon in Las Vegas, and he insisted that we could have jobs in the production end of the family business if we wanted them.

•••

Twenty-four hours later the four of us wandered into The Sahara on the Las Vegas strip. Alex contacted his ex-wife who first cussed him out, then offered us the glamorous position of stapling magazine pages together! At least it was a new scene. A few days later we rented a one-room studio apartment in downtown Las Vegas. We settled in and began our new lives.

One afternoon as I was napping by the pool, I suddenly heard a voice behind me say: "Want to share a joint?" See, my English had not improved much since my days in Los Angeles with Dean, but I thought it had! And I was sure I had heard correctly. I looked up and saw rippling muscles under tan skin.

"¿Qué dices? What did jou said, Baby?"

"I just assumed you smoked reefer," he said sincerely.

"Oh, jeah, is what I thin jou say. Maybe I try it...if jou twisted my harm, honey..." I was proud to have become so fluent in this strange language, and I flashed him a huge smile.

In a second he had taken my arm and flipped me over like a pancake. "Wah-h-h?! Whathufuck?" I said. I hadn't seen that coming at all, and for a second I thought I had been busted or something.

"You said I should twist your arm! I didn't hurt you, did I? I'm a karate instructor. My name is Dennis." His teeth were blinding white through his smile.

"Well, jou better chill out, Penis!"

"*Dennis!* My name is Dennis," he insisted. (Why do they all think it's so cute to toss women around? And why the hell do I like it?)

Anyway, we did smoke a joint together. Dennis was actually a nice guy, super beautiful, and we started meeting every day by the pool and visiting. I thought he was highly intelligent, even though I didn't know what the hell he was saying ninety-nine percent of the time. After a week he asked me to move in with him. I said I would have to talk to my girlfriend about it. That sort of threw him for a loop!

I had not had a boyfriend or been with a man in well over two years by now, and as I said before, I wasn't really gay. I loved Flaca deeply; she meant so much to me and had been such an important part of my life. But lately I had been missing just being with a guy — maybe unconsciously that's why I called him Penis! I was dreading the inevitable discussion with Flaca, but I felt that I needed a change. And maybe Dennis would just be temporary, I told myself. Maybe it wouldn't work out, but I wanted to try.

A few days later I sat down with Flaca. She knew there was something serious going on inside my head. She was no fool. She felt I was beginning to withdraw. She was prepared for whatever dilemma I felt I was in and she was ready to be there for me, to offer sage advice, to forgive me any transgression, to promise to love me forever. But she wasn't ready for this.

"Dennis has asked me to move in with him, Flaca," I cut straight to the point.

She didn't quite get it. "Dennis, the muscle-head by the pool? Why, to cook and clean for him?" She thought she was being amusing, but I knew she was about to enter a huge state of denial.

"No, my love, it's more than that."

This was going to be harder than I thought. I could see that she was starting to tremble, but still refused to believe what she was hearing. Flaca knew that, at most, I was only bisexual. I would never be completely gay as she was. But Flaca and I didn't just swap recipes and try on hats. We traded thoughts and added substance to each other's lives. We were able to be more than intimate with each other; it was as if we could see into each other's soul. I was all Flaca ever wanted or needed in a relationship. She was more than I had ever had, but she was not all that I needed.

My eyes filled with tears as I held her hands in mine and tried to explain these thoughts to her. It occurred to me that I had never been able to talk this way with Juan or Dean, and I began to doubt why on earth I would want to leave this beautiful, intelligent woman with whom I could share my deepest thoughts without being laughed at, ignored, misunderstood or slapped, merely for a hard dick suspended from a nice set of abs.

Something even I didn't really understand was pushing me into this decision. Perhaps it was a problem of identity; maybe the idea of being gay bothered me more than the actual reality ever could. Perhaps it was society's conditioning that dictates what our tastes are supposed to be, individuality be damned. Perhaps it was a chemical, biological need to be with a man. I didn't know then, and I don't know now. More than likely it was not one or the other, but a pinch of one and a dash of another.

"What did I do wrong?" Flaca begged.

"The only thing you did wrong was to fall in love with me, *mi vida*, nothing more."

"Then why are you leaving me, why? I can't bear this!" She was crying uncontrollably.

I couldn't bear it either, so I tore myself away from her tight grasp and ran out the door, sobbing and gasping for breath. *Ciao mi vida, mi amor, mi Flaquita!* Why was I doing this? I ran to Dennis's apartment and stood outside the door, my face in my hands. To this day the sadness and guilt of what I did to her overwhelms me.

··· 16 ···

I collected my thoughts for a minute and decided it wouldn't be fair to Flaca to end it this way, so I went back to our apartment to try to explain myself better and to beg for her understanding.

The door was still open, as I had left it. "Uh-oh," I thought to myself as I called out her name. No answer! I went into the bathroom and there she was lying in the tub, her wrists and arms slashed and bleeding, tears streaming down her face. I called an ambulance and they came in about two seconds and bandaged her up. The cuts were not deep enough to require a call to the police or even a hospital visit, but I was horrified. I stayed with her another hour or two and held her and tried to explain that I hadn't stopped loving her.

By the time I left her, she had calmed down and, though she was still terribly sad, she let me walk out the door.

But a short while into life with Dennis, I realized that I had made a huge mistake. Under each rippling layer of beefy muscle there was only another layer of muscle. Living with Dennis was like living with a steroid-enriched "super child." Forget anything closely resembling a heartfelt conversation—we didn't even speak the same language! Looking back, the time I spent with Flaca was so beautiful. Yet the only thing "Penis" had to offer me was a night out on the town, singing pub songs under the neon lights of the Las Vegas strip, with the constant ping-ping-ping of the slot machines, which never quieted twenty-four hours a day.

As I grew more and more depressed, I considered begging Flaca to take me back, but I kept hesitating, waiting to see what—if anything—would happen next. Maybe Penis would grow a brain cell and surprise me with a thought, any thought, any day now. Maybe my brain cells would be irretrievably damaged, and I could drift through the rest of my life in a state of blissful dementia with What's-His-Name.

One night at Dennis's apartment, he and I were sitting at a little metal table with the linoleum top—which was our dining table—and playing poker. We had been drinking scotch for two days. Dennis's hand beat my hand, and as he was raking in his winnings we both started to laugh hysterically. But my laughter stopped abruptly and without any warning at all, I began to sob. I got up from the table and stumbled to Flaca's apartment, opened the unlocked door, crawled into bed with her and went to sleep.

Flaca was the first person in my life whom I felt had a genuine regard for me as a complete individual. She accepted the entire package: the stubborn, irresponsible and shallow package, as well as whatever my good points are. Before Flaca, I had only known the overdone theatrics of my mother and Dean, both so full of fanfare and high drama that I was always on guard.

It never occurred to me that I might have a chance to be with someone who let me just be who I was. With Flaca, simple, everyday activities that brought me great satisfaction and self-worth were noticed, encouraged even. When I got a new shower curtain I didn't have to wait two months before she noticed; no subtle change I made was unappreciated, and it was nice to be respected and praised for my own choices instead of being kicked or punched for thinking without permission. Besides, if Flaca kicked, at least I had a fair shot at kicking back.

We did have one knock-down, drag-out fight that ended with me locking her out of the apartment! Later, I peeked out the window to find a picnic setting for two. Flaca was stretched out on a lawn chair on the patio, gesturing for me to come enjoy my surprise. There were a couple of steaks on a grill, several beautiful potted plants, a half bottle of whiskey and two mugs. It was a great set-up, but none of it belonged to us. She went shopping *(or shall I say, shop-lifting! Did I mention that Flaca had no boundaries??)* along the neighborhood, picking and choosing items as she pleased.

Flaca had a capable quality about her; when she said she'd handle something, you could just relax in the knowledge that she would — consequences and all. It was a healthy, spiritually nourishing relationship. When I went back to Flaca, I'm sorry to say that I treated Dennis as very disposable, because as fast as I let him into my life, I pushed him out of it. I thought, "Oh well, *c'est la vie!* He'll find another girl who isn't a 'lesbo'...or bisexual...or bipolar!" In other words, he would be better off without me.

• • •

About six weeks after I had left Penis, Flaca's mother, Jovita, showed up in Las Vegas. Jovita had once been an elegant woman, with puffy hair and designer clothes, although she was built like a whiskey barrel on a pair of misappropriated pencil legs. Like Flaca, she had endured many years of being homeless in Mexico since gambling away their fortune and becoming a drunk, but she had stayed in touch with her daughter, and was drawn to Vegas like a fly to honey.

Needless to say, she did not approve of Flaca's "lifestyle" and had been greatly disappointed to hear from Alex that Flaca and I had gotten back together. She said our relationship was "sterile" and abnormal. I couldn't stand her, but since she had no place to go, we found another complex with a larger furnished apartment and let her and Alex move in with us.

Those days were truly hellacious; there was not a moment of silence between the put-downs and the bickering. Jovita drank to excess, which of course we all did, but she was way over the top—ugly!

Otherwise, however, our lives were slowly returning to normal, when I began to get an old familiar feeling. Mostly in the mornings.... kind of sick feeling....Wendy's French fries were starting to gross me out....

I was pregnant again.

We talked to one of our hooker friends who gave us the name of a clinic. I talked to Penis about his "fatherly obligations," but he said he had no way of knowing who the father was and wasn't about to pay a cent. So Flaca and I handled it alone.

We scraped together some money and took a bus to the clinic. I told Flaca I'd go in the back office alone but nobody there spoke a word of Spanish. The doctor came in and gave me a shot that didn't even affect me as much as a good shot of tequila would have. I tried explaining that I wasn't at all "locally anesthetized," but they didn't seem to understand until I began to scream bloody murder.

I was yelling and kicking until Flaca rushed in to find out what the fuck they were doing to me. She explained to the doctor that I had a high tolerance for medications and was not sufficiently deadened. He explained that he had a low tolerance for our inability to afford more medication and told me to shut the hell up and quit scaring away the other clients or he would stop in mid-procedure and send me home. He was already halfway done.

The doctor finished quickly and I was ushered, shattered and weeping, out the back door and into a taxi. Flaca took me back to our room and put me in bed. A few hours later I woke up in a pool of sticky blood. It seemed only seconds after Flaca said she was calling an ambulance that I was being lifted onto a stretcher. The paramedics told Flaca that I had a raging infection. She sat next to me in my hospital room all that night, waiting for the penicillin to kick in. The next morning I was feeling well enough to walk, barely, and we snuck out of the hospital through a side door.

For the moment I needed some first-aid supplies and some medication, but we were completely broke. I didn't know how we were going to get the prescription filled and I started to cry. "Flaca, how are we going to pay for the stuff I need?"

"Are we as broke as the time we got into a fist fight over a Big Mac? We're not sleeping under a bridge this time, my love, we'll make it," she said with a wink. Then she left, saying she'd be right back. She called a couple of hours later from downtown. It was a collect call and I knew instantly what that meant.

She was in jail for grand theft Kotex!

I sat up and scanned the room for something to sell to bail her out. Alex came in from the kitchen to ask, "Was that Desiree?"

I climbed out of bed as quickly as I could and mumbled back, "Yeah. She's going to be a little late."

"How late?" he asked.

"Two to five...Don't let your mother know! She didn't have the money to get the things we needed and she got busted," I said, afraid to meet his eye.

"You mean the things *you* needed!" The voice came from the other room. Jovita had overheard. "To think that Desiree actually believes in you. She thinks the world of you—I don't see why! Maybe now she'll shed her rose-colored glasses!"

"Yeah, right. You think you're in some kind of position to be condescending to me? I don't think so. If anybody around here needs to lose some glasses it's the ones you keep overflowing with cheap rum!"

•••

"So what can we do to get her out of jail?" Alex tried to change the subject back to the problem at hand, "We don't have any money, do we?" He looked at his mother, a half bottle of rum next to her chair.

"No, I—I spent the last of my money last night...."

"Why am I not surprised?" I rolled my eyes.

Jovita wanted me to go to the jail to see how we could free Flaca, but I was in more pain than ever and I refused. So she decided to take the matter into her own hands and marched herself down there.

Two hours later Flaca called again from the jail. I lay on the bed and listened to what she had to say. Jovita had also been arrested and was in the cell across from Flaca because she was in the States illegally, and boy was she pissed! She and Flaca were both going to be deported to Mexico. When I told Alex, he was flustered and didn't know what to do.

But I knew exactly what to do. Our apartment had come furnished — pretty nicely furnished, actually. I grabbed a lamp and took it outside to the street. I came back with a few dollars. Alex started grabbing shit left and right as well. In no time, the apartment was completely empty and we had a wad of cash.

Five days later, Flaca and Jovita were boarded onto a rusted-out prison bus and driven to the Mexican border. Alex and I had collected enough money to get a completely disgusting place, just steps from the bus stop in Mexicali, Mexico. We waited for the bus to arrive with Jovita and Flaca. Then the four of us had twenty-four hours to decide which way to flop, because in twenty-four hours we would run out of cash and we'd have to leave the Mexican motel room.

But twenty-four hours is plenty of time to spend in a sardine can with a woman that considered me the spawn of Satan. Jovita held me solely responsible for the present condition of her life. She planted herself on the ratty naugahide couch and played solitaire while slamming Cuba Libres.

I playfully tapped her on the shoulder. "Who's winning?"

She rolled her eyes and blasted me with smog from the nasty Lark cigarettes she smoked. I was about this close to letting the snotty bitch have it—Pow! Right in the kisser! I was sick of her always bitching and I had some issues to make clear.

Flaca cut me short and dragged me out on the stairwell to smoke a joint. "She deserves no respect when she acts like that, Flaca," I fumed.

"She's under a lot of strain right now, María. Give her some slack. Think of how she used to be. What she really should be." We both knew that the woman inside that room was far from the socialite she had once been. Even in the protective darkness of the barely-lit staircase, I could see Flaca's words were more for herself than for me.

"Okay, Flaca. I'll let it go. But only for you," I said.

We went back in and settled on the bed for a nap. Being stoned did little to melt the tension in the room for either of us. Alex sat in front of the television—apparently he had become a new fan of professional wrestling—and Jovita was in the shower. It was almost midnight.

Flaca turned to Alex. "Where's mamá going at this hour?"

"Fuck if I know. What am I, a mind reader?" he said flatly.

By this time the four of us had endured several hours together, which was impressive considering the amount of animosity that had been charging around the room like a lightning bolt.

Jovita had been in the shower for so long that Flaca finally decided to check on her. When I heard all the yelling, I ran to the bathroom and found Flaca in a full-fledged fistfight with her drunken mother. I yanked the two apart and tossed Jovita back under the water. Flaca had slap marks all over both cheeks.

"She's officially freaked out," Flaca said in disbelief.

"No shit, Sherlock," I replied.

I started to lead her out of the room when her mother started screaming like a madwoman. We both spun around. She was stark naked; her eyes were fixed and glazed. "Look at my body! I'm every bit as attractive as you are! I could have any man I want. I could get laid as easily as you!"

"There's no contest going on, you stupid drunk bitch, so dry off and get dressed," I said with disgust.

"Do you think she's really flipped?" Flaca was pulling on her hair; she did that when she was stressed.

"No, she'll sleep it off. She needs to blow off some steam," I suggested. Flaca was yanking on her hair with both hands now. I led her back into the tiny living room and sat with her.

Half an hour later, Jovita made a dramatic entrance wearing a red dress and a gash of ruby red lipstick across her wrinkled lips. "I'm going out now!" she managed to croak while emptying her umpteenth drink. She pranced toward the door like a gorilla imitating a Clydesdale.

Flaca tried to stop her, but all that got her was another swat across the face. Again, I separated the two and told Flaca's mom to get the fuck out as I pushed her into the hall. Alex pretended not to notice the violent outbreak two feet from where he was sitting, as if one more loaded gun joining the argument wasn't a good idea right now.

"Maybe she needs to prove something to herself. Maybe she's just lonely," Flaca offered.

"Maybe she needs more rum!" I corrected. Still, I was deeply impressed that in spite of her mother's abuse, Flaca was worried about Jovita's safety and didn't want her out on the streets alone, especially in a dangerous Mexican border town. We ended up following the swaying nutcase around for hours before she cooled off enough to be led home like a mule. I considered myself quite generous for letting her back in.

Alex's former mother-in-law, Jackie—who had often taken a load off his shoulders by helping to look after Jovita—wired him some money so that Jovita could have a one-way ticket back to Vegas. Back in those days, it was easier to cross the border illegally than it is today. When asked, "Ma'am, are you a U. S. Citizen?" all you had to say was "Yep!" and you were good to go. That was how we all crossed.

Once we were on the U. S. side again, Alex decided to go on his merry way and Flaca and I hitchhiked to Los Angeles, hoping to find folks from my days with Dean to put us up until we could find a more permanent place to stay. The Salvation Army was always an option, too.

Beto on a "trip"

··· 17 ···

Flaca and I spent our first few days in L. A. outside the 7-Eleven in my old neighborhood. We were sleeping under a little tree next to the convenience store, trying to hide ourselves so that the manager wouldn't kick us out. We panhandled money for a hotdog or smokes, hoping for a miracle—or whatever we could get. Actually I was hoping that someone from my "Dean days" would stop in and recognize me, since I didn't have the courage to knock on my old neighbors' doors and say, "Hey, can we move into your house? I'm not with Dean anymore so he's not beating me, but now I'm with a girl and we're doing the gay thing and we're homeless."

I imagined what would be going through their heads: "God, Girl, are you ever gonna learn?" They would think I should get a job, which of course was true – but that was easier said than done, with no car and no clothes and no English. Up until now, my career had been "Survival 101," and I wasn't trained for anything else.

After way too many hours of this, I was starting to panic. I was very hungry, very uncomfortable, and very scared. All of a sudden: BOOM! I had been asking so much for a miracle and it finally came through for us. I heard my name being called from the other side of the parking lot where we were living.

"Is that woman talking to me?" I asked Flaca anxiously. "I don't want to look. Describe her to me...is she in any kind of uniform?" I was freaking out.

Flaca sneaked a glance and whispered to me very slyly, "She's dressed in a 'mom' uniform. She's short. She's fat. She's kind of old. She looks extremely dangerous. Look out, María! She's coming to get you!" She was a little too amused with herself and giggled like a little girl.

"María, *chica*, get yo' head up, *porque* I know it's you!" The woman was Theresa, the mother of one of Dean's friends. We told her our story and she immediately had the perfect solution. Her sister had rented a room in a boarding house for a month and then ended up staying somewhere else. Theresa had the key and the place was a pre-paid deal. It looked to me like Theresa had just shit a miracle for us.

Theresa took us to the house where we would be staying, handed us a joint as a housewarming present, and bid us farewell. Our smiles were so big we could have oxidized our own earrings! A sliding glass door in the back of the house led directly to our room. It was cold and musty, but it was free. And it had walls! And a bathroom! What a luxury! We were pretty high and I remember feeling strange, almost paranoid, nestling into someone's home without even meeting them.

"Have you ever done this before?" I asked Flaca. "Maybe the owner is uptight or something. You think I should put this joint out? I don't want to blow a month of no rent."

Just then, we heard the front door slam, followed by a child's giggle. Flaca and I looked at each other, eyes wide. We never considered that a kid might be living in this dump. I stubbed the joint out on my jeans and then wiped at the black smudge. We stood up and tried to look presentable, or at least, not too scary.

A young woman entered the room and did not seem very much surprised or at all bothered at the sight of two strangers in her home. Her name was Chayo, and the child's voice we had heard belonged to her daughter, Erica. We explained to her about Theresa's sister and the situation. She said "No problem!" and then asked us if we would be having dinner with her and Erica that evening. Flaca and I looked at each other in disbelief. Our luck was once again swinging in the other direction. Blue skies and clear sailing ahead!

During the next month or so the three of us became pretty close friends, and Chayo proved to be a person with a very generous nature. As for the pot, she only asked that we hold off until Erica was asleep at night. Chayo had a husband, but we only saw him twice. He had another girlfriend somewhere and he pretty much stayed with her except to come back for more clothes in the middle of the night. One night I heard someone rummaging around our stuff on the floor of our room. I thought it must be the husband looking for more clothes. I wasn't even half awake, and I just dozed off again. Then I heard Flaca scream! I turned on the light and it turned out to be a crazed kid on PCP attacking Flaca. The two of us managed to wrestle him out the door and call the cops. After that, our month was almost up anyway, so we went ahead and moved out.

We stayed in L.A. another two months. Los Angeles is not an easy place to get around in without a car or a bus pass, both of which cost money. Desperate for cash, we called an old friend in Mexico, a guy called Vato B, to see if he could help us out, only to hear that he was actually in Los Angeles! We got his local phone number and called him up. Boy, had we hit the jackpot — or so we thought. He had a little house with a few pounds of marijuana in it, and a car. And, he even offered us a job, babysitting his stash while he went to Mexico for a "quick trip."

The first thing we did was move in, lock up the house, and grab the car for a joyride! But we only made it five miles down the road when we heard the sirens of cop cars behind us. We were getting pulled over — and we were smoking a joint as big as a cigar, Cheech & Chong style! We tried to put it away as fast as we could, and we opened the windows to dispel the odor. Nonetheless, we were definitely in big trouble. We were stoned illegal aliens with no license, no insurance, no registration — not to mention, we had been speeding, and the car had been stolen!

We were driven with great fanfare to the Sybil Brown Correctional Facility for Women, where we were stripped and subjected to a body cavity search by a huge prison guard dyke wearing rubber gloves. Flaca and I were held for five miserably long days before we were even allowed a phone call.

We managed to get a hold of the original owner of the car, who turned out to be Vato B's cousin. After we explained our well-intentioned misunderstanding, the charges were finally dropped. Apparently, Vato B had borrowed the car for a few hours, but never returned it. His cousin, pissed that his car was still gone and unable to contact Vato B, reported the car as stolen. A few days later, Vato B was in Mexico, and we were stopped driving the car.

Having no other charges with which to hold us, we were released. Because there is such a huge Hispanic population in L.A., no one even thought to ask us for papers, so we were not faced with another deportation.

Once again free, Flaca and I decided that we had had enough of Los Angeles. Flaca wanted to return to Las Vegas, but I wanted to try some place with fewer bad memories — or, failing that, I wouldn't have minded going back to Mexico City. We had quite a discussion about it. I felt that Vegas would be another dead end—we had done Las Vegas nearly to death. "There's no way I'm going back there!" I told Flaca.

• • •

•••

On our way to Las Vegas (Flaca could be very persuasive!) we were picked up by a couple who were traveling with their four-year-old son in an old beat-up station wagon.

They seemed pretty cool at first, and we were happy to get a ride. Once we were in the car, they lit up a joint and started smoking. The car got so full of smoke that their son was getting stoned. At one point the kid climbed into the back of the station wagon and came back to the middle set of seats where Flaca and I were sitting. In his tiny little hand he was holding a Playboy magazine. He began flipping through the pages and giggling, and at one point he took the long, loose end of his belt and pulled on it, miming a hard-on! The parents didn't think anything of it, but it bothered the hell out of me!

Then the kid climbed into the front seat and sat on his mother's lap, facing her. He tried to lean in and kiss her but she pushed him away from her. This game continued for a while, but the mother was so stoned that she didn't realize how hard she was pushing him, and actually threw him into the dashboard of the car. Flaca and I made the father pull over and let us out. I still have nightmares about that poor child.

After that incident, I was reflective. I have never wanted children of my own; there are far too many children born who end up unwanted and neglected, and I knew how that felt from my own childhood. I suppose I feel so strongly about this issue because I adore other people's children, but I know myself well enough to know that my life is not stable enough on any level to want to subject a child to it.

We finally made it to Vegas, where we were welcomed by neon lights that lit up the night sky as if it were daylight, and the constant ping-ping-pinging of the slot machines that could drive a person insane enough to lose everything they owned just so they could quit and go home.

But Las Vegas at that time was a smorgasbord for street-hustlers, pickpockets, prostitutes...and us. Meals were cheap if not free, and money came and went from one person's pocket to another like the tide. We hung out with friends we'd made the last time, except for Penis, of course. We got high and roamed the strip in the twenty-four-hour-a-day party that was Sin City.

•••

We came across many friends we had known from Mexico. One of them was our old boss Beto. Some people called him Rojo, which means red, because his hair was a shiny coppery brown. Beto was big-time in the import business, and a flagrantly wealthy man. He wore dress shirts with collars pressed and sharp enough to carve a turkey with, and gold chains big enough to tow a Buick. His cigarettes were filterless, and his bottles of Chivas were as bottomless as his generosity —*if* you were on his good side. He had a tight little white ass that was greatly admired by women. And, he was a great fuck. Even Flaca had agreed on that issue, which surprised the hell out of me! Apparently it had been a one-time deal.

I had always been fond of Beto. He had a presence about him, even without his usual entourage. His physical appearance was like peaches and cream with smooth ivory skin and that gorgeous hair. When the weather would change without warning or if his mood took a new direction, his cheeks would break out in ruddy splotches. And, mmm, those grape-green eyes!

He was as cuddly as a barracuda, though, and this element of danger drew women to him. It also didn't hurt to know that Beto took very good care of his friends. If Beto gave you a little work, it could easily mean a grand or so for a couple of days of your time—but if things went wrong, a few days could become a long vacation in the nastiest blood-stained cell you could imagine. Still, we asked Beto to take us along on his next trip.

Amazingly enough, the next trip was to Mexico City....

Flaca in Las Vegas

⋯ 18 ⋯

With a free trip in the offing, we decided to leave Vegas behind and move back to Mexico City. After all, the only difference for us in making the move was the language. We traveled light, so we just picked up and left.

I had always adored the little cabin that I'd lived in when I first came to Mexico, so we decided to check out whether there would be one available. Ironically, Flaca and I were able to get the same cabin that I had shared with Juan. Out of the seven, "mine" was the only one available! So I thought it was meant to be.

Juan, I found out, had deteriorated so much that he had been institutionalized, and had been there for a few years. I wasn't too surprised, but I felt for him all the same. I remembered what being in a mental facility was like, and I wouldn't wish it on anyone, sane or insane.

I went to *Torremolinos* to see if any of my old friends were still around. Manolo was there and was so happy to see me that he begged me to come back to work for him! I remembered those carefree days, the happy nights of waitressing and partying. Since our runs with Beto were to be pretty sporadic, I thought, "Why not?" so I accepted his job offer. Manolo had not changed at all, but he did notice Flaca by my side. He looked at me and whispered, "Looks like things have changed a bit for you!"

The little cabin was still beautifully furnished with those wonderful antiques, but I felt it was lacking something. I felt my life was lacking something, and I turned to Flaca for support.

"What is it, my love? What's troubling you?" she said.

"There is something I want, Flaca…something the two of us have never been able to have, and it's starting to really upset me. I can't stop thinking about it."

Her face went ashen; I could tell she was afraid to ask what it was, but she thought she knew. But that wasn't possible, was it?

"María, that's a huge responsibility! I don't know how you think we could handle what it is you are wanting!"

"I know it would make it more difficult to just pick up and take off, I know that. But this cabin seems so empty with just the two of us, so bare. I'm ready to settle down a little bit. I'm tired of being always on the go, always on the run. This is something I really want!"

She thought very seriously for a few moments. Then, with a tear forming in her eye, she asked who I would choose to be the father.

"*Father?* What father? I want some little knick-knacks, some pretty little vases and things to set around the apartment, to make it homier! I'm tired of feeling like I was born from a potato in the ground and my only home is the dirt! You thought I wanted a baby?" We both started to scream and snort with laughter until snot shot out of our noses! We laughed till it hurt, and then we kept on laughing.

She suddenly turned serious and said, "No, come on, María. We can't afford to shop for stuff like that; we can barely eat half the time. And I know from experience how that stuff starts to make you feel a false sense of security...comfortable, like you're 'somebody' because of what you have, not for who you are." Her voice got very quiet and small, "And then your father dies and you lose it all..."

I grabbed her and hugged her. "I knew this would be difficult for you, Flaca, and that's why I had such a hard time asking you. But it would mean so much to me. I would feel like maybe we could breathe a little, feel more like a couple with some roots, like our lives are not always in transition, temporary."

"But everything *is* temporary, my love." Hearing her say that scared me a little, and made me sad. She could see that I didn't want to hear that just now.

"Well, how about some 'temporary' knick-knacks bought with 'temporary' money?" I offered. I had to try to convince her.

"I don't know, *mi vida*, let me think about it. Vases, huh?" She looked around the little cabin, then back at me, her expression doubtful.

I was hopeful. I was falling back into that old "work and party" routine with the guys at *Torremolinos*. But Flaca was beginning to get depressed about everything. She was bored, I wasn't there enough, and nothing felt right. She thought I was slipping away from her.

And she was right.

One morning I came home from work—and the subsequent all-night party with the guys—to find she had cut her wrists again: not too bad, but worse than before. Was it the cabin or was it me that kept driving my lovers insane?

I didn't know what to do. Depression and suicidal thoughts were starting to take hold of Flaca, body and soul. I didn't want to assume the responsibility for another suicide attempt. I felt so helpless and (I'm sorry to say) restless. I could barely take care of myself, much less be responsible for someone else.

Despite all that Flaca and I had endured together, I realized that I had spent three beautiful years with her, but I was ready for another change in my life. I adored her with all my heart and I knew I was going to miss her tremendously. But the fact was: I wasn't gay. I found in the drug runs an excuse to separate from her. I didn't know how to make a clean break, so I did the best I knew at that time. I wanted to split up without hurting her, knowing in my heart that in a different place and time we'd be forever friends. But boy, I felt so guilty.

Beto was about to take off on another run, and I needed time to think. So I left Flaca and took off with Beto alone. It wasn't easy; nothing like that ever is. But it wasn't too hard, either. Beto was becoming pretty attractive to me. I had been poor and on the road so much, I was sick of it. I wanted a better life; I wanted to be able to go to a restaurant and not have to walk the check. I wanted to drive from point A to point B in my own car; I didn't want to have to hitch-hike, putting my life in danger just to get across town. I wanted pretty clothes.

We went to Beto's hometown of Tampico, Mexico at the end of this particular run. We sat in a bar drinking our inhibitions to smithereens. Beto was no idiot—he had seen how I looked at him, and I'm sure he knew what I wanted. He said that we could go to Texas together before returning to Mexico City. I said that sounded great, but in the back of my mind I was thinking that only the first part sounded great. I had no intention of returning to Mexico City.

Beto had started calling me *nenita*, little girl. He didn't know how much I wanted to be called that by a man. Not since before I was two years old had I been called that. We drove to the Texas border, his strong arm around my shoulders. It had been so long since I had heard that name, so long since I had felt the protection of a man. We got to the border and my anxiety heightened with each rotation of the wheels of the car as we inched closer to the customs screening point on the Texas side.

Beto cracked his window for the stone-faced customs official as if it were all an inconvenience.

"American citizen?" the man asked.

"Yep," Beto yawned as he answered.

"What about you, Miss?"

"Me, too," I swallowed hard, sure that I would throw up all over the dash. I held my breath. The customs agent walked around inspecting the car and the plates, then waved us through. Beto drove on, pulling me closer into his chest and caressing my hair.

I never would have believed at that moment that I would be doing this for many years to come, as mindlessly as tying my shoes. Eventually I almost became convinced that I *was* a U.S. citizen. After so many crossings, I remember thinking, "Can't they tell I must be a citizen by the way I know what I'm doing?" Little did I know at the time that I would eventually stay in Austin, Texas, longer than I had lived in Argentina...or anywhere else for that matter!

We drove to Austin where Beto had just rented a house. I was growing more and more attached to Beto, and I found myself hoping that he was feeling the same way. I felt comfortable in his arms, and safe in spite of the mind-numbingly dangerous occupation we now pursued.

While Beto made another quick run by himself, he asked me to stay and decorate his house for him. He said it needed a "woman's touch." A woman's touch! I had almost forgotten I was a woman, with all the dirty blue jeans and torn T-shirts and flannel Flaca and I had managed to come up with. Beto gave me a fistful of cash, plopped me in his Corvette and sent me off to the furniture store.

Four days and two delivery truckloads later, I had a "shake and bake" home that announced a "woman's touch" with a shout! I went out and bought some feminine clothes and high heels and plopped myself down on my lacy ass and told myself, "This is it, Baby! This is where you belong." I had my knick-knacks, and so much more. I felt coveted, secure, pretty and wealthy. It was the biggest head-rush ever. But I couldn't stop thinking about Flaca, still alone in the cabin with taped-up wrists. She was going through a very difficult time, but only in part because of me. I didn't know how to tell her that I still loved her and wanted to be there for her, but it had to be by long distance. It just had to be.

When I didn't allow my thoughts to center on her, Beto's absence gave me dangerous time to let my thoughts and feelings drift.

I hadn't spoken to Dean in four years and I was beginning to wonder how he was doing. Despite our rough relationship, I always loved him. We'd always had our fun times. I picked up the phone and tracked him down through his parents. We had a pretty decent conversation, although it didn't sound like his life had changed one iota since the old days. He was happy to hear from me, at least he said he was, and he was encouraged by the news that I wasn't with Flaca. He liked her, but could never understand how two girls could be in love. I didn't tell him that that ability had been beaten into me.

...

During my first two years with Beto, I spoke with Dean three times and even saw him once, when I took the opportunity to visit him at his parents' house in Mexico City during one of my runs. He wasn't at all surprised that I had become so strong. As a matter of fact, he mocked my security as though I had been unable to see that it had been there all along. I knew enough to keep our visit short and sweet, and when I started to notice Dean's eyes gaining a little too much sparkle for me, I made my apologies and left.

As my taxi pulled away from his house he smiled at me—a warm, genuine smile that spoke of a happily shared past life together, and nothing more than loving good wishes for an old friend. The setting sun shone on his hair, and as the glint from it obscured my view completely, the taxi turned the corner. I had the strange feeling that this would be my last memory of Dean. His lifestyle always kept me worried throughout the years, and I knew that if he didn't change he wouldn't live long.

...

The same, however, could have been said of me. The fairy tale I shared with Beto began to turn into a nightmare, as we became immersed in the drugs and all the chaos that comes with that. We thought we were on top of the world. We were actually on top of a never-dormant volcano, but we had no idea. It really is amazing the way you actually become the drug. You truly are what you put in your body.

When the clubs closed down for the night, the party moved to our house until nine or ten in the morning, or whenever the coke ran out. Then we would pop downers and smoke pot to slow down the shakes and allow us to sleep. This went on for three years.

I remember watching Beto in astonishment as he charismatically wove a web around people, feeding off their praise and admiration. Deep down he was a kind person, but it was too easy for him to live the role of a self-indulgent playboy who refused to grow up. But the more drugs I consumed, the less I noticed this side of him.

··· 19 ···

*O*nly two months into our relationship, Beto started getting rough with me physically, adding to the already growing verbal and psychological abuse. I knew he was fucking around on me, too, because he was pretty sloppy about hiding it.

One sober morning, I called Flaca out of the blue. We hadn't spoken in some time, but we were able to clear the air. Thank God she let me be best friends with her again, even though it was from a distance. From then on we were in constant contact, like friends are. I told her that I missed her and that nobody would ever take her place.

Beto and I were cultivating a biting hostility towards each other as a result of the drugs and his controlling behavior. And he was becoming more and more paranoid — the true sign of a guilty conscience! One night, after Beto, his friend Forrest, and I had finished a marathon session of snorting coke, Beto flipped out completely. Forrest, whom I had just met, was very polite to me, but I knew that even accepting a light from him or letting him fix me a drink would be misinterpreted by Beto. So I just took care of myself and refused any overt kindness. I could see Beto's ruddy complexion darkening as the night wore on, though. He grew ominously quiet, staring first at Forrest, then at me. "He just needs more blow," I thought. "I'll just get him some more and he'll chill out."

But we had depleted the entire stock. I tried to explain to Beto that we should just pop some downers and try to get some sleep, but he slapped my face against the wall before I was able to finish the sentence.

Then he started running around the house, ripping the stereo speakers apart and overturning chairs as he searched for the "cat." "Where is it, *pinche pendeja*? Tell me what you did with it!" He was freaking out.

Forrest started to panic and tried to make his way to the door. I called out to him and begged him to stay and help me, but Beto lost it. He started thrashing me and tearing at my pants, pulling them down to humiliate me and demonstrate his power over me.

Again, he demanded to know what I had done with the "cat." He said he knew I had stashed it in my underwear!

Forrest just stood silently watching as this terrible spectacle unfolded. "What cat?" he mouthed to me, confused.

"We don't have a cat! I don't know what the fuck he's talking about!" I cried.

I begged Forrest to leave and call the police. Suddenly, Beto punched me squarely in the face, and I collapsed on the floor. He bolted upstairs and I ran, unthinking, into the bathroom. Forrest took this chance to tear out of the house.

I could hear Beto as he stomped back down the stairs. He heard the click when I pushed in the lock on the bathroom door and the house immediately fell silent. I presumed that Beto, like a hunter in the woods, had stopped in his tracks, his ears tuned to any movement. I prayed he would calm down. Then all of a sudden, the tape player rewound itself and started over, blaring through the coverless speakers.

I heard Beto outside the bathroom door, and I cowered in the tub. My head was pulsating from the drugs, the music and the fear, and I was positive I would die of fright long before Beto made his way in to kill me. The door splintered into flying fragments as Beto's foot came bursting through, a gun in his hand. He burst in and was startled by his own reflection in the bathroom mirror. His face was gleaming with sweat and his pupils were dancing so fast I doubt he knew what he was seeing. He knew I was there, though, and he told me to get up and come to him.

He held me in his arms, almost like a lover. He was shaky and completely gone. He held the gun to my temple and described his hallucinations as they were appearing before his eyes. Through his description I was able to learn that the "cat" was drugs. He had been looking for more drugs! We slid slowly to the cold floor and stayed that way for hours, the gun always pressed against my temple.

Whenever he returned to the subject of the "cat," Beto would kick or slap me. They were the only times the gun left my head. I watched all this in the floor-length mirror, and I knew that this picture would probably be the last image my eyes ever saw, if not due to a bullet to the brain, then from the drugs I had ingested or the slams from my head hitting the marble tiles. Several times I began to black out, and I whispered to Beto to please call an ambulance.

• • •

He hit me again. He tilted my face up and stared at the purple waves developing across it, and then he said he would drive me to the emergency room. In Beto's car on the way there, I remembered Dean's message to me when he had been deported from Cuernavaca and had called me in Buenos Aires. "Man, is Texas a drag, María. I hope you never have to go there."

There was only one doctor on duty that spoke Spanish that night. The nurses made Beto wait in the waiting room while they led me to the back to see the doctor. When the doctor saw me with no shoes, no sweater and the obvious injuries to my face and head, he just held me. Instantly I broke down and told him everything about the weeks and weeks of non-stop drugging and how terrified I was of my boyfriend.

The doctor told me I had a severe concussion brought on by Beto's blows and the slams to the marble floor. I was cautioned on how easy it was to overdose. "You will not live," the doctor told me, "if you do not change your life completely, and change it now."

He told me that he knew someone who would help me, who would take good care of me. While in the back room with the doctor, I heard Beto asking the nurses how much longer I would be in there. They lied to him and said that I had already exited out the back door and that I was long gone. I was taken to a women's shelter to stay while I put my life together. There I met ladies who had endured for years what I had survived that night. One woman had a three month-old baby with a cast on its leg. I didn't want to ask how that had happened.

It should have made me not ever consider going back.

Beto and me, flying high...

··· 20 ···

After a week in the shelter, I decided that a healthy life wasn't for me. So I escaped. I stood at a pay phone outside the Safeway supermarket, impatiently waiting for Beto to pick me up. I know! After all the care those nice, sweet people gave me, it's hard to imagine how I could have run away from them to return to the person who abused me. But I wanted to hear Beto's explanation, to receive his apologies. I just couldn't leave it alone; I was anxious to make up. Of course we did, and he showered me with gifts for days afterward and told me he didn't know why it had happened—end of subject.

Soon afterward, we went to Mexico to visit my sister and Flaca. As it turned out, I was deposited at my sister's for safekeeping and Flaca was allowed over only per Beto's express instructions.

This whole trip was a disaster. When I arrived at Alejandra's house I immediately came down with the flu. A visit to the doctor revealed that the bug I had been infected with would eventually grow to become a small human child. I couldn't believe it. My mind was reeling. Beto had always talked about us starting a family, but he was living in a fantasy world. How on earth could Beto and I raise a baby successfully to adulthood, without killing or misplacing it somewhere along the way?

I phoned Beto and gave him the joyous news. He was elated. I knew he would be. I turned to my sister for support, and she described for me the zero probabilities of having a normal, healthy baby, considering all the substances swirling around my poisoned system. Then she digressed to various other facets of my lifestyle and the dangers inherent therein. "Oh," I said.

I went to a clinic in Mexico City and cried a sobbing farewell to my third would-be child. I told Beto that I had had a miscarriage. I didn't know if he would be understanding, concerned, or absolutely furious. After we hung up the phone, he jumped on the next plane back and comforted me so sweetly I couldn't believe it, which made my guilt multiply.

It must have been a great strain on Beto to lose his child and to have to be nice all at the same time, because that night he and Flaca got into a huge fight over me. I had said something, I no longer remember what it was, and Beto told me to shut up. That was actually sweet for Beto. Flaca sprang to my defense, Beto sprang for her jugular, and they fought. This was, of course, late in the night, and Alejandra was awakened. She entered her living room just in time to witness the explosion of her beautiful glass wet bar. Beto demanded that she throw Flaca out, Flaca pleaded for her to evict the foul-tempered Beto, Alejandra threw up her hands and went back to bed, and I sat and cried. It was, after all, just another typical night in the life of María.

After a while I began getting tired of Beto always being "the man with the plan." It made me feel inferior to him, powerless. So I thought, "Why shouldn't I arrange my own deals?" I called Flaca and Yuri, we met in Mexico City, and I gave them the details of my plan. Then I sent them off to Oaxaca to make the pick up.

They rented a car and left it strategically hidden just outside of the checkpoints. They went down to the row of tin-roofed shacks where the *indios* lived and filled up the order. There were soldiers scattered all over the top of the mountain where most people would drive or walk. My two friends managed to forge into the brush carrying bags on their heads, circumventing all the areas patrolled by the soldiers. The stressful drive back wore them out, and they decided to catch some sleep at a rest stop.

Two men with guns and badges demanding to search their car awakened them. Yuri and Flaca panicked, but didn't know what to do. Reluctantly but obediently they got out of the car, sure they would be going to a Mexican prison. They were terrified. But the officers, if that's what they were, were not at all interested in searching the vehicle. One of the men took Yuri and held him apart as he was forced to listen to the stomach-churning sounds of the other one brutally raping my Flaca: my sweet, intelligent ex-lover screamed and fought the best she could, but she was no match for this big greasy maniac. The "cops" had thrown the car keys into the treetops.

When the men finally took off, Yuri hot-wired the car and drove to the nearest town to report the crime. "Yes, that sounds just like two of our officers," the station cop told them without apology. Nothing was ever done about it.

Flaca came bolting through the door much later than I had anticipated, of course, and I was worried sick. I was sure they had been busted, but they showed up with all the reefer. Flaca's face was almost unrecognizable, and she was covered in sweat and dirt. All she said was that she needed a shower, and she repeated this over and over. I could tell she had been crying, and I knew something had gone terribly wrong. She fled to the bathroom, and all I could hear was the steaming hot water and soft sobs. Yuri explained it all to me, how those fucking pigs had wounded a beautiful person that night. They hurt my friend, and it broke my heart. I decided to stay in Mexico a little bit longer to comfort and support her.

When I returned to Austin that next week, I immediately got into a fight with Beto. Of course. The level of passion was so intense between the two of us that I had started to get turned on by his brutal treatment, because our reunions were equally passionate. It was really more addicting than the mountains of drugs could ever be. By this time I was taking eight or ten Valiums a day to counteract the rest of what I was doing, and my judgment was a little impaired, to say the least.

Meanwhile, I had pot to get rid of. Beto couldn't believe what I had been able to do without him, but he also offered to help sell the buds for me. He said he knew a guy in Houston who was buying, so off we headed. On the way out of town, Beto said he just needed to stop at the bank to make a deposit to cover the rent check he had written. No big deal, right?

Walking around the block seems to turn into a big deal in my life, and this quick stop at the bank was no different. I watched the teller's bewildered expression through the glass of the drive-through booth as she spoke with her supervisor. "It's not that difficult, Honey, just stick it in the drawer and give us a deposit slip." I thought with growing impatience.

After a ridiculous amount of time for such a simple transaction, Beto held the call button down, "Hey Ma'am, what's taking you so long?"

"Um, there seems to be a counterfeit bill among your hundreds, and, um, we'll need to see you in the office." The teller was nervous and suspicious, not sure what to expect from us.

Beto gave her an unworried smile and reached for the door handle of my blue 1979 Mustang. "Great! Fucking great! This is just what we need," I hissed, as Beto got out of the car and headed for the main building. Just then I glimpsed two suits in my side rear-view mirror approaching the car.

The next few weeks, months, were a disaster. My stash was stolen, Beto had to rat on the people who gave him bad money, then was deported. Our apartment was being watched so I couldn't go home. At some point I realized I absolutely had to find another way to live.

Puppy Hot!!! I love you!

··· 21 ···

I stayed in the bizarre little world of Ranje, a German friend who was willing to take me in, and hoped for the best. To ease my boredom and to give me a little much-needed affection, I found a puppy for sale in the classified ads section of the newspaper—a small Yorkshire Terrier. I called the number that was listed and went to check it out. I fell in love with the tiny thing at once, and so I asked the owners if they would take a check. They did, and I named the sweet little thing Puppy Hot — "Puppy" for obvious reasons, and "Hot" for reasons that are obvious if you know the type of check I gave them! I loved Puppy Hot and, more importantly, Puppy Hot loved me.

But every wrong-doing has its consequences, and I eventually ended up in a 'hot-check' class from having written one too many. As I sat there listening to my classmates explain why they were forced to write "insufficient funds" checks—like, they needed to buy diapers for their baby or to feed their family – when it was my turn, I couldn't help but feel embarrassed.

"And you, María?" the instructor asked me. "Why did you write a hot check?"

As I told the class about my loneliness and why I needed a dog, everyone erupted in laughter when I explained to them the meaning of my poor little puppy's name.

I started cleaning houses to scrape up more money. "Everything is temporary," I heard Flaca's voice saying, back at the little cabin in Mexico City. Everything *is* temporary. I looked at my hands in a toilet bowl and stared at where I had only recently had beautiful fake fingernails. "Knick-knacks," I told myself.

Meanwhile, Beto was flown to New York City and wired up like a transistor radio. All he had to do was to pretend to be just joking around with the guy and ask him what was up with giving him a fake bill. An extremely attractive undercover agent—made to look like an everyday hippie-type—accompanied him. The undercover agent and Beto checked into a hotel and waited to conduct some business with the "bad guy."

When they met, Beto punched the guy playfully and called him a puss for handing him play money. The guy was pretty full of himself, and was actually proud of what he had been able to "pull off." He started mouthing off full speed, spilling all the beans. A minute later the hippie undercover guy pulled out the cuffs and took the "bad guy" away. Easy as that.

For the three months while the trial went on, we were bitterly reminded of what the poor life felt like, yet again. Our friends obviously backed off like we carried the plague. If you consider police surveillance a plague—and they did—then they were right. We had it! We had to call in every morning and say, "Hello! We're clean and here at home. How are you? Have a nice day! Thanks for everything!"

Beto got a job slapping together meatball sandwiches at a pub in the mall, and I was still scrubbing toilets. We rented a little room from an ad in the paper. I remember that after a while we noticed that the woman who owned the house left her three year-old-daughter alone all day. Putting a chair by the phone and setting out the can opener for her kid was what she considered "acceptable parenting skills." We reported the lady and took off.

We found an efficiency apartment that I thought was adorable. It couldn't have been more than three hundred square feet, but it was so cozy. It had a view of the section of the Colorado River, which flows through the center of Austin and is locally called "Town Lake." Nonetheless, I was becoming more and more disillusioned with Beto and his fucked-up world. We had lost a lot of friends and associates through this disaster, and I was, once again, preparing for change. The trial was drawing to a close and we were facing deportation.

Three months after Beto got busted, there was a knock at our door in the middle of the afternoon. We had been napping, so I took my time arriving to open the door. The trial was over and agents were here to inform us that it was time for our voluntary departure from the United States. We had to shell out the money for our own tickets, otherwise it would be a five-year waiting period before we were allowed to return. We were given twenty four hours to leave.

Beto claimed to have a few loose ends to tie up around town, so he said he would meet me in the morning in San Antonio. Puppy Hot and I arrived early and waited for Beto. We waited longer for Beto. They made the final boarding call, but Beto was nowhere to be seen. Puppy Hot and I got on the plane, they shut the doors and we took off.

• • •

I came back across the border a few days later. With Flaca. (Of course we were U.S. citizens at the checkpoints).

Sitting on my little balcony with the view of Town Lake, Flaca swung a leg over a lawn chair and looked out. "What's that?" she asked.

"My backyard," I replied, "Like it?"

"I see what you mean about Austin, María. I'm glad I decided to come with you. It's beautiful." A breeze lifted off the water a few hundred feet away and the wind chimes on the balcony played their relaxing random melody.

"Beto said it would be a month or two before he makes it back here— he's trying to build the business back up, running non-stop deals. Until he gets back, you know you're welcome to stay here, Flaca."

"And after?" she asked, sounding far away.

"You know we'll have to get you your own place when he comes home, the way you two get along." I knew she was jealous of Beto, she blamed him for stealing me away from her. In a way, she liked him, too—after all, we had all been friends once — but everything is temporary.

"Do you remember that first run to New York with all the suitcases? Remember Miami? It was so romantic, María." She was definitely feeling nostalgic for the way we had once been.

"Remember Las Vegas and Los Angeles, Flaca? Remember the women's correctional facility?" Maybe a jolt of a harder reality would add focus to her selective memory.

"Yeah, well..."

We finally got a call from Beto two months later. He had regained his stature with his old connections and was coming home with a sizeable stash. He wanted us to meet him in Kingsville, Texas, and pick him up. Flaca, Puppy Hot and I headed out to collect him.

We waited more than two hours but Beto never arrived. We shrugged our shoulders and headed back to Austin. Near San Antonio we had a blowout of one of the tires. We were stranded at around four in the morning along the highway. I wanted to run into the bushes and hide, because that's the first instinct of an illegal alien in trouble. My brilliant Flaca wouldn't hear of it—she flagged down a car with four guys who could easily have been lumberjacks. We stood helplessly by in our hot pants and halter-tops, not knowing if they were discussing who gets who or how to change the tire! They turned out to be extremely gracious, and miraculously, they fixed our flat for us.

When we walked through the door the phone was ringing off the hook. Beto had made it across the border all right, but had been pulled over at a checkpoint. The cop noticed that Beto's nostrils looked like they had been rolled in flour. He had only been arrested for marijuana though, because the little amount of anything else Beto had on his person had already been sort of "processed." I think the cop was operating alone because he took the opportunity to keep the pot and to let Beto go, unreported. By now, nothing surprised me in this crooked world.

He showed up at the front door not long afterwards. His pockets were much lighter and the pot had been confiscated, but at least he was not behind bars. He was not at all put off by the incident. He just jumped right back in, wheeling and dealing on the phone.

I was really enjoying a life with less stress for once. I was planning the rest of my life, but Beto's intensity clashed dramatically with my picture of this future. Still, power can be intoxicating and addicting, and I agreed to make one last trip for Beto, swearing that after this one, I would be done for good.

⋯ 22 ⋯

The group this time consisted of myself, Beto, Flaca, Tammy (Flaca had somehow stolen her away from her boyfriend, Ronny, and was now dating her), a guy named Boo, and, ironically, Flaca's mother Jovita. It wasn't even that Jovita needed money; back in Las Vegas, a casino door had fallen off its hinges and crashed down onto her foot, and Jovita had won a substantial settlement as a result. She was the last person I would have expected to join our little army, but that former millionaire socialite looked to be our perfect cover.

As was our custom, we drove to the border and left the car on the American side for our return trip. It was not difficult, once on the Mexican side, to find someone to take us the rest of the way for a small fee. We met at the airport in Mexico City. We had agreed that everyone would travel solo, except for Tammy and Boo, and me and Puppy Hot. We thought we would look less suspicious that way.

We left Mexico City in the early evening, and as I shifted back into my seat on the plane, I could still smell the perm solution in my hair that changed my looks. Boo was an old friend of Beto's, and had been in and out of prison many times. This alone should have told me that this man was a walking calamity. A slight man with deep pockmarks on his face and a noticeable gap between his two front teeth, Boo was a nervous little guy, and that bothered me. He was too shifty.

We flew to Oaxaca and rented a couple of bungalows at a fabulous lodge on the edge of the mountains. It was so high up that, when you sat out on the balcony of the little restaurant, it seemed like you could reach out and touch the clouds. In spite of traveling singly, shrouded in mystery, once in town we hung out together and were seen all over the place in each others' company. Not too smart. Beto was always loud and boastful wherever he went, and at night in the discos he was anything but subtle. We each, I think, stood out in our own special way from any of the locals, and we attracted attention everywhere we went. Singly we were obvious, but together we practically cried out for attention. But we didn't realize that until much later.

The little mountain village of Oaxaca was where the Indians harvested, sold and competed with each other in the marijuana industry. To avoid police surveillance, they would wait until dark and then hike to the caves where they kept their cache of pot. There, it was weighed and bundled up for the trek back to the car the following night.

It was always a relief to see Beto after this part of the deal. Once this aspect of the venture was accomplished, we would always party like there was no tomorrow...as there very well might not have been! And anyway—a throbbing hang-over gave you something to focus on while crossing the border.

We all met for breakfast the next morning. Boo, returning to his usual state of panic, couldn't find his identification card anywhere. "What do I say at the *aduanales*?" he begged, his eyes filled with terror. Beto calmly told him everything would be all right. He explained that all he needed to do was to speak to them in their own language, slip a few bills in their pockets, and that would be that. He could do it, no problem! I wasn't confident in Boo's ability to assure anyone of anything. I started to worry, which is a very dangerous thing in this line of work.

The Oaxaca airport is not much bigger than a porta-potty, so we had to work hard to appear casual and indifferent. The place has the pent-up atmosphere of an elevator. You find yourself taking shallow breaths for fear of depleting the room's oxygen.

We all assumed our assigned roles: Jovita was reading a book, Beto was flirting with a waitress by the dessert cart, Tammy and Boo were sitting in silence as many married couples tend to do once the honeymoon is over. These were all good signs.

My anxiety was low until I looked down at Puppy Hot. He yapped...no big deal. But then he yapped again. I looked down at him. He had started recognizing all his friends scattered around, the people he knew so well, and he wanted to say, "Hey, Beto, why don't you come and play with me? Hey Tammy, rub my belly!"

"Oh, shit!" I said under my breath. I'd forgotten to brief the dog! All I could do was pray that nobody would notice or would understand the meaning behind his eager expression.

I rose and headed outside with Puppy Hot to find a place for him to pee. By the time Puppy Hot had finished sniffing around, chasing bugs and peeing, it was time to board the plane. I went directly to my seat. So far, so good.

Puppy Hot was worn out and fell asleep in my lap. I gave my cohorts a good objective evaluation. Nobody would believe that the well-dressed elderly socialite had a bag stuffed almost to bursting with some of the most beautiful marijuana buds in all Mexico. And who could guess that Tammy was the lover of Flaca and not Boo's wife? Who would speculate that Beto and I rubbed elbows with the laid-back rich folks in the Texas hill country?

No one. Except, possibly, that fat man who was drilling a hole in my head with his eyes, and completely ignoring his newspaper! Beads of sweat popped out on my palms and my heart did a belly-flop against my spleen.

I considered that maybe he was just being a dirty old man—but that didn't fit with the intensity of his stare. I ignored him as best I could, but I could feel that his gaze never left me. I traced the outline of my lips with a finger, looking innocent and unruffled. I examined my hair for split-ends; I did anything I could think of to occupy myself and to look carefree. When I had performed every trick of innocence I had ever studied for, I was left with one last alternative to make him stop staring. I smiled at him. But his face grew even more grim and menacing.

Puppy Hot awoke and started to bark again. Now all eyes in the vicinity of my seat were on me, and this did nothing to quell the rising apprehension I was feeling inside. Then the airline steward, alerted to the sound, came over to visit the cute little puppy in my lap. "Oh, I remember you!" said the steward. I could have punched him for that alone, but he had to go on, "You flew with us last week. You've been in Oaxaca all this time? How did you like it? Where are you from?"

I wanted to scream to him to go away and stop drawing attention to me, but of course I couldn't. As politely as I could, I conveyed the message that now wasn't the best time for a question and answer session. Paranoia was running rampant in my wildly racing mind, and it was all I could do to keep my face from twitching. The old fat guy with the penetrating gaze continued his vigil. I searched the plane again with my eyes. I saw that Tammy was holding up pretty well, carrying on a conversation with the air in front of Boo's ashen face. Boo's expression was a dead give-away, though, and he was ignoring Tammy completely. "Stop it, you jerk!" I hissed under my breath. "Listen to your pretty blonde wife and stop looking so guilty!"

Still the man stared.

I spent the rest of the flight praying, hoping against hope that my supplications were being received at the correct destination. I had long since learned to leave out the expletives when talking to God, and I had begun to get a better response.

Sometimes.

The plane finally landed in Nuevo Laredo, a Mexico/Texas bordertown, just across the Rio Grande where we had hidden our car. I nervously approached customs, and just about released my bladder when I was simply waved through. My victory was short lived when I saw that Boo had been taken to the side, and I watched as he shakily dealt with the customs agent. I couldn't believe the asshole hadn't just offered the man a bill and gone on his way. His reaction didn't correlate with the misplaced I.D. story I overheard him telling the agent. He was pointing the finger at himself in a big way. Popping his knuckles, smacking his gum with sonic intensity and shifting his weight nonstop.

I tried to look around casually as I took my bag from the conveyor belt, scanning for the fat man. There he was, in all his piggish reverie, and we were all in his sight now. He looked like he was ready to pounce, his eyes darting from me to Boo, to Tammy, resting on Tammy a minute, looking her up and down—oops—then to me again. What a pig!

Up ahead, Beto's voice boomed in the cramped baggage claim. He was drunk and happy, already celebrating his latest victory. Jovita looked like nothing more than a tired grandmother whose stiletto heels were killing her. Flaca looked cool as a cucumber, the perfect solo traveler concerned only with getting through the routine and looking for a taxi to take her any number of dull places. They made it out fine.

I was moving closer to the baggage claim myself when Boo comes up and bumps into me, a little too obviously. He whispers that I have his claim stub for "the suitcase" and he mistakenly has mine. We were fucked. I took out my claim stub and made like I had accidentally dropped it on the floor. Boo did the same with his, but just as we released them an elderly man saw what happened and lurched toward us, trying to do the gallant thing by picking our tickets up for us. I gave him a death stare—it wouldn't have taken much of one to be effective—and he hobbled off. Boo and I bent to the floor and switched tickets. I retrieved my bag and turned to look towards Tammy. She was checking her hair in a mirror, completely clueless that there was any danger. I got a porter to take my bag, shifted Puppy Hot in my arms, and turned towards the exit.

Then it happened. I shoved my cleavage into an armpit high cop who requested a search of my suitcase.

Yanking my bag open with great pleasure, the young cop was obviously very proud of himself. He was frantically tossing my stuff in the air, desperate to find anything inappropriate or illegal, all the while failing to notice that the clothing he was discarding belonged not to one young lady but to a group of people.

Weird vibes rippled all over me like a wave. I was left with an abrupt apology and a heap of clothes strewn about the floor. It took every nerve in my body to replace the clothing neatly and with an air of nonchalance. Then I noticed a great deal of commotion going on a few feet away. The cops were trying to locate a screwdriver to pry open Tammy and Boo's suitcases! And the head honcho in charge was my old admirer, the fat man. My only thought was to leave them to their doom and walk discretely out the exit to find Beto and Flaca.

Just then Puppy Hot, who was now on the ground at my feet, hikes his little leg to pee! Knowing I wouldn't look all too innocent if I dragged him behind me on his leash, leaving a yellow stream across the baggage claim area, I had no choice but to act cool while I let him do his thing.

I strolled out the exit door and made my way to the first cab in the long line of taxis waiting outside. I gave the driver my bag and opened the rear door. I put Puppy Hot on the seat and climbed in. As I was reaching for the door handle I felt a sharp tug on my scalp. The short cop had my hair wrapped around his hand and he was pulling me from the seat. I landed flat on my ass on the curb.

He hauled me into the airport, cursing me and really roughing me up. I had been able to grab Puppy Hot and I held him close to me, asking over and over what I had done wrong, still playing innocent. He yelled to me to stop lying—the other guy had already squealed that my boyfriend was the "ring leader" of this smuggling operation.

That fucking Boo! No bamboo shoots under the nails, no Chinese water torture, not even a mild case of martyrdom, taking the blame himself. I knew from the moment I saw him that he was a piece of shit! In less than two minutes he had spilled everything! I shot death rays from my eyes in his direction. His eyes bulged out of his pockmarked face like a squished frog on the highway.

There were a couple of well-to-do newlyweds at the airport arriving from some other destination, and a newspaper photographer was there to snap pictures of the happy couple. When the photographer saw all the commotion, he dropped the newlyweds' story and started shooting us instead. His photo of the three of us — Boo, Tammy and yours truly — made the front cover of the paper along with a headline mentioning thirty kilos of marijuana smuggled in suitcases.

The fat-ass from the plane was in the center of all the commotion, barking orders and making sure everyone knew that he was the man in charge. The three of us and Puppy Hot were crammed into the back of an LTD. Puppy Hot growled and showed his tiny puppy teeth in an attempt to protect me. The two assholes up front threatened to toss him out the window, and I pulled him tighter to my chest. All the way to the jail we were barraged with questions, threatened with life terms and worse.

··· 23 ···

We arrived at a small courthouse complex with disgustingly filthy jail facilities. The cement walls were splattered with blood, and rats and Volkswagen-size cockroaches with armored backs flew about the cells, landing on our arms and faces. In our holding area Tammy and I could hear Boo being beaten. His moans sounded muffled and small compared to the noise made by the brutal punches. We heard him beg for them not to put the plastic bag over his head again. I wished that I were the one delivering those blows to the bastard, but at the same time it made me fear for my own well-being.

When it was my turn they were only slightly less physical with me, but they threatened to make tacos out of Puppy Hot. I cooperated a little and played dumb a lot. No matter what I told them I got the same response: a couple of backhanded slaps and a few kidney punches. They knew I was keeping information from them. They were well-experienced with drug smugglers and they knew that we must have a lot more information than we were giving up.

The fat man told me they were taking me to all the expensive hotels in town until we found my associates. He knew they were here and we were going to find them.

As we left to go on this mad search, I decided I would give them physical descriptions that were far off from Beto and the others. They only had me because I had still been there when Boo squealed; the other three had already left the airport baggage claim area.

At the first hotel I was shoved up to the front desk. The fat man ordered me to describe my friends, which I did in all their imaginary detail. But the fat man was ready for this ploy as well, and he told me to try again, this time with the truth. He tried to grab Puppy Hot from me. At each hotel I gave a pretty good description of Flaca's mother. At the last hotel of the night the clerk told us that a woman matching the mother's description had just checked out suddenly, not even staying the night.

I was relieved that Beto, Flaca and Jovita had apparently made it, but I wondered how much more difficult this would make things for Puppy Hot and me. We returned to the jail. Tammy was lying on the floor of her cell smoking a cigarette when I was shoved in. She thought they had taken me out to kill me, she said. She passed me her smoke. She looked anything but freaked out, so I thanked the dumb bitch for her concern.

Tammy and I were the only women in the place. In our holding area there was just a cell for us women, and a separate one for the men, which was four times larger and crammed with about twenty guys. Each cell had a desk in front of it, just outside the bars. There was a tiny upstairs office where the doctor brought Tammy and me for inspection. They wondered if we could also be dealing heroin and the doctor was supposed to administer a "junkie test."

Tammy had old track marks like road maps along her arms and under her tits, but the young doctor took one look at our terrorized faces and said, "No, these girls are not addicts."

The next day an attorney came to represent Tammy. As I saw her being led away to meet with her lawyer, I yelled out, "Hey, what about me?"

"What about you?" he asked in an irritated tone.

"I'm María, Sir! Is Beto not going to help me, too?"

"Oh my God," he said, "You're María? Beto has been looking for you. Let me tell him that you're here."

Apparently, Beto and the others didn't even know that I had been arrested along with Tammy and Boo. After all, I hadn't been carrying any of the pot. They thought I was just lying low or unable to find them.

The nightmare of the public declarations in the Mexican court began. We had to appear before the judge and kiss-ass big time. They asked me to translate for Tammy since the lawyer didn't speak English, she didn't speak a word of Spanish, and they had no other translator. It was up to me to defend us and make the puzzle pieces fit. That was the only part of this miserable experience that was in any way funny. Tammy had no idea of what was being said by the judge, by the officers, or by Boo and me. She took the whole translation thing extremely seriously, which of course worked in our favor, but it wouldn't have mattered if she were reciting nursery rhymes, because I was making her story match ours, regardless of what she said.

The fun part was extremely short-lived, however. Our attorney went into the judge's chambers and we stood up to meet him when he returned. "Bad news," he told us, "I can't believe it, but this judge doesn't want any money. No *mordidas* (bribes), no 'donations', nothing. You are to be transported to La Loma Prison." His eyes wouldn't meet ours, but I put my Puppy Hot in his hands to give to Beto and Flaca. I didn't know if I would ever see my little Puppy Hot again. I wept openly as I handed him over.

We were immediately taken to a patrol car and driven off, Tammy asking every two minutes what was being said, what was going to happen to us. We didn't have any answers.

La Loma had a rough reputation, and its maximum occupancy of seven hundred inmates was actually double that. But Beto had somehow arranged for Tammy and me to be in one of the best cells. Now that's something not every girl can brag about! Boo wasn't so lucky, however, and we later learned he was put into solitary confinement and forced to stay on his knees for days at a time.

Tammy and I had a cellmate named Sofia. She was like the underworld version of a sorority sister. Sofia and her brother had been dealing coke and were nabbed at the train station. Her brother had been allowed out to go scrape up the money to pay the fines. It had been four years.

Sofia had found her own way to survive in this hell-hole, and it was not by accident that she was in one of the best cells. She performed "favors" for the guards for certain benefits and had attained an elevated status within the system. Nobody bothered her in any way. She had a couch, her own bathroom, two hot plates to cook on, and a window, and her cell was left unlocked until midnight. That they locked it at all was probably her idea, not theirs; it helped to keep the horny bastards away when she wanted to sleep.

After the midnight lock-up the place got very eerie. The prison was built like a square, all four corners having towers with armed guards keeping watch. To stay awake and alert at night, they would whistle to each other non-stop throughout the night. If one guard didn't respond, they knew he was asleep or something had happened. At night the guards would come in stinking drunk, wanting a piece of ass.

Our attorney had held some kind of public office and had a lot of connections. We made sure all the guards knew this, and as a result they never abused us too badly. They also knew that we had money and connections of our own, so when we told them "no," they listened. Still, it was a prison, and a bad one at that. It was scary, dirty, depressing, and boring to the point of making you truly "stir crazy." We had it a lot better than most other inmates, but believe me, it was no motel!

After we'd been at La Loma for four days, the lawyer came to us and said that he had been able to work out a "financial arrangement," but only two of us would be released. They didn't care which one stayed, but they were adamant on this point, and it didn't take a rocket scientist to realize that Boo would be the fall guy. This was a Monday, and the lawyer said that Tammy and I would be released on Saturday. I told the lawyer to make sure that it was no later than Saturday, because I would kill myself if I had to stay longer than that.

Friday came and went with no word from the attorney. I was beginning to worry as Saturday came, and we entered the afternoon hours before the damned attorney finally showed up. He explained that more money had been required to prevent my deportation to Argentina, but it was taken care of, the money had changed hands, and the deal was closed. Tammy and I were to be released into his custody that day!

We jumped into the lawyer's car to go back to the States. I sat between the lawyer and Tammy, praying that I wouldn't be asked anything by the border guards that would keep me from crossing one more time. My stress level wasn't a hundred percent…it was a million percent! I was skinny, depressed and terrified, and I had no real hope for a brighter tomorrow.

The lawyer drove us to a hotel across the border to meet Beto, Flaca, Jovita and my Puppy Hot! Beto had a big party waiting for us in the hotel room. He apologized for the extra time it had taken to extricate us from La Loma.

"Never again," I swore to myself. "I am never going to jail again."

• • •

Book Two

Serenity

"I picked up my leg, moved it forward, and set it back down again."

Me and Pixie

My Flaca on the beach in Mexico

··· 24 ···

The next day we drove back to the wonderful Texas hill country with its lakes, rivers and abundant wildflowers, back to Austin, back to my cozy little apartment on Town Lake.

Flaca had rented a place nearby and Beto took an apartment in north Austin after I told him I would never live again so close to all the action in his life. He could hardly argue with me, after all I had been through. I got a job waiting tables through a new friend named Luis whose family owned a Mexican restaurant.

I determined to clean up my life; other people seemed to live quite happily without drug runs across the border, imprisonment and beatings on a regular basis. And I thought I'd like to give it a try.

I had a great time working at the restaurant, the whole family treated me like one of their own, and, just as I had at *Torremolinos* in Mexico City, I made friends with many of the customers and with one other waiter in particular.

His name was Fernando and he had come to Austin from Monterrey, Mexico. He was honest and intelligent, a person of truly great integrity, and someone who, over the years, has proven to be a loyal friend. Fernando has come to be like a brother to me; he is one of the most trustworthy people I have ever come across.

There were also the musicians who liked to frequent the place, like legendary musician Stevie Ray Vaughn, Marcia Ball, and countless others. Little did I know at the time that these two would be the first of so many great musicians I would be fortunate to know. No wonder Austin is called the "Live Music Capital of the World!" I can testify to that, and enjoy every single one of them.

During my first Christmas on my own I found myself with nothing much to do during the holidays. Beto pleaded with me to go with him to Mexico for the holidays. No way, I told him.

At the apartment complex I had noticed Nevada plates on a car in the parking lot and I wondered if the driver was familiar with my old stomping ground. One day I happened to be outside when that car pulled up and parked. A beautiful blond guy got out of the car and I decided that I would introduce myself. Or die! After all, we were neighbors, and this is Texas. In Texas neighbors talk to each other.

His name was Dale Johnson. He was obviously someone who worked and lived outdoors: his skin was tan, his body toned, and his ass was tight and round.

We spoke briefly about Las Vegas but we obviously knew the town from different sides and from different angles. Dale was a thrill seeker, not a thrill victim as I had been. He scratched Puppy Hot's ears as we talked, but he caught me scoping out his posterior and we both grinned. He had a great smile! I grabbed Puppy Hot and, as I turned to go, I said, "If you have no plans Christmas Eve, stop by for a drink." I didn't think he would, but you never know.

I was still pretty tied to Beto emotionally, although I knew I needed to start moving away from him and his lifestyle. I was rarely interested in any other guy, or girl for that matter; my obsession with Beto overrode any long-term interest in anyone else. But I found myself thinking about Dale a lot, and I made mental notes of when he came and went, what chicks he had over to his place and how often. I wasn't actually stalking him, just noticing and not forgetting.

I was pleasantly surprised when Dale did show up on Christmas Eve. He even brought a bottle of J&B. "Now that's my kind of man," I told Puppy Hot! We had a couple of drinks, but it was a little awkward because my English was still pretty iffy and Dale didn't even speak high school level Spanish. Still, I was thrilled he had come.

When he left I went over to Ranje's. It was midnight and she was dragging a huge Christmas tree up her stairs. I enjoyed some eggnog and a brief visit in the twisted winter wonderland of Ranje's version of Christmas before flying back to my cozy nest on Town Lake around two o'clock on Christmas morning.

I spent Christmas Day with Tammy's loser junkie ex-boyfriend Ronny. He lay on the floor, scratching himself and asking me every twenty minutes for a joint.

"Got crabs, Ronny?" I asked, disgusted by his relentless scratching.

"No, it's the smack," he replied.

I kept Puppy Hot on my lap, covered with a blanket, and tried to ignore him the rest of the morning. Just another traditional Christmas holiday at María's!

Beto wanted to see me. He missed me, life was unbearable without me—so he said! —the same old crap. I met him long enough to get into a huge argument over my independence and my new-found friends and lifestyle. Then I began to wonder who he was fucking and after several obviously false statements I began to figure out that it was Tammy.

Tammy and Flaca had broken up right after we got out of prison and Flaca had returned to Mexico City. I got ahold of Tammy and invited her to come over and party. I gave her a ton of coke, which got her to start talking. (I'm not manipulative – no, not at all.)

After she admitted to everything, I no longer pretended to be the caring friend who wanted to console her for the guilt she felt for betraying me. I got so mad that we started to fight. She ran out of the apartment. I followed her. She flew to her car; I got to mine first, and crashed into her car in the parking lot as she was trying to make her escape. Then I beat the shit out of her for what she had done behind my back. Later, Beto would beat her worse than I did for having spilled the beans.

Beto kept begging me to take him back. We stood outside talking, shuffling our feet around in the grass: he pleaded with me to come back to him, and I refused to have anything more to do with him. Then I brought up the matter of the eleven thousand dollars of Beto's money that was in a safety deposit box under my name at the bank. "What do you think would be a fair split, Beto? I mean, considering you were fucking Tammy behind my back, considering all the beatings, considering I went to prison for you—what do you think would be fair?"

"Split? The hell I'm splitting anything with you! That's my money and you damn well know it!"

Beto's face was turning all sorts of unpleasant colors, and I began to consider whether it wouldn't be better to just give him the money to get him out of my life. Wanting to put an end to this, I got in the car with him to go downtown to the bank. Before I had even put the car in gear, he lunged over and grabbed my neck and started choking me. I flailed my arms, trying to reach for the door latch. Getting away from Beto for just a brief instant, I threw myself from the car.

I saw a maintenance man on the lawn and I ran towards him, Beto following right behind me. The man radioed for the police and in his defense he did his best to keep Beto at bay, but eventually Beto grabbed ahold of me and started punching and kicking me. The maintenance man, not knowing how else to help and not really wanting to get beat up in my place, backed off and looked around desperately for the police. Beto's rage was terrifying to anyone, and I can't fault the poor guy for not doing more.

Dale heard the commotion from his apartment and looked out his door. It didn't take him long to figure out what was going on and run down to where we were. The moment Beto saw big, tall, muscular Dale coming down at him like an angry god from Mount Olympus, he backed off to see what Dale was going to do. Dale gently grabbed me in his strong arms and Beto moved further aside for a moment. Dale told me, while staring Beto down into a whimpering puppy, not to worry, that nothing like this would ever happen to me again.

The police arrived to find that the situation had pretty much been controlled. Beto tried to toss a few insults at Dale to egg him on, but Dale ignored him completely and kept me at his side. The police told Beto to take off, which he did, looking over his shoulder at me enfolded in the arms of some unfamiliar blonde god.

A couple of hours later, though, Beto returned, knocking on my door, ready to teach me a lesson on how not to treat him again. But this time I was ready for him. I had gone to the bank and I met him at the door with a huge fistful of cash. His face was red and splotchy and he started to say something. I walked towards the open door and he saw as my eyes focused past him to the balcony overlooking the yard and the lake.

"NO!" he screamed as I flung my hand out over the railing and released the whole eleven thousand dollars to the wind! He never finished his sentence. He dashed down the stairs, grabbing at the bills that floated and drifted in the wind like confetti. I watched him for a minute, rather proud of myself, and then I remembered it was time for my soap opera. I locked the door.

Some time later, after tempers had cooled, I told Beto that I honestly had no desire to make up with him. My life was beginning to change and I liked that change. I would not repeat the mistakes of the past. Moreover, I recommended to Beto that he should consider one of his past mistakes and revisit it: he should be nicer to Tammy than he had ever been to me.

He passed his tongue over his lips and looked out towards the lake.

"What is it, Beto?" I could see he wanted to tell me something.

"Tammy left," he said. "She hopped a bus to Miami because the situation here got so fucked up." He looked back at me, to gauge my reaction, to let me see his. His eyes were dull and his expression pitiful. He was obviously wounded and he wanted some comforting words from me.

"Oh," I said, and I shut the door.

Since my last three years had been so brutal and disruptive, I reveled in setting up house and going to work at a real job. I felt independent and responsible. I gave thanks for every day that no one died or went to the hospital; for every day that no one with a badge came to my front door; for every day that simply passed quietly from morning to night, filled with simple conversation and good clean work.

Me and Dale, watching the fireworks on the 4th of July

Dale washing windows on a "high-riser"

··· 25 ···

I returned to my old goal of learning ten words of English a day, and in no time I was blazing past that to learning twenty words and being able to apply them in a conversation. I also used my ability to read people's meaning in their eyes to grasp some of the finer points.

Flaca was back in Mexico, Tammy was in Miami, Boo was still in prison, Dean was God-knows-where, and Beto was fading, slowly, into the past. My new life had begun. Oh, I still partied a little, to be sure, but the wild days were on hold.

I wrote to Boo in prison and told him I was praying for him and that I was leaving my old life behind. As time passes, all those crazy events got buried under the everyday "normal" memories that began to pile up on top, and after a while I even wondered if those things really happened to me. Even though the trauma is ingrained in me forever, to some extent my past began to feel like a bad dream.

Dale asked me to dinner one night and I agreed. After a dinner of sushi I stuffed his nostrils with coke and we ended up paddling down the Colorado River at four in the morning. It all seemed so "right." He was a perfect gentleman, and I felt comfortable in his protective company. We started seeing each other regularly. Not dating, but just hanging out as friends, doing things together. I knew that Dale was still seeing other women, and I was still feeling too much of the effects of my experience with Beto to consider jumping into another relationship. I was literally afraid of people — and can you blame me?

Two weeks later, though, I showed up to work at the restaurant and Luis came up to me. He told me that his family was worried about my green card status and about how much trouble they would be in if I were caught. The INS had begun a crackdown on many of the restaurants in Austin and they were sure to be inspected soon. Mexican restaurants in particular seemed to be the targets. He told me that I needed to find some way to become legal, or I would have to leave.

That night I went to see Dale. As I said, Dale and I were really just friends, and new ones at that. But after explaining my situation, I abruptly proposed to him, and I threw in a two thousand dollar offer to cushion the blow. He didn't say yes, but he didn't say no, either! Dale and I lived next door to each other, and he had a habit of talking to himself when he was alone. I went home, got a glass, and held it to the wall. I could hear him going back and forth, asking "Should I? Shouldn't I? Should I?" Eventually I went to bed.

Three days later Dale called me and asked if I'd meet him at the courthouse on his lunch hour. I was stunned! If Domino's can make, bake and deliver a pizza in thirty minutes, why couldn't I become "Mrs. Dale Johnson" in the same amount of time? It was the perfect Shake-n-Bake wedding. I hung up the phone and jumped in the shower, threw on whatever clothes were lying around—overalls, but they were white!—and dashed downtown to the courthouse.

As I neared the courthouse, I zeroed-in on my husband-to-be as he leaned against the building, wearing a wild Hawaiian print shirt and eating an apple — my knight in shining armor, my green card in tight Levi's! We strolled into the courthouse and found the office of the Justice of the Peace. I started to get nervous—maybe it was being in a courthouse, maybe it was being once again before a judge, or maybe it was because I was getting *married*!

My English flew around in my head like a bird that gets into your house and smashes itself into every window trying to get out. As the judge began, I started repeating everything he said, whether it was to me, to Dale, or to the bailiff. People started giggling. "Do you, María, take this man..."

"Does jou, María, took that man..." I would repeat (I didn't know I was supposed to wait!).

Dale was in hysterics, the judge couldn't keep a straight face to save his life, and I was almost in tears with frustration, fear, and excitement. I didn't know what anybody was saying, including myself! The judge had to repeat himself because everyone was laughing so loud, and complete strangers were walking in from the hallway to see what all the noise was, which only made me more incoherent. It was a disaster, albeit a funny one. When I finally made it through the ceremony everyone cheered, including the judge! I was married!

The months went by and our friendship grew closer. It was April 6, 1987 when we got married and by the next Christmas Eve, change was in the air. Dale insisted on giving me one of my presents early. This was a sweet gesture, and not unusual for him. It was a small box, and I was shocked to see an elegantly designed ring with a two-carat diamond in the center! It was as big as a doorknob, I thought, just a pretty bauble, so I said, "Gee, thanks, Dale," and I left it in the box and set it on the coffee table.

I turned to him to ask where he wanted to go for dinner, and I was surprised that his face had fallen and his shoulders slouched. "What's the matter, Dale?"

"Don't you know what that ring means?" he asked, his voice sounding just like a little boy's.

"It's a Christmas present," I said, puzzled by his reaction.

"It's a *wedding ring*, María. I'm telling you that I want us to really think of ourselves as a married couple—I love you!"

"Do you mean that rock is *real*? I don't believe it!" I hugged and kissed him.

To be fair, I really didn't know that a diamond signified marriage! In Argentina the custom is to exchange gold bands. I wasn't aware of the American tradition. Plus, no one had ever given me a present like that, so expensive. Dale literally had so little money at the time that he had taken out a loan. But then I received this wonderful, beautiful, emotional present! I was so shocked that if I had been in a chair I would have gone over backwards – but needless to say, we considered ourselves "officially married" from that moment on.

And when people say the first year of marriage is so hard, I have to disagree! Mine was a piece of cake! Part of our success may have been due to the fact that we couldn't speak the same language so it was hard for us to fight. But to this day, Dale teases me about that two thousand dollar offer that I threw in to try and sweeten the deal, when I didn't even have one dollar at the time! Needless to say, he never got it from me.

To start off our life as a "real" married couple, we bought a house in the Austin neighborhood called Travis Heights. I was still a waitress, and Dale started his own company doing high-rise window washing and building maintenance downtown. He was one of those guys hanging from the thirtieth floor! His company grew very rapidly and was profitable from the very start.

Three years later he sold the company, made more money, rolled in more money that his father used to give him yearly as a gift, and then he opened *another* company that turned out to be as successful as the first one. All of a sudden, kaboom! We were rich.

There were no expectations of me as a wife: no cooking, no ironing, none of that. There was just Dale and me, living together in this incredibly peaceful existence that allowed us to let our imaginations soar. Dale taught me to structure my time, to get things done early and promptly, so we could party. Dale thought about the future: stocks and bonds, investments, retirement. My attitude was "party today, vacation tomorrow!" We were a good match.

He spoiled me like I was a little princess. In the movies, women show their husbands something in a store window and the next morning it's next to them on the night table. In the movies, women mention to their husbands that they've never seen snow and the next day they're on the way to Lake Tahoe. In the movies, women take their husbands home to meet their family and the husband takes them on a shopping spree with no limits. Well, those breakfast-in-bed husbands don't only exist in the movies.

Mine was named Dale Johnson!

Most importantly, Dale was the only man in my life who not only gave me security by putting a roof over my head that I could truly call 'home.' He also listened to me, didn't judge me, and gave me the freedom to be who I am. For all of that and more, I adored him, loved him, respected him, and to this day, still thank him.

We began spending all our time together on different projects. We refurbished a couple of houses, we traveled, we exercised together, and we traveled even more. It was like a fantasy life.

"Dale, want to go to Jamaica?"

"Again? We just got back."

"Yeah, but didn't you like it there?"

"Good point, let's go!" And we would be off. It quickly became a way of life for us. And it was all legal. One day Dale bought his own plane, and then it was a different beach every weekend, or some island where we could go exploring.

Our house in Travis Heights was a fairytale pink and white, a sort of New Orleans-style affair in a beautiful neighborhood. We had a white picket fence and animals romping all over, including my little Puppy Hot. Dale insisted that I didn't have to work, but I've never liked to stay still, so I started a cleaning business, cleaning four houses a day. It was hard but satisfying work, and it felt good to have my own income. I also drove to Tyler, Texas to buy tons of roses, which I would sell on Guadalupe Street near the University of Texas, along with corn on the cob, apples and lemonade. For the first time in my life, everything was going great.

Little Sissy, winking at the camera

Patchouli and Mamacita

··· 26 ···

Beto wouldn't allow himself to be removed from my life, not that simply. I couldn't say that he was stalking me, but it wasn't far off from that. He said he just wanted to stay friends. It took a while for that to be possible, but it did eventually happen.

I had no need and no desire for any romantic attachment with Beto. He knew that, and more importantly Dale knew that. If he was on his good behavior, Beto was allowed to visit. Dale was not the jealous type at all, and he trusted me.

Slowly, all three of us reached a comfortable point with each other.

Beto was seeing a tragically sexy dancer from one of Austin's fanciest topless nightclubs. Unfortunately, he felt he needed to increase his smuggling to shower this woman with expensive vacations and trinkets. The way he was going seemed a little too hasty to me, and a lot too risky. I was worried. But it was out of my hands, after all, and thank God this time I wasn't involved.

Meanwhile, I was enjoying married life. I was also enjoying just having any life at all where I didn't have to cower in the corner for speaking my mind. I had my circle of friends from work, but most importantly I had Dale. With Dale I kept up with all the physical activities; we rode bikes, lifted weights, went camping and hiking — all the things I had once considered "stupid." And I was loving every minute of it.

We were just coming in from one of these activities one day when I heard on the answering machine the words:

"María, call me. Dean's dead—they found him outside of Mexico City with a bullet in his head and he had no eyes. They identified him by one of the malamutes. The dog was still there with him two weeks later. Can you believe it? Call me."

It was Dean's aunt.

All I can remember is gasping and crying at the same time and Dale telling me to breathe deeply. Dean had been a bastard to me sometimes, but he had been my first great passionate love, and the memories of those times never fade. Maybe that's why we stay in those relationships long after the good part is gone.

And I remembered Dean the last time I had seen him in Mexico City — his smile as I drove off in the taxi, the way the sun shone on his hair as I turned the corner. I thought of those beautiful dark blue eyes that had so mesmerized me, that had looked at me—at least once—with love.

And now they were gone, gouged out by some drug dealer probably, his body, the body that had held me, and yes, beaten me, dumped in the desert outside Mexico City. It was too personal, too horrible for me to take in.

I will always miss Dean. And I have forgiven him for the sad moments when his temper made him do mean things to me. Now I understand what drugs and alcohol can do to an unstable mind. He wasn't a mean person. He was just lost.

I love you, Dean. You will always be a sweet memory in my life. And all those adventures in our life that we shared unfortunately took your life too soon. I hope you're at peace now, and when I re-read the letters that you used to send me when we were young lovers, I can see that you were a wounded little puppy trying to portray yourself as a big bad wolf. Are you in Heaven now? Please don't get in trouble with the cops. Bye, Gorgeous....

•••

Had it not been for Dale I know that I would not have survived the following days and weeks. Dale had a psychology degree which came in handy to help me with my grieving.

Still, while things were picture-perfect with Dale, I was slowly starting to grow bored. Beto had been talking a lot with Flaca, and frequently they would conference me in. The three of us would talk for hours about the old days, and several times we came dangerously close to agreeing to do another deal, but I would eventually blow it off.

One night Beto and I went out and did a mountain of coke. We got into a great conversation, though a fucked-up one, and I told him, "Beto, man, you know I love you. But you worry me — you can't keep doing this. You've got a kid on the way now, and things aren't always going to work out in your favor." I begged him to slow down on the trafficking. Dean had been on my mind, and I worried that a similar fate would befall Beto.

He told me he would always be careful, he had always been careful, and besides, smuggling was all he knew. How would he support the child as a busboy?

We shared a couple of sweet moments holding hands and I went home. "Don't worry about me, María, I'm a survivor!"

Beto's pregnant girlfriend was the kind of woman that made you want to announce her arrival into a room with "Attention, K-Mart Shoppers!" She wasn't sure how she felt about me, and she was always distant. Fine with me, I thought.

About two months after I'd heard of Dean's death, I was sitting at home rather drunk, when someone started pounding on the door. It was late at night, Dale was out, and this type of thing didn't normally happen in our neighborhood; people around there practically went to bed at six-thirty! I staggered to the door and opened it to peep out through the crack. Beto's girlfriend pushed her way in and started yelling hysterically.

"Someone killed his brother, Chacho…and they think Beto's dead, too!"

"What?!" I couldn't believe what she was saying, and for a moment I figured it was some kind of ploy to get me out of Beto's life for good. But she went on, "Jovita was there with them, in Oaxaca—someone came into the room and shot Chacho to bits! Nobody can find Beto. María, I don't know the family — you have to get in touch with them."

Tears streaming down my face, I picked up the phone.

Needless to say, Beto's mother was devastated: two of her sons, gone in the same instant; one definitely dead and the other probably dead as well. I called Jovita, and she filled me in on the details. As she told it to me, it was three a.m., and she heard gun blasts in Chacho's bungalow. She looked through the window but saw nothing. She contacted the front desk, and the guy there said she should get the fuck out of there, which she did. That was all she knew for certain.

Within two months I had lost two of the most important people in my life. First Dean, and now, most likely Beto, too, who to this day has never resurfaced. He faded away, which in a way is worse—for a long time we all kept expecting him to pop up at any moment.

A few months later my stepfather died in Argentina. I decided to go home. I was filled with sadness during those days, and to top it all off, I learned that my nephew, Mariano, developed a brain tumor and was scheduled for surgery the day after my arrival. Afterwards we got the appalling news that the tumor had affected his optical nerve and left him blind.

When I returned from Argentina I arrived at the airport in San Antonio. Airports still make me nervous as hell; all those years of drug running are permanently ingrained in my psyche, and I was in a needless panic as I stood there all alone. Dale had seen me from a distance and watched as my face started to show the strain of all those haunting memories from my previous life. He made his way to me and just held me for the longest time. He knew what was going through my mind and he knew how to stop it. Any other man would have just said, "Good, you're back. Let's go home." Dale knew to hold me.

...

Things were great with Dale, I can't say that they weren't. But you know me — I started, after eight years together, to get itchy feet.

The first six years of life with Dale had been so beautiful that I guess I started to get scared. Nothing in my life had ever lasted too long, especially the happy moments. So I proceeded to destroy all the love that I had. Years seven and eight were tough. Dale had met me when I was 100 pounds, an illegal alien, and a drug addict. I had been so dependent upon him. But now I had become more independent. I was starting to change.

Dale and I started to clash as his little bird began to fly. I had new dreams for myself, which he sometimes belittled and didn't fully support. Even though he could be extremely critical, we rarely fought, and we never argued. We had a very amicable divorce, and today we are the best of friends. I still always go to him for advice. I guess it's just that our relationship evolved into something else. It's still as comfortable as ever, and I will always love him.

··· 27 ···

The divorce was painful, but I had even more tears to shed.

One day in 1995, when Puppy Hot was nine years old, I noticed that he wasn't acting normally. He seemed to be in pain, and didn't want to drink. I took him immediately to the vet. They performed a series of tests and told me that my little Puppy Hot was suffering from kidney malfunction. I told them to do whatever they had to do to keep him alive. We began a grueling series of treatments that included hydrating my poor baby with injections of fluids under the skin and administering a lot of other medications. For his treatments, I had to drive Puppy Hot to a specialist in College Station, Texas. In the last report, the doctor wrote that the dog's owner was in denial about the seriousness of the condition. I realized that it was selfish of me to continue, and I finally agreed to put Puppy Hot to sleep.

I went to the vet's office in Austin to say goodbye to my little buddy, my constant companion and loving friend. I was too upset to stay with Puppy Hot and to hold him. I couldn't stop thinking of how much he had meant to me throughout all these years. After he died, I just curled up on the couch for I don't know how many tearful days. I missed him so much. I had Puppy Hot cremated and I bought a beautiful ceramic jar for his ashes. It was very hard to say goodbye to my little friend, but in a way he will always be with me.

After the divorce I found a very small run-down house only seven blocks from Dale. Thank God I saved the money I made in cleaning houses, plus the money Dale gave me in the divorce settlement. Although I still had a roof over my head, I went back to being broke. I didn't even have an A/C unit. The house was a tiny piece of shit which must have been almost illegal on the tiny lot it was on, but I could see through the rough and long-abused exterior a fine skeleton that would one day exude, if not real charm, then a fine character. But for now, all I had was my bed, my television and my new puppy, Mamacita, a tiny teacup Yorkie.

To make money I was cleaning houses all the time. I didn't know what more I could do, what other occupation I could get myself into, but I knew I needed to make more money. The house, in its current condition, was terribly depressing and uncomfortable, but at least I owned it outright. It would not be until many years later that I would even consider allowing myself to fall into the "American" condition of indebtedness, a notion that still causes me extreme panic.

After some time I got fed up with cleaning up after other people, not knowing what to do with my life and living in an uncomfortable little shack.

So one day a solution came to me (desperation can be a great motivator). Before our divorce Dale had given me a brand new car, so I drove it to Laredo, Texas, on the border of Mexico. I found some wrought-iron furniture, some tables and chairs and stuff, and I traded my car for it. I saw potential in selling it back in Austin. Then I bought an old beat-up Ford F-150, which was the only thing I could find to haul all that crap back home. And, it gave me a vehicle.

Driving down South Lamar I saw a little run-down place in front of an old trailer park, and a little sign in front that said "For Lease." I went inside to inquire and found a little ninety-year-old lady who asked me how much I could afford. I told her I couldn't pay more than $500 a month, so she agreed. Little did I know what the future held in store for me on that very spot, and what a fateful day that was.

It was right there and then that I opened my very first business: a tiny import/gift shop that I called, out of the blue, "Curiosity That Killed The Cat."

A friend of mine and I painted the shop in bright colors and it looked pretty cute, pretty funky. I ran the shop for about a year and a half until I started to have panic attacks due to this boring and sedentary occupation. Contrasted with my previous bohemian lifestyle, sitting day in and day out in that little shop filled with metal and glass began to eat away at me, and most days the meager sales barely covered the bills. The only month that was any good was December because of Christmas. The other months I was just getting by, going crazy from sitting in that damn shop all day.

And all through this time, whiskey and I were still a couple. I was very conscientious about doing my hardest at work, but I always made sure that Happy Hour was a big part of my life. I could still drink a half a bottle of whiskey in one night, no problem.

One day my nephew, José—Alejandra's son—arrived at my house after backpacking in Europe. José wanted to stay in the States instead of going back to Argentina, so I told him he could live with me for a while. He soon started to make friends in town, and one friend in particular starting paying attention to me. His name was Alvaro. He was also Argentinean, and he was beautiful like a Greek statue, with gorgeous green eyes and golden hair that fell in soft ringlets.

Oh, did I mention that he was fifteen years younger than I was? By this time I was 36, and he was 21.

For nine months we flirted with the idea of starting a little romance, then we decided to go for it, and four months later we were married!

We put a lot of thought into planning the wedding, which was going to be fantastic. We had rented two cabins in a charming little town called Wimberley, about forty-five minutes from Austin. They were cozy in their decor and filled with all kinds of wonderful and colorful artwork. We didn't have much money so all our friends pitched in, including my friend Teresa, who was working for a top designer florist in Austin at the time. She arranged the flowers herself: gorgeous arrangements of soft pink and ivory roses.

Alvaro and I were to be married on a Saturday, so we rented the cabins Friday night so that we could stay the night and be ready for the ceremony in the morning. We spent Friday night decorating and celebrating in a little pre-wedding party (I could always still find an excuse to party!).

But like anything you try to plan out to a tee, something always goes wrong. My wedding day was no exception.

An old friend of mine named Shirley had agreed to play the harp for the ceremony on Saturday, but had to play another engagement Friday night in San Antonio, so she wasn't going to be able to make it to our little decorating-fest. But at the last minute her other gig was cancelled, so she decided to come out after all.

Apparently she got lost on the way, and she called me from her cell phone screaming and yelling, saying I was stupid to have a wedding so far out in the country and that there's no way she was going to play at my "fucking" wedding! This was, like, ten-thirty the night before my wedding, and I was in the cabin with all my girlfriends, and my artist friend Michael, drinking and dancing.

I hung up the phone and started to cry.

Just then there was a knock on the door. It was a cop, and he was saying that he was with the INS. He said he wanted to check my papers, and that he was going to deport me *immediately*. I was half drunk and already crying because of stupid Shirley canceling, so I just grabbed my little Mamacita and held her close. Memories of jail and deportation filled me with terror and everything began to swim around in my head and to go black. At that moment the cop pulled out a boom box, put on some disco music and started to take off his clothes!

It took me a few moments to realize what was happening, and even then I was still pretty upset. But then I finally said, "Well, maybe it would've been worth it to be busted by this cutie!" Everyone burst out laughing, and between sobs, I did, too.

The day of my wedding was October 12th. It was a beautiful day. We found a guy somewhere who played the guitar, so I did have music in spite of Shirley. As the wedding march began to play, Mamacita, who was also all dressed up for the occasion, walked down the aisle—which was a little path in the lawn. She pranced ahead of me as if she had rehearsed it a million times before. I made '*Mammi's* gown with a very fancy g-string of mine with beautiful pearls, and I added a pink bow and a few mini-roses. Needless to say, she and I were a beautiful match! Even Mamacita felt special as she wagged her little tail. She knew she was looking good!

Alvaro looked beautiful in his tuxedo. My dress was simple but adorable. I was in ivory satin with just a touch of beading and sequins, and my girlfriends did a fantastic job with my hair and make-up. The flowers were beautiful, the candles were lit, and everything was perfect, despite the fact that I was so hung over that I was worried I would lean over and throw up!

The ceremony went really well, although Alvaro's mom made it clear to everyone there that she thought her son should be taking his first communion, not getting married. I was mortified, to say the least, and at that time I thought her unbelievably rude. But today I look back and think that if I had a son who married a 36-year-old drunk, I would have shot her! (His poor mother!) But overall the wedding—I should say "party"—was a success.

Everything else was so romantic; we must have had fifty candles on each side of the aisle and flowers everywhere. There was no wind at all, so the candles all stayed lit, but there were a million mosquitoes. If you look back at the wedding video, it's really funny because everyone is slapping themselves like crazy. There were mountains of food that my girlfriends had made. It's amazing how well everything came together considering how drunk we were the night before.

After the ceremony it was time to continue the party! I remember a blur of dancing and drinking, and then it was time to cut the cake. By then I had been "celebrating" so much that I tried to drink my unity candle, thinking it was a cocktail. The funny thing is that Alvaro was—and still is—what people call a "teetotaler"; he didn't drink at all. I'm sure my behavior embarrassed him, but we were so in love at the time he didn't say anything. I knew that my drinking was out of place and out of control, but who likes to admit it, right?

When I first saw our wedding suite, I almost cried. The girls had put rose petals all over the bed and there were dozens of candles. But when Alvaro and I climbed into the bed, I looked through the window and saw a Peeping Tom! I didn't know who it was, but I found out later that some local teenage troublemakers had invaded our cabin area. They were helping themselves to the beer when someone realized that they weren't part of our party and chased them off.

Later that night, after almost everyone had left, gone to bed or passed out, my friend Michael decided to walk down the wooded path to the hot tub, which was about a five-minute walk through the woods. The tub was built into a wooden deck that had no railings and jutted out over a ravine filled with trees, rocks, and cactus. This must have been around three in the morning, and he stayed there about forty-five minutes. He got out of the hot tub soaking wet and attempted to get his clothes back on. But being so wet, and having been drinking since about ten o'clock that morning, his pants got hung up on his wet legs and he fumbled, then teetered, and finally fell face first off the edge of the deck. He fell about fifteen feet and landed with his bare chest in a huge clump of cactus. He also broke his right foot and badly sprained and cut his left knee. How he made it back to the cabins remains a mystery, even to him.

• • •

• • •

Alvaro and I tried to make the best out of our relationship, but it was difficult. Both of us worked sixteen-hour days, seven days a week — except Alvaro would sneak off every now and then on Sundays to race his motorcycle. He was a wonderful carpenter and fine wood craftsman. He could build a spiral staircase from scratch and do many other things beautifully. He had a strong boyish quality and he liked to play kind of rough, in a well-intentioned way. He was always punching me in the arm or pinching me somewhere, until I was almost black and blue from affection. The fifteen-year difference between us was starting to show.

The first Taco Trailer

··· 28 ···

The little import shop, "Curiosity" wasn't doing that well, so we decided to open a convenience store in the same location. We sold all the wrought iron in a big parking lot sale and Alvaro built all kinds of shelves inside the shop. We stocked it with toilet paper and light bulbs and cans of food and all that shit, but the hours were long and the profit was very low.

We named the store "Sugar and Spice" and we made it look like an old-fashioned general store. Michael painted it inside and outside, and added a cutout border around the front with painted representations of fruits, vegetables and different products.

Alvaro worked construction every day until two. I would wake up at five-thirty in the morning and go to the grocery store to get whatever we needed to restock the shelves at Sugar and Spice, then stay there until two when Alvaro would come and work until ten-thirty at night. By then, of course, I was exhausted and by the time he got home I was usually asleep, but he, with his youthful energy, would be ready for fooling around.

All day at the store I would sit and eat Fritos and then an ice cream and then more Fritos, and I put on thirty pounds. Alvaro was working construction, so he was tan and muscular, but my own morale and self-image were going to hell.

Everybody who knows me knows that I have such a soft spot in my heart for animals. I love them like crazy, and when one comes into my life it becomes a part of my family. I had loved Puppy Hot with all of my heart, and after he died Mamacita had helped to comfort me. But I wanted to give Mamacita a little friend, too. So one Christmas, Alvaro and I decided it would be a good idea to give her a little companion of her own, since he and I were working all the time. We brought home a little Yorkshire Terrier who we named Patchouli, and they became instant friends!

I have always liked little dogs, especially Yorkies because they're so adorable. Like all Yorkies, Patchouli was very tiny. Mamacita was silver, and he was black with a blonde head. We named him Patchouli because it's one of my favorite scents. He was very shy and took on the personality of the "step-child," always deferring to Mamacita to call the shots, maybe because *Mammi* was so demanding. It could be that he just knew his place. Even though Mamacita was only three pounds, she always outshone him. I like to think that *Patchou* just knew how to treat women well!

It was also at this time that Sissy came into our lives. Sissy was a black and white toy fox terrier, who must have been about eleven years old by the time that I met her. She had belonged to an old lady and had been very well cared for all of her life. When the old lady died, her boyfriend inherited Sissy.

The boyfriend didn't have much money, apparently, and he was one of the tenants in the trailer park behind Sugar and Spice. We didn't really know each other (we had only chatted a couple of times) but one day he said he had to go to Dallas for four days and he asked me if I would watch the dog. I was surprised that someone would ask a virtual stranger to take care of their dog. But I agreed; anything I can do to help a four-legged creature, I am happy to do! His instructions were to just go once a day and let her out to pee.

The first time I went to the trailer I saw the horrible condition that the poor doggie was living in, and noticed that all the man had left her for her to eat was a plate of spaghetti – not exactly a healthy diet for a dog, and who knows how long it had been sitting there? Even the water in her bowl was dirty. I let her out to pee, and with a broken heart, I put her back in the trailer. Later on when I returned again to let her out the second time, she talked to me with those beautiful brown eyes, begging me not to leave her there. I swear to God, she didn't need to talk. When I went home I couldn't stop thinking about her. So first thing the next morning when I let her out, I thought, "Well, I'm lonely at the store, and she's lonely in the trailer. I'll just take her to the store with me. We can keep each other company."

I did and she was very sweet. I had a little green rocking chair at the store, and she would hop up in the chair with me. As I chatted with customers we would munch on Cheetos, M&Ms and ice cream, and in a short time she became very protective of me. I had noticed that Sissy had a terrible cough, so I took her to the vet. I was told that there was something wrong with her trachea, undoubtedly from birth. The vet gave her some medicine to make it a little better and Sissy didn't cough quite so much afterwards. Also, we gave her a much needed shampoo bath, with generous amounts of suds!

That night as I was taking her back to the trailer, she suddenly stopped in her tracks. Then she ran back to the store, parked her booty down and looked at me like, "No way I'm leaving this place." So I looked at her and I said, "Say no more, Girlfriend. This is your new house!" She became a store fixture.

When I came back the next day, I was surprised to see that she had thrown herself quite a party to celebrate. She had gotten chips and candies and pulled them up into the chair and had eaten them! There was partially eaten food and candy all over the store. Needless to say she had also had some little bathroom accidents! Trying to open the store that morning took a little bit of work as I cleaned up the mess. You could tell that she knew that she had done something wrong. But I didn't scold her; I just rearranged the shelving order of all the food to make sure Sissy couldn't get to it again and put all the toilet paper, paper towels on bottom shelves, maybe hoping she could clean her own butt next time!

The days kept passing, with no news from her "dad." Alvaro, Sissy and I had developed a very strong bond. We were approaching day fifteen when finally this "gentleman" came back to pick her up.

The guy called to her to follow him, which she started to do. It was obvious she wasn't very excited about the idea. As they headed out the door and back to the trailer park, I started to cry. I missed her instantly and felt sorry for her bad luck.

She followed him about half way back to the trailer, then fifteen seconds later she turned and bolted back to the store and raced back to me. It was clear that she had adopted me. I talked to the guy and said, "You can't even take care of this dog — are you sure you want her?"

He said, "What, do *you* want her?"

"Sure I do," I said. So he let me have her, and of course I really came to love her. Sissy lived in the convenience store until we closed it down, and then she moved into the house with us.

Then, a couple of weeks after Sissy joined the family, we had another surprise. Into the store walked a girl with a tiny orange Chihuahua about one year old. She wasn't very nice to him, and to make him sit down she would step on his back! I wanted to send her front teeth to the back of her neck! But I kept my composure and said to her, "It doesn't look like you really like that dog."

She told me that it had been given to her as a present and that, no, she didn't really care for it. Well, I never liked Chihuahuas either, but you know me—if it's hard to love, I love it even more.

"Why don't you give it to me, then?" I offered. I couldn't believe the words were coming out of my mouth; I needed another dog like a hole in the head. But my heart went out to his sad little face. The girl looked a little shocked at first, but I could tell she was considering it.

She left with him that day, but then three days later Alvaro called me from the store to say that we were now the proud parents of a tan and white Chihuahua. His name was Pixie.

Pixie was so shy! You could tell he was abused, because when we first got him, you couldn't make eye contact with him; he would look away and put his tail between his legs. I took him to the house just to keep him until I could find a good home for him, but he and Patchouli got along so well, we decided to let him stay.

•••

But my love for animals doesn't stop with the four-legged and furry kind....

One day as I was leaving the store and going to my house with a friend, we drove past an itty-bitty something on the yellow line in the middle of the street. We couldn't tell what it was, but it appeared to be moving. "What the hell is that?" we both wondered.

Then I figured it out. "It's a little bird!" I exclaimed. I almost slammed on my brakes! We turned around immediately and I picked up the little bird and took him home.

At first I put him in a little ornamental cage that I had, but then I noticed that he had little bugs crawling all over him. There were so many that they were in his eyes and climbing out of his beak. I filled the kitchen sink with warm water (he was too hurt to fly away) and very gently began to rinse them off. After a few minutes the little bird began to revive and become more alert.

Because I'm a "city girl," however, I didn't really know what to do next. He was so scrawny he looked like he was at death's door. I didn't want him to starve to death, but I had no idea what to feed him. I called Alvaro, who had grown up on a ranch in Argentina. I thought that if anyone would know the answer it would be him.

"Alvaro, what do you feed little birds?" I asked him.

He paused for a second, then answered, "Why, Mari?"

I was anxious. "Just tell me what you feed little birds, Alvaro!"

"First just tell me *why*, and then I'll tell you what you feed them."

"*Because,* when I was leaving the convenience store today, I found a little injured bird in the middle of the road!"

"*Where* did you find the bird?" he continued.

"What does that matter?!" I was losing my patience, but he wouldn't let up.

"Just tell me in what road you found him."

"But what does that matter?"

"Just tell me the road!"

"You're pissing me off!" I yelled at him. "It was on fucking West Mary Street, so what?!"

"Because…on the way to the store today…I ran over a little bird on West Mary!"

"Oh, my God!" I couldn't believe it. First Alvaro runs over it—then I rescue it. The absurdity of the coincidence made us both start to laugh.

Still, it was actually the perfect metaphor for our relationship, and the relationship I've had with all the men in my life. I couldn't clean up my own messes, but I was more than willing to help clean up theirs.

After that I started to take the little bird to the convenience store with me every day. Because he couldn't fly, he had to walk around. Everywhere

I went, there was Sissy behind me, and the little bird behind Sissy! He seemed to think he was a little dog, just like her! Stranger still, sometimes I would be sitting in the old green rocking chair and he would climb all the way up my leg and up to my shoulder and would sit there just by my neck. I couldn't believe it! I fell in love with my little bird who thought he was a dog.

When my shift was over, I would tell Alvaro, "Please watch the little bird, please take care of him."

"Yeah, sure, Mari," he would say, but he didn't take his babysitting duties as seriously as I did. The little bird survived for a couple of weeks under our care, but one afternoon Alvaro called me to say that the little bird had left.

"What do you mean, he *left?*" I yelled.

"He took off," Alvaro responded, rather unconcerned. He explained that he had gone outside the store with the little bird and was talking with a customer, but that when he looked again he couldn't find the bird. I immediately went to the store to help look for it, but we couldn't find it anywhere.

Two days after the disappearance of my little bird, we discovered that he had drowned in the little pond next to the store. Apparently while Alvaro was visiting with the customer, the bird had walked over to the pond to get a drink and it had fallen in and drowned. When any of my pets die, I am completely devastated, and this little bird was no exception. I fell into a very big sadness that lasted for weeks.

··· 29 ···

Sugar and Spice was not a big money maker, and the hours were long and tiring. Some of the tenants from the trailer park on the property behind the store added a lot of color to the daily goings-on at the store, to say the least. When I first arrived at this property and opened Curiosity, the trailer park was quite dangerous. The park's ninety-year-old owner was afraid to even collect the rent from the residents. People would just pull in, park, and set up, staying for as long as they wanted, sometimes without ever paying at all. There were drug deals going on, police coming in and out. It was a nightmare.

When the old lady died, the property passed to her son and his wife, who really put things back in order. I never really had any problems with the people in the park, myself, when I had Curiosity. But after I opened the convenience store I began to have regular contact with all of them. They would ask me to front them beer and cigarettes. Usually I would.

For this reason most of them liked me and we got along great. The landlords liked me because I always paid my rent and I was always making improvements to the place. Still, as I have said, the hours were long and the profit just wasn't there. And, to top it all off, my relationship with Alvaro was deteriorating. We were both unhappy, and I knew I needed a change.

Then tax time rolled around. I had the money set aside to pay the taxes on my business (the taxes I owed were more money than I used to earn in a whole year!), but I was so tired of the daily grind of the store—and tired of cleaning other people's toilets on the side just to get by—that it just didn't seem fair. I knew that I had to come up with something else.

Once again, desperation drove me to another innovation. I decided to file an extension on my taxes and I took a huge leap into the scary black void called "hope." I thought about what new business I could do and I figured, "Well, everybody has to eat." So I decided to open up a taco stand. Never mind that I didn't even know how to cook.

I took that money I had saved and used it for a down payment on a little trailer. A *really* little trailer. I had it painted on the outside to look like a little Mexican casita, complete with chickens in the yard, a clay tile roof, pots of geraniums, and a portrait of my poor little dead bird. I parked it in the courtyard next to the store. I bought eggs, butter and cheese, brought in pots and pans from my house, and started to sell tacos (my first taco burned like Joan of Arc!). A friend of mine suggested that I call it "Taco Xpress." I didn't love it, but the name stuck.

Almost immediately I felt that I had just signed my own death warrant. Sales those first two weeks didn't even top seventeen dollars a day. When someone wanted a taco I would dash next door and cook it, and when someone wanted to buy a coke or a roll of toilet paper I would fly out of the trailer and into the convenience store, ring them up, throw the change at them and run back to the trailer. I was just about in tears at what my life had become. The old security I'd had with Dale seemed distant and remote, like a thing I once dreamed.

They say that there is always a light at the end of the tunnel, always a silver lining to each dark cloud.

Whatever the explanation, one day in the middle of my third month of cooking tacos, an angel intervened on my behalf: a food critic for the local newspaper stopped at the store to buy I don't know what, maybe a soda, and, being somewhat hungry and in a hurry, ordered a taco "to go." This resulted in a glowing review of the "funky new taco stand on South Lamar," and the road to my future took a u-turn. I felt like I'd been discovered by a Hollywood agent!

My sales shot up to two, three hundred a day, then more. *Much* more! Lines began to form and people began to talk. I hired extra help, both in the store and for the taco stand.

•••

In the early days of the little taco trailer, the business just hadn't been there, so I was able to call my girlfriends to come and play canasta with me. But my canasta days were long gone! I hired a girl to help me cook; then two months later I hired another one. My life, and my family, was starting to expand.

It didn't take long for me to realize that, as cute as it was, Sugar and Spice sucked. Six months after opening the taco trailer, the decision to close the store, after a year and a half of frustration and penny-pinching, felt like both a blessing and another leap into the abyss. Converting the space, yet

•••

again, to accommodate an indoor restaurant was the most expensive business undertaking yet. Now I had to contend with contractors, electricians, plumbers, health department regulations, fire department codes, city this and city that, vent hoods, handicap facilities, and huge, mounting expenses.

I was ecstatic about my success, but I began to worry. What if it's all a fluke, a cruel cosmic joke? What if people stop coming to buy tacos? What if I fail again? Before, it was "nothing ventured, nothing gained." Before, I was a kid with my whole life ahead of me. Before, things could only get better. Now—I was investing thousands of dollars into a sand castle that might, at any moment, crumble in the lapping tide, lost forever. But I couldn't turn back. The pool was full and I needed to dive in, or never get in the water at all and let my feet burn!

There was a brief transitional time while we were converting the space from a convenience store to a restaurant. We were trying to sell out of what little product we had left: four or five off-brands of cigarettes, a few six-packs of beer, a half-dozen cans of spaghetti, maybe one cake mix, stuff like that.

One morning, we had some men working on the air conditioning unit outside and Alvaro and I were rearranging the shelves, moving furniture around to figure out how best to maximize the space with the materials we had. I wanted to move the main counter in the front of the store from one side to the other, but we had installed a panic button under the counter that was directly tied in to the police station. I told Alvaro to just cut the wire so we could move the counter. He said the police would come, but I said if he just cut the wire and didn't push the button, it would be fine. So with a quick inhalation of breath and a wince, he chopped the wire in two. No alarms, no flashing lights, nothing.

We had just started to slide the heavy counter across the floor when one of the A/C men came in and asked for Alvaro's help with something outside, so I was left alone. Several minutes later, a couple stumbled into the store, drunk and arguing with one another. They made their way towards the back of the store to the glass coolers. The man was begging the woman to buy him a six-pack of beer and she was sloppily pushing him away and swatting at him. After a minute she relented, swung the glass door open and retrieved a cold six-pack. They had made it halfway back to the counter when the woman saw me. "You got a bathroom here?" she slurred.

"What?" I could barely understand her.

"A bathroom? A toilet? You got one?" I swear she only had two teeth in her mouth.

"No, no public restroom," I replied, rather curtly. I didn't want to have to clean up some chick's vomit on top of everything else I had to do, and I wanted them out as soon as possible.

"Uh-oh," she said. She set the six-pack down on the cement floor, squatted, and proceeded to pee all over the beer, the floor and herself! She had so much pee and it came out so hard that it sounded like a cow emptying its bladder instead of a human being!

"What the fuck?" I yelled. The back door opened and Alvaro ran in with the A/C guys, while simultaneously two cops raced through the front door with pistols drawn, answering the call from the disconnected panic button.

Like a well-rehearsed movie scene, everyone in the room stopped and said at the same time, "What's going on?" The police hauled the couple away for public intoxication and public lewdness, and as I went to the back of the store for the mop and mop-bucket, I thought how happy I would be to see the end of Sugar and Spice.

··· 30 ···

My relationship with my landlords remained great; they were always supportive of my little businesses and helped me with all of my endeavors. They were so generous that they let me park my trailer next to my building with no extra rent. I considered them to be family.

Once the convenience store closed, I excitedly started decorating my new restaurant. I added murals to create a funky yet homey atmosphere. We painted an old pot-bellied stove in one corner, shelves full of objects, pots and pans hanging next to the grill, and a cozy sleeping cat on top of a cabinet. Taco Xpress didn't turn out to be a crumbling sand castle after all, but continued to grow and become more and more successful.

And I couldn't believe that I was still going after a year and a half! For the first time, I didn't have to shut my business down again to open something else. If I had, the next thing would probably have been a mortuary; I was running out of ideas! But thank God, this one worked!

And the reviews! I was getting so many reviews in papers, magazines and on the Internet, and not one of them was in any way bad. One of the first reviews, written by *Austin Chronicle* food editor Virginia Wood, proclaimed me "South Austin's Taco Queen," and the name stuck.

The restaurant was starting to make good money, but there were still expenses, taxes, and plenty of unforeseen mini-disasters. As great as things were going, I was still new to the restaurant business, and I had many trials to overcome and lessons to learn along the way.

One day, as my friends and I were busy working on building a stage in the outdoor patio area and painting murals on the wall, a man in a wheelchair arrived outside the front door, opened it, and struggled to get his chair over the two-inch high threshold. Seeing that he was not having an easy time of it, I went to him and offered to help him.

He said, "No, I want to be able to do it by myself! You need a ramp."

I said, "I'm sorry, Sir, I'd be happy to, but I have people in wheelchairs coming in all the time without problems. I didn't know I needed one."

He became very agitated and he said, "You have money to pay that artist to paint a mural outside, and money to build a stage on your patio, so you must have money to make your restaurant handicap accessible!"

The City of Austin had given me a certificate of occupancy. I thought I was already in compliance with everything, so his anger caught me by surprise. The guy parked himself in the middle of the doorway, took off his shirt to show all the customers how twisted his body was, and started yelling. No customers could come in, and no one could leave! He was really making a scene and accusing me of being an uncaring, money-hungry bitch. I was genuinely very upset by this. I told him about my nephew who went blind at the age of fourteen, but got married, graduated from college and even played sports, and also has a *great* attitude and is a great inspiration to others – so why did *he* have to have such a bad attitude, when I was trying everything I could to be helpful to him.

"The fact that you are in a wheelchair is not an excuse to be an asshole," I told him.

There were about fifteen customers in the restaurant, and each of them took my side against the guy. One customer got up to leave and the guy wouldn't move to let him out the door. The customer said, "Will you let me leave?" and the guy said, "No, you can't leave here until I get some satisfaction." The customer tried to push his way through and the wheelchair guy tried to pin him in the doorway! The customer then lost his balance and *fell* through the doorway. I was terribly upset at this point, and didn't know what to do. Then the customer got up and yelled at the guy that two could play that game and that he was going to sue the guy for causing his accident!

Everybody started arguing with the guy in the wheelchair, and finally I told him I was going to call the police. He said, "Are you refusing to serve me?" and I said, "You're damn right I am refusing to serve you. I want you completely off of my property, *sir*." Finally he left, spewing curses at me.

I was totally sympathetic to his feelings on the matter, but nothing could separate him from his anger, even after I had agreed to put in a ramp.

A few days later I left the restaurant to go pick up Alvaro for lunch, when I noticed one of my employees driving behind me, trying to wave me down. I stopped my car to see what he wanted.

He said, "María! María! You have to come back to the restaurant! They're all there with signs – they won't let anybody in!"

"*Who* is there?" I asked.

"The wheelchair people, the wheelchair people!" he cried.

"Oh, my God..."

We flew back to the restaurant, and the sight that met me was unbelievable! There were about twenty-five people in wheelchairs, four police cars, and customers who couldn't get through the line of chairs. Our wheelchair-bound customer from the other day and his friends were posting flyers on the building and on the cars outside saying that I discriminated against them.

I was being picketed!

I parked in the middle of the parking lot, threw open my door and jumped out of the car. I was furious! After all, I had four employees in there who needed to work in order to make a living. The situation was escalating very quickly. I started yelling at the people in the wheelchairs, and one of the cops came over to me, saying, "Excuse me! Excuse me!"

Apparently the police thought I must be a monster to have all these poor handicapped people angry with me.

I said to the officer, "Won't you at least listen to my side of the story?" Then I started to cry. He calmed down a little, too, and did listen to me. By the end of it he was completely on my side, and asked me how I wanted to deal with the situation.

"What can I do?" I said. "This guy and his friends are ruining my business, even though I am trying to be considerate. I told them I would put in a ramp but they refuse to listen to me."

"Well, we can call for a bus to take them all away for trespassing," the officer offered.

Oh God, that would look great on the news! "No, no, I don't want to be mean to them, but I don't want them back here if they're going to have this attitude."

• • •

So, with the police behind me, I decided to try and talk to the guy one more time. I said, "Look, Dude, unless you stop this picketing, you are not welcome here now or ever. I'm willing to drop all of this and forget what happened, but you need to knock it off."

The group eventually left, but the guy was still angry, and unfortunately he didn't stop his vendetta against me. During the next month he would park outside of Taco Xpress and bad-mouth me to my customers. Not knowing what to do, I called a lawyer to help me stop this madness. He talked to the guy and told him, "Look, María is not a bad person. Why are you doing this to her?"

It turns out what he really wanted to be able to come back to Taco Xpress as a customer. He thought he was unwelcome there. I finally told my lawyer that he was welcome to come back. A week later he and a group of his friends showed up and we were able to make peace once and for all. We even took a photo together, my arms extended to embrace all of their wheelchairs.

•••

That wasn't the only problem I encountered. As time went on and the restaurant got busier and busier, some of the people in the trailer park behind me began to change their attitude towards me from supportive to negative. When the outdoor stage was completed I started having live music on the weekends. Some of the neighbors called the police about the noise and the parking, giving me all kinds of shit.

When I first started having musicians play at the restaurant, a Swiss musician who used to be a friend of mine asked if he could play there. That would have been fine, except for the fact that he played very loud heavy metal music. I wanted more mellow music, and said, "Look, dude, I wouldn't have a problem, but this is a restaurant and people want to talk. It's not a concert stage. Also, I don't want to disturb all the people living in the back."

Apparently this pissed him off, because who do you think was the first person to start a petition in the trailer park about the noise from the music at the restaurant? Bingo.

At that same time, I was having a huge problem with the electric breakers going off all the time. I had to throw away many, many pounds of spoiled meat and eggs every day because the coolers wouldn't stay on. I couldn't understand it, and I was spending a fortune on electricians to come out and tell me that there was nothing wrong.

I had just hired my friend Fernando, my friend who had waited tables with me at the Mexican restaurant in Austin, to manage Taco Xpress. He was working one day when the breakers went off. He raced outside, just in time to see the Swiss guy running away from the breaker box! That little sucker was responsible for costing me thousands of dollars over the previous couple of weeks! Now I was furious! Fernando and I called the cops. There was not a lot they could do, but they did get him to confess, and they made him apologize to me. I bought a padlock for the breaker box that afternoon.

Through all of these incidents, I have become good friends with all the police in the area. Sometimes I can't believe it, considering the fear and loathing I held for them from my past. If you had told me twenty years ago that I would be friends with cops and would enjoy hanging out with them, I would have said you were smoking something wacky!

Taco Xpress has, from the beginning, been a hangout for local musicians, as well as some pretty big celebrities from all fields. One wall in the restaurant is dedicated to celebrity autographs, and after only five years there was barely space left to write on.

One of my old friends in Austin is the great musician Alejandro Escovedo. But there was a time, during the era of the convenience store, when he needed a little extra cash, so he helped me behind the counter. We were probably the only convenience store who had a great musician working the register!

Of course, when I opened the restaurant, he happily played with his band on our stage in the courtyard. Every year during the famous South By Southwest Music Festival, which draws musicians and record label scouts from around the world, Alejandro organizes the day of concerts at the restaurant, which always features not only Alejandro and his band, but names like Ian Moore, Stephen Bruton, Will Sexton and other fantastic bands and musicians from around the country. We usually feature eight or nine musicians or bands in a huge one-day-only concert.

• • •

One day, musician and good friend, Stephen Bruton, pulled up outside the restaurant just after we had closed for the evening. He came in and asked if it was too late to order some tacos, and I said that for him I would go ahead and do it. Once his order was ready he asked me to come out to the car and meet his friend, so I said, "Sure, why not?" My friend Michael, who was there visiting, watched as I went out to meet Stephen's friend. I went over to his BMW and in the passenger seat was some lady with bright red hair.

He said, "María, this is my friend Bonnie. She's staying at my house while she's in town, and I told her she *had* to try your tacos."

"Hi, Bonnie," I said, not thinking she was anybody I should recognize.

"Hi," she said in a friendly way. I went back into the restaurant, and found my friend Michael about to explode.

"María," he said, "don't you know who that *was?*"

"Yeah, that's Stephen's friend Bonnie. What's the big deal?"

"*Big deal?* You're playing her CD right now in the restaurant! That's Bonnie Raitt!"

"Oh, my God!" I cried out. One of my favorite singers, and I didn't even recognize her! Well, that's just like me, and maybe that's why musicians all feel so comfortable in my restaurant—because I don't know who the hell they are and I treat them like anybody else. I never knew it when Bob Dylan and Sean Penn were there, they just sat in the corner, and my customers or my employees told me later who they were. I guess I'm glad I didn't recognize them at the time because I probably would have embarrassed myself somehow.

··· 31 ···

As time went by the restaurant became more and more popular. There were lines out the door and down the sidewalk: hippies in tie-dyed T-Shirts, yuppies in suits and Izod shirts, pierced punks, bikers, joggers, cops, construction workers and grandparents with their families — all kinds of people standing in line, side by side, waiting to order my tacos. People would park in the grass, on the sidewalks, down in the next block.

In 1997 or '98 I received a call from Flaca. She said she had, for the past ten years, been thinking about wanting a baby.

"What?!" I said to her, I was amazed! I thought we had always been pretty much on the same page about that subject. But now, she told me, she had definitely decided to get pregnant.

"How?" I asked. "With who?"

She said she had thought about it a long time and had finally gone to Yuri with her decision. After all, they had been friends since they were teenagers and he had agreed to be a part of it (if you know what I mean).

She called back only three short months later to tell me she was pregnant. A month after the baby was born, Alvaro and I flew to Mexico to visit my super-gay Flaca who now was a mom! She named the boy Axel. Axel was one of the prettiest baby boys I had ever seen.

We stayed at a beautiful historic hotel in Oaxtepec called The Hacienda, which was built in the 1700s and had been a real hacienda. It had beautifully manicured grounds, and five swimming pools with waterfalls and ponds linking them together. We had a great visit with my brand new little "nephew." It was so odd, though, to think of Flaca as a mother and to see her breast-feeding this perfect little baby. If you had removed the baby from her arms, you never would have known she had ever been pregnant: she was still so skinny! I wish I had been able to see her with her little round belly. But she glowed; she was so happy to be a mom.

Alvaro and I returned to Austin after a week and got back into our separate routines. But as good as things were in the restaurant, the same could not be said for the situation at home. Alvaro was still working construction, and I was at the restaurant all day, every day. Being around food all day,

I never managed to work off those extra pounds. And why bother? I was too tired when I got home to be much of a wife to "my little husband," as I liked to call him. I was feeling my years, and in the midst of the excitement and hubbub of the restaurant, I was inwardly becoming more and more depressed. Once again, I needed change. But what? And how? What could I do that would not blow apart the success and the financial security that was finally coming to me?

Then, one day it came to me. Actually, it came to Alvaro. "I want to move, Mari," he said.

"Well, where do you want to go?" I asked.

"We need another house, a better house, *our* house." And I realized that Alvaro did not feel like this was his home, it was *my* house from *my* settlement with *my* first husband. And even though we had added a second story and loft, the house was just a little too bohemian to really be comfortable.

Still, I didn't see how we could afford the time or the money to move at this point in our lives. I said, "And you're gonna buy it with your good looks?"

As I've said before, I have never considered buying anything on credit. I have always felt that if you want something and you have the money for it, you buy it. Otherwise you don't buy it. You don't live beyond your means. And though the restaurant was doing well and Alvaro was working, the real estate market in Austin was skyrocketing, and I had a lot of expenses.

But the idea wouldn't go away; now that Alvaro had suggested it, it wouldn't leave the forefront of my thoughts. "A new house, a better house, *our* house" kept echoing in my mind. Eventually a swimming pool was added to this imaginary house, and I could feel the cool water on my skin after a hard day at the restaurant. I tend to be a bit compulsive by nature—well, okay, I am *completely* obsessive/compulsive—so I obsessed.

A few days later Alvaro called me. "Mari! You won't believe it! There are some old customers from the convenience store who are going to put their house up for sale, and it's right behind the restaurant. And it's big, Mari, and it has lots of land!"

I was still in my PJs, but I jumped in the car anyway and drove to the house, which was on the street only a block away from my restaurant.

Alvaro had been right. It was a great house: all stone, built in 1948. Its original owner had named the house "Sunnyside," and the name was elegantly carved into a cornerstone near the front door. It seemed a perfect name for the place, and it gave me hope for my marriage and for the future. The property it was on looked like a park—you could barely see the end of the land, which was fully landscaped with rose gardens, flowering fruit trees, huge, ancient oaks and pecan trees. The inside was another story!

So I talked to the owner, then I went back home and began to think. How could I manage this? It was crazy, wasn't it? But it would be great for our marriage to have our own place and to make our own memories. But how could we afford it? It was too risky. I never had credit in my life, and neither did Alvaro. I couldn't imagine that anybody would lend us a quarter of a million dollars, which was the asking price. I pictured myself on the sidewalks of Las Vegas, of that girl I used to be, and I just knew that any bank person looking at me would see her, too. And then in my mind's eye I saw again a swimming pool in that huge, park-like backyard, surrounded by the fragrant scent of all those flowers.

We had to try.

Putting our house on the market wasn't as difficult as I had imagined. As I said earlier, it was in a rather prestigious neighborhood, and Alvaro and I had put a lot of work into it. I found a customer who was in real estate, and she came to appraise the house. I almost shit when she came back and said all she thought we could ask was two hundred and forty thousand dollars! I called the owner of Sunnyside and told him not even to put up a "For Sale" sign: I was going to buy his house!

Our old house was on the market just a few days and I already had two offers, and more people were still coming by to see the house. Also, at this time my sister Margarita was in Austin visiting me, and when I would go to the restaurant to work, Margarita would sit quietly in a corner of my house and show it to any realtor or prospective buyer.

My poor dog Sissy's condition was getting worse with age. She still had that terrible cough, caused by the deformed trachea, but now very often when she would cough, she would also fart like a sailor. I came home one day and my sister said that I had to do something with Sissy, take her to work with me or just somehow get her out of the house during the day.

"Why?" I asked her.

"Because when people come to look at the house and Sissy and I are downstairs, the people hear her cough and fart, and I'm afraid they are thinking that it is me! I'm too embarrassed to stay here any more!"

Then a lady named Virginia fell out of the heavens and into my lap. We loved each other immediately. She was an older-than-middle-aged lady who liked to drink and was just getting a nasty divorce from her well to-do husband. He had to buy her a house, and she wasn't too concerned about what he had to pay. She paid every penny of the asking price, and on top of that bought almost every piece of furniture I had in the house! And *pap, pap, pap!* The deal was done!

Closing the deal on the new house was another story altogether.

I went to the owner with my realtor. I had a contract and ten thousand dollars in earnest money, all of which he eagerly accepted. Later that night, though, he called to say that he wasn't sure he wanted to go through with the deal, that it hadn't been on the market yet, and that I had put too much pressure on him to sell it. I told him, "Dude, you cannot do that, we have a contract!"

"Actually, we don't," he said.

I started to get a sick feeling in my stomach.

He went on, "It is my mother who actually owns the house, and she still lives out of the country, so we don't really have a contract. The house is not even in my name, so the contract is not valid."

"Wait a minute, you fucker," I said, "if you signed this contract and took my ten thousand and you don't have the right to do it, I'm going to charge you with fraud, you piece of shit." So I had to get a lawyer.

Right away I found Tom Hutchison, a loud, aggressive man who stood something like six foot, seven inches tall. But to me he was a precious angel. He called me "Coochie-Coochie" and he took such great care of me, I really trusted him. We became great friends, and he would come often to Taco Xpress to eat or to visit in the few months that we knew each other.

So with Tom by my side I went to the owner and I said, "You have two choices: you can sell the house to me, or I'm going to press charges." So he talked to his mother and she agreed to sell. Everything was set — or so I thought!

By law I bought the house and it was mine, but they were still living there and they wouldn't leave. The problem, they said, was that the kids were still in school and they didn't have anywhere else to go, combined with this excuse and that excuse. On top of that, Virginia wanted to move into *my* old house. We had to go to court to get a legal eviction.

The day we were to appear in court, Tom called me at home and said, "It's me, Coochie-Coochie. Listen, I'm really sorry to have to tell you this, but I have another really important case and I won't be able to be with you in court today."

"What?" I said, "What am I going to do?"

"Don't worry, Coochie-Coochie, my partner Ross, whom you know, is going to fill in for me. He's completely up-to-date and it's an easy win on your part. You don't really need me there, but this other client does."

Well, what could I do? So I called Dale and my friend Michael, and they both agreed to go with us for moral support. We were scheduled to appear at eleven o'clock in the morning before the District Judge. We met Ross in the parking lot and entered the courthouse together. My heart was racing, and I was wishing that Tom could have walked in with me. I looked around, and on the far side of the courtroom I was shocked to see Tom Hutchison!

"Tom! You made it!" I cried.

"Yeah, I was able to postpone the other case after all, just for you, Coochie-Coochie!" I can't tell you how relieved and how happy I felt!

At eleven o'clock, on the dot, we were called into the courtroom. We entered the small room and were seated before the empty judge's bench. We were the first and only people in the room. A moment later the judge entered the room, very regal in his black robes. He sat and quickly scanned the room, his eyes stopping on me.

For an instant my heart fluttered, but calmed just as quickly when the judge said, "You're not cooking tacos today, María?" He was one of my customers! (This was one of the first times I started to get the sensation that I was becoming well known in the community – or at least South Austin!).

And while I was feeling better and better about the outcome of this miserable situation, I looked over at the owner, who was sinking deeper and deeper into the wooden bench. When the judge asked him for some documents, he fumbled and mumbled, finally saying that he must have left them at home. The judge ordered him to go home and retrieve those papers, and that he better be quick about it. The guy slipped out of the courtroom, leaving us there alone with the judge.

"How's it going, Tom?" The judge asked my gentle giant of an attorney. "Have you been up lately?"

"Just last weekend, Your Honor."

As it turned out, both the judge and Tom were pilots and flew their own planes, and sometimes saw each other at the small airfield where they kept their birds. Well, that was perfect, because so was Dale! So for the next forty-five minutes, the three of them talked about flying, all the places they had been, and all their near misses and high dramas in the air.

Finally, the guy returned with whatever papers he was supposed to have. The judge scanned them for a brief second and then found in my favor. Done. There was an order of eviction and the judge told me to enjoy my new home.

(A very sad note: Two weeks later we were all devastated to hear on the news that my gentle giant, my sweet gruff lawyer, Tom, had taken his new wife and two kids flying for Mother's Day and had crashed in the beautiful Texas hill country. All four of them died, burned beyond recognition.)

At eight o'clock in the morning on May 1st, three months after the guy had signed the sales contract—and the day set by the judge in the eviction order—I arrived at my new house with some of the girls from my restaurant. I was expecting to have to clean like mad before bringing in what things I had that Virginia did not buy: clothes, dishes, personal items, etc.

To my extreme dismay, the guy's wife, his brother, and his two kids were all still sound asleep. Almost nothing had been removed from the house, and certainly nothing had been cleaned. When I re-entered Earth's orbit, I grabbed my girls and got to work. Apparently the guy had been arrested the night before and was still in jail. The wife and brother had been up all night trying to get him out, and they had, of course, planned on waiting until the last microsecond to start packing and moving out — an event which, because of the arrest, never happened at all.

I was exhausted from having spent so much time packing my own stuff and furious about this turn of events, so the girls and I just start throwing the families' belongings into the front yard as fast as we could. Alvaro was on his way with another truckload of our things. It was only just before the mountain of rubbish in the front yard began to obscure every inch of grass that the family, rubbing their bloodshot eyes, reluctantly began to pitch in and help. The two boys were pulling toys out of Mount Rubbish and were playing in the driveway.

Eventually, the house was emptied and, much later, completely disinfected. I was free to move in!

My first priority, after getting settled, was to eradicate them and bring in my own flavor. My friend Michael and I walked through the house with a color deck of paint chips and a sketchpad. He said that definitely the kitchen should be targeted first. I looked at him and said, "What are you talking about? Look at this place! There is no 'first.' We have to do the whole thing and we have to do it yesterday."

"I see..." replied Michael.

Thus began four months of renovation: knocking down walls, ripping up tile, painting, faux finishing, putting in graceful archways and French doors throughout the interior, and initiating a frantic, compulsive race to buy out every antique shop in the vicinity. Because of all the dogs, I was hesitant to put any type of rug or carpet on the hardwood floors, so Michael painted oriental carpets, very softly and subtly, on the ceilings!

And the swimming pool! Our friend Johnny Walker (yes, that's really his name!) had a pool company, and it was not long before the bulldozers, Johnny and his workmen had come and gone and left us with a crystal clear blue oasis in the center of the vast park-like rear lawn. It was surrounded by roses, flowering fruit and ornamental trees, bougainvillea, Mexican petunias, hibiscus, and exuded peace and tranquility. Finally my vision had become reality! As Michael would later say, we turned a four-bedroom cottage into a two-bedroom mini-mansion.

•••

A month later Alvaro and I divorced.

What was intended to relieve the pressures in our marriage had only added to them, the age gap became an un-crossable chasm, and Alvaro now, more than ever, wanted children. His vision of the new house turned out to be quite different from mine; he saw himself in that beautiful yard racing remote-controlled cars with his kids, playing soccer, digging for fishing worms, and I'm not sure what else.

All the renovations to make the house livable were all paid for by me, with money from the sale of the old house and the restaurant income. Alvaro could have pitched in, but he had just bought his third motocross bike. Well, irreconcilable differences happen; I loved him too much to deny him his dreams, so I suggested to him that it might be better for him to find someone his own age. Of course our divorce was very friendly.

Now I was in a big, new house, and all alone for the first time in my life. I had always been able to move from one bad relationship directly into another one. This time I had no one waiting in the wings, and I was forced to confront many fears and issues. Michael told me that if I allowed myself the opportunity I would not only learn to deal with being alone, he guaranteed me that I would actually really love it. I was more than skeptical; I felt sure he was out of his vodka-marinated mind!

The following months did prove to be very difficult. The house, though beautiful now, seemed to me to be little different from the hotel in the movie, *The Shining*: bigger than I could manage alone, bigger than I could ever feel comfortable in. It was actually scary—at night especially—and as I looked out the windows, the rear of the house seemed to be a dark hiding place for all kinds of real or imagined monsters. I remember standing at one end of the house looking through the living room, the dining room, the long hallway extending from that and all the way to the far wall of the last bedroom, and it simply terrified me. The next day I called Dale and he bought me a shotgun and some ammunition, which I kept under my bed for a very long time. I also had one of my cop/friend/customers come to the house to tell me what I could do to make the place safer.

I was still overweight, my self-esteem was very low, my new house filled me with fear and anxiety, but the restaurant continued to grow and to do well.

A couple of months later Alvaro and I tried to reconcile. He moved back in, but in our case, the old saying was true: you really can't go home again. Alvaro wanted to turn the backyard into a motocross circuit, and I said no way! I got tired—again—of picking up his underwear from the floor and cleaning up after him, and he was tired that I never had free time to be with him. The same old reasons we grew apart in the first place were still there. So for the next year and a half we would reconcile, break up, reconcile again, and each time it became clearer and clearer that we just didn't have what it takes to be together. Eventually Alvaro did re-marry, but not to me! He married someone his own age, and they are very happy together.

I started going to another shrink, and he was very good with dealing with the here and now. I began to focus on my fears and to start dealing with them one by one.

I decided to rent the back bedroom to a friend, so I would have some company in the house, which was great for a while. I was becoming comfortable within myself and within my house. The best times were when my roommate was away and I could start to relax, to keep the house as I wanted to, to do what I wanted to, when I wanted to — in other words, to enjoy just being alone with myself. This is one of the biggest breakthroughs of my life: to feel the power of not needing!

My life was occupied with the restaurant and my friends, hard work and good, quiet times with my menagerie, which came to include three chickens, two roosters, two peacocks, four dogs, two parakeets and my new favorite: a Military Macaw named Guacamaya, who, at only one year old, was already having long, hysterically funny conversations with herself. "Guaca, Guaca, Guaca! Pretty bird! Wow, wow, wow, Guaca! Whassup, Guaca! Guaca, Guaca, Guaca!" I found her endearing and wonderfully funny. Life was good indeed.

One day my roommate and I were dashing about town in my little VW bug, when the car automatically and without explanation pulled into a fancy foreign car lot. When we left an hour later, the bug did not, and the car parked in the driveway of my house was now a shiny sliver of obsidian: a black Jaguar.

Marrying Alvaro ...

⋯ 32 ⋯

Throughout all the years, Flaca remained a constant in my life. Through my marriages to Dale and to Alvaro, Flaca was my friend and confidante. We spoke at least twice a week, without fail.

Flaca had loved Alvaro, but she was happy to hear that I had chosen to be on my own and doing what was right for me. During one of our routine conversations, Flaca said, "María, *mijita*, I found a lump on my boob. I gotta go see some fucking doctor to get it taken out." I, myself, had had three surgeries over the past three years—one per year!—for the exact same thing, and all of them had been benign.

"Flaca, *no te preocupes*, not to worry. I get a fucking lump every time I sneeze. They'll take it out and you'll be fine, you'll see."

A week later, my phone rang. It was Alex, her brother. Flaca had been scheduled for surgery that day and he was supposed to call me to let me know how she was doing after they removed the lump. "María, Flaca just got out of surgery. She wanted me to tell you that it was cancer. They cut her breast off."

I couldn't believe it. I was devastated for my poor Flaca. "How is she, Alex? Is she depressed?"

"Yeah, she's depressed," he said. "She doesn't want to talk right now."

"Tell her that I love her and that I'm coming to see her —."

"María," he said, "the good news is that they got it all. It was localized on her breast." I sighed with relief. My Flaca was boobless, but she was going to live.

A few days later Flaca called me. I reassured her telling her that it was all going to be all right. She was coming to terms with her new figure. "Ah, María. What's one less tit? I never had much of a rack anyway...." She laughed, and I laughed with her.

⋯

Christmas was nearing and although I was becoming more and more at peace with myself, I knew Christmas alone would be depressing. I got a hold of my friend Michael, who was also alone, and made a proposition. "Why don't we go somewhere? Let's take a trip!" I urged.

"Sounds great! Where do you want to go?" He was all ears.

"Oh, I don't know...I was thinking Cuba."

"What? Can we go there? We *can't* go there. We can not go to Cuba!"

"Oh, don't be such a wimp —"

"Well how do we get there, María?"

"Simple. We fly to Mexico City, we buy a ticket to Havana, and we get on the plane. When we are staying over in Mexico City, maybe you can meet Flaca."

"There's no way! I could never —" He tried to protest, but he's no match for me!

• • •

Returning to Mexico City was a great feeling. I had called Flaca. She met us in our hotel room at the airport, and she brought Yuri and Axel, who was now two years old. Michael immediately dubbed him "Super Axel." He's a beautiful boy, sharp as a tack, and extremely sweet-natured.

But I had not really been prepared for Flaca's appearance. The chemotherapy had left her thinner than ever, and she wore a large, brightly colored bandana over her nearly bald head.

"You wanna see my scar?" she asked as she lifted her shirt to show me. "Yep, it's gone," I tried to make light of the absence of her left breast, trying to cover the deep wave of emotion that swept over me.

Images of my mother came back to me, that old terror of surgery and cancer caused my face to flush, and memories of all those nights lying next to Flaca, years ago when we were practically kids, caused me pangs of sadness and remorse.

• • •

I had loved this woman. I loved her still in many ways, as I still loved Dale, and Alvaro, but differently, because with Flaca I had really shared some of the lowest times, some of the times that will never fade from memory. And with women it is also different, especially when it's the first woman, the first time.

Anyway, we talked, all of us, late into the night, and I remember that at one point Axel had fallen asleep. Flaca rested her bald head on his little chest and he automatically raised his two-year-old arms to caress and to hold his sick mother, and I realized that he must do this often — this gesture was habitual — and it broke my heart for both of them.

The next morning Michael and I headed for our departure gate at the airport in Mexico City. The plane was large, a Mexicana Airlines 747, which wasn't even half full. Two hours later we were making our approach to Havana's tiny airport, the runway lined with waving palm trees. We touched down, and Michael and I looked at each other. It felt like we were being naughty, and we practically squealed with excitement and anticipation. It was a little strange, setting foot on forbidden soil, and there were Cuban soldiers with rifles at every exit.

We went through customs, and as we had been instructed. We asked—in Spanish—the customs agent not to stamp our passports. "Of course," he said in perfect English, stamping, instead, a loose paper form that we were to keep with our passports, but could discard before arriving again on American soil. He asked us each a few questions about the purpose of our visit, things like that, and all so charmingly and courteously that Michael and I both thought he was trying to pick us up. He had the eyes so many Cubans had, that startling clear green. In America he could have been a model, he was so beautiful. Once through customs, Michael and I looked at each other and knew, without saying a word, that we were about to have a real adventure.

Before we had left Austin, I had gotten a call from crazy Ranje, my dear friend who had given me shelter during my Beto days. She had moved to her native Germany several years before, and she said she wanted me to meet her for the holidays, so she decided to hook up with us in Cuba.

Ranje showed up late to meet us at the airport and was extremely angry.

"What's wrong, Ranje?" I asked.

Her pale blue eyes were icy and a filterless cigarette hung from her lower lip, swinging back and forth like a metronome as she let loose her tirade.

"These fucking people! They've lost my bag, all my clothes, my toiletries, my pot, everything! I've been coming back every day and all they do is give me the runaround! I've been here eleven days already and I'm *pissed off!*" She wore her blond hair in tiny curls, and it seemed that the tight coils wound even tighter as she spoke, pulling her features into a terrifying mask.

"What?" I could hardly keep my voice down, "You tried to bring pot to Cuba from Germany? What were you thinking?!"

"You're one to talk," she said, "and besides, I do it every year. I always do it."

"Ranje, that was many years ago for me. I was a kid, and I learned my lessons! You must be crazy!"

"What I am is pissed off. Come on, let's get a damn taxi. There's nothing more I can do today." She strutted off like a giant blonde turkey having seizures, followed by billowing black smoke, almost comical if you forgot about that terrifying part. Michael and I picked up our bags and reluctantly followed her.

Welcome to Cuba...your adventure is waiting!

We grabbed a taxi and took off through the poor outskirts of the city of Havana, which is also poor, of course. The natives call it La Habana, and in spite of the total poverty of its people, one sees instantly that this was once a very wealthy and very beautiful city. The once magestic mansions are crumbling now, and most have been subdivided into apartments. We asked the taxi driver if we were going to pass Fidel Castro's home on the way, and he laughed out loud.

"El Presidente does not have a house, per se," he told us in Spanish, "at least not that anyone knows about. His location is always kept secret."

I was rather surprised by this fact, but upon consideration I could see that for Castro, this was undoubtedly a necessary means of survival.

• • •

We arrived at the home Ranje had arranged for us to stay in. There are many fine and beautiful hotels in Havana, all full of visitors from around the world (including the U.S.!) but Ranje had always stayed at this house, called a "casa particular," which was owned and operated by two elderly sisters, Georgina and Elena. The two sisters had a townhouse with three or four bedrooms, and they rented out two of the rooms to foreigners, so Michael got a room and Ranje and I shared the other.

Each room had its own private bath, which seemed quite comfortably appointed, but we almost turned around and returned to the airport when it was explained to us that the sewer systems of Cuba are not advanced enough to handle the disposal of any kind of paper! Michael was almost hysterical over this grave embarrassment, and asked what people were supposed to do with the used toilet paper.

"You just put it in the wastebasket, and the ladies take it out to the garbage can each morning," we were told.

"No way!" he cried. "I'm not going to use the toilet all week!"

Well, he did. We all did. When in Rome...!

Late that afternoon we all went down to Old Havana, the heart of the city and truly a beautiful historic district, swarming with tourists and locals alike. We learned that the locals are not allowed in any hotel or restaurant unless they are employees of that business, and to enforce that law there are armed guards at every entrance. Panhandling is not allowed, and punishments are severe. After walking for hours, taking in as many sights as possible, we returned to our rooms for dinner.

The next day we returned to Old Havana and had a blast, walking the narrow old streets, talking to the natives, stopping for a beer or mixed drink at the famous Hemingway bar—which had been a favorite haunt of the famous author—or any one of the other quaint and charming establishments. Around sunset we made our way back to the home of the sisters for dinner. Elena did most of the cooking, and Georgina did most of the drinking. I bought her more than one bottle of rum in the few days we were there. The meals were simple, but delicious and fresh, with fried bananas or *plantains*, chicken, wonderful eggs with onion and tomato for breakfast, all very expertly prepared.

Ranje had already planned our evening for us, and we said no thank you. "Well, what do you want to do?" she asked as if irritated. I looked at Michael, and I knew what he wanted to do without asking.

"Michael would like to see some of the local color — he wants to go to a gay bar," I told her. The sisters nodded their acceptance.

"And you?" she asked.

"I'm not feeling too well, probably exhaustion," I said truthfully. "I think I'll just stay in tonight."

"Come on, María," Ranje railed, "if you are going to stay here a month, like me, you can stay in one night. But you only have a week to see Cuba! You need to get out!"

"I'm not going out, tonight, Ranje. You go wherever you want, pretend like I'm not here. Please."

"Oh, all right!" She sounded defeated.

Michael went out, surely having the time of his life (or perhaps, floating face-down in the waters off the Malecon, although I prayed not). Ranje had gone out, and I sat on my narrow cot with an intoxicated Georgina, listening to first-hand stories of the revolution. I was fascinated!

Georgina seemed a sweet grandmotherly-type woman, handsome but not pretty, and when she kissed you, which she did often, she would take your face in both hands and her lips, like butterflies, would criss-cross your entire face. But her whispered tales revealed a strong teenage girl who had carried a rifle, had shot and killed many people in a war of ideals, had set off bombs to blow up buildings and bridges in her own homeland.

She, too, had served time in jail. She had sat, fascinated and intense, in a small room and been included in conversations with Fidel Castro and with the famous Che Guevara. She showed me a deep indentation on her left thigh, the scar of a wound caused by the many brutal kicks from a soldier of the opposing side. Soft, sad Cuban love songs from a radio down the street wafted through the open French doors coming off the stone balcony outside the bedroom. The air was warm and fragrant with honeysuckle and exotic tropicals, and I was intoxicated by the moment.

In each block in this neighborhood, as in all residential areas, there are armed patrol guards, so we kept our voices to a whisper at night, and the lights were kept low. No matter how drunk Georgina became, no matter how exciting the story she was telling, her voice never raised above a whisper.

The next morning I awoke and made my way to the kitchen. Michael was there, safe and sound, with his newfound Cuban boyfriend, William, who was muscular and handsome. They were drinking coffee and smoking cigarettes. Ranje followed a few minutes later, anxious and ready to start the day — by sitting around for an hour, then making plans till late afternoon, then changing them at the last moment.

Michael and I started making our own plans for the day and were about to call for a taxi when William suggested we hire his friend's car for twenty dollars a day plus food and gas. We agreed.

The friend, named Medardo, arrived an hour later in a green 1954 Chevy, and had also brought the man William called his father. Michael and I were skeptical. Ranje said we would all die now for sure. But off we went, into the beautiful Cuban countryside, the tropical coastal flatland turning quickly to yellow fields of sugar cane set in rich black earth, and then to emerald green mountain forests.

The car was a classic, but of course they cannot import American replacement parts, so most of the engine is rigged. Going up steep hills we would all have to get out to lighten the load, and more than once we would all have to push from behind to make it. It was also a dangerous proposition for Medardo, William and the "father," because it was against the law to taxi tourists without a permit, which of course they could not afford to acquire. It was decided that if we were stopped, I would be the sister of Medardo, Michael would be my husband, and Ranje his sister. Fortunately we were never stopped because Michael and William remained in a lip-lock for four days and that would have been hard to explain.

Although it was a beautiful country it was also very sad. I was buying food for almost every stranger and for the poor dogs I would come across. One day in Old Havana a large young woman stopped us on the street and begged us to buy her some powdered milk for her baby. We agreed, and we followed her to the corner store, where we had to stand in line for a long time. We felt so sorry for her that we bought her two small sacks of powdered milk, at eight dollars each!

That was shocking because we had just discovered from a bicycle taxi driver we had hired that the average income for a high school teacher is about fourteen dollars a month. A doctor in Cuba makes about thirty dollars a month! How they live is just unfathomable, and it explains why Medardo was willing to take such risks for us to hire him; the eighty dollars we paid him for four days, plus food and drink, must have seemed like a fortune.

After five days, I had had enough. It was just too sad, and I couldn't get that last image of Flaca and little Axel out of my mind. I talked to Michael, who was really sad to leave William, but agreed to return to Mexico two days early just for me. He and William would have to part anyway, and another two days together would only make it more difficult. The "father" had already said that he was afraid William would try to escape by raft to the states to look for Michael.

We hired Medardo one last time the next morning to drive us to the airport. When we got there, our Cuban "family" was afraid to enter the airport; they had never been inside it before in their entire lives! But we talked them into accompanying us as far as the painted line on the floor across which no Cuban citizen is allowed. Michael and William were both wiping tears from their eyes, Ranje gave us both a big hug, and Medardo and the "father" waved us good-bye. Minutes later we were on the nearly empty plane headed for Mexico City, back to civilization, flush toilets where you can happily wave adios to toilet paper, and back to Flaca.

From the airport in Mexico City we took a taxi for the one-hour trip to Flaca's village, called Oaxtepec, nestled in the foothills of the volcano Popotecatepetl (which had just erupted the week before, spewing soot and ash on the opposite side of the huge mountain from Flaca's little casita).

Arriving at Flaca's just felt right to me. It was where I wanted to be right now, where I felt I should be. Little Axel was in the yard playing with his only friends: two little Indian boys and a goat. We spent all afternoon together, Michael, Axel, Flaca and myself, talking, playing and just relaxing. Immediately Cuba seemed a distant memory, distinct in detail, yet very removed in time.

• • •

That night, after Axel went to sleep, the three of us stayed up and partied till the early hours. Flaca was still in pain from her mastectomy, and always kept her left arm pressed to her side. The more we partied the more she seemed to give in to this posture, and the sight of her like this was too alien for me to accept. That night I slept in the bed with Flaca and little Axel, and my mind flooded with ancient memories, until finally I was able to drift off to sleep.

The next morning we got up, showered, dressed, and went to the Hacienda hotel for breakfast. This was the same Hacienda where Alvaro and I had stayed when we had gone to visit Flaca two years before, but Michael had only seen pictures of it and was thrilled to visit it in person. That afternoon we boarded a big luxury bus for Mexico City. The bus had a television mounted near the front and was showing an American movie about Manuel Noriega, in which Fidel Castro was one of the characters portrayed. That was fun, because now we felt like authorities, after Georgina's whispered late night stories.

Michael, aka "Vaselina"

Fernando and me

··· 33 ···

$\mathcal{B}$ack at the restaurant, I had started to serve an old favorite recipe from Argentina, called a *chimichuri* salsa, made with cilantro, chilies, and vinegar. It quickly became really popular, so I thought I would begin to sell it in jars. I found someone to bottle it and to do the nutritional breakdown and all that stuff required to market a product like that.

Then we needed a label, so I went to Michael. He came up with the idea to make a portrait of me, with my arms extended like Evita Peron addressing her people, with the flag of Argentina behind me. The finished piece of artwork looked great. We made the labels, and people liked it so much that we decided to make tee shirts with the same design. They sold out almost immediately and we had to make more! Eventually I was getting reports back from customers that they had seen people wearing the shirts as far away as Mexico and Hawaii!

I also had the honor of being approached by Whole Foods Market, who asked me if they could carry my *chimichurri* sauce in their flagship store in Austin! Of course that made me *so* proud.

One day Michael and I were talking in the patio of the restaurant with his cousin. We were all in a great mood, laughing and joking around. Michael said, "You know, María, wouldn't it be funny to make a huge statue of you, using the design from the labels and the tee shirts, that we could put on the roof of the restaurant?"

"That's not funny, Michael," I said. "That's a *great* idea! Why don't you do it?"

Later, I began to have some doubts about how this would be received by the public; I could just hear people saying "Who does she think she is?" behind my back. I'm not very comfortable with self-promotion considering all I have done in my past. But Michael assured me that people would love it, so I gave the go-ahead. About a month and a half later there was a twenty-foot wide, twelve-foot tall statue of me, from the waist up and arms outstretched, atop my roof. I called it the "Monster María." We dress her up for different holidays.

True to Michael's word, "Monster María" quickly became a South Austin landmark, people using it as a reference when giving directions to other people: "Oh, I live about three blocks from the giant María," or "Turn left after the giant María." It even appeared in a television commercial for the local Time Warner cable company, with me in front mimicking the same "Evita" gesture. And now *that* image has been transferred to several of the city buses in wrap-around billboard fashion, my face in front of Taco Xpress, arms open wide!

Because of all this, I sometimes have complete strangers coming up to me and calling me by name. It even happened in the airport in San Antonio! At a movie theatre, I presented my ticket to the usher girl inside the entrance. She took my ticket and said, "Thanks, María." It would be a strange sensation for anyone, I'm sure, but there was a time in my past where such recognition would have sent me flying off to another country for safety!

··· 34 ···

Learning the English language remains an ongoing endeavor for me, and because of gaps in my knowledge, I have come up with some hysterical bloopers all my friends have come to call "María-isms." For example, one day when shopping with Michael, I wanted to look at some new sheets and pillow cases, so I suggested that we run over to Bed, Bath and Behind and then maybe to Linens and Shit.

Another evening we had decided to stay at home and rent a movie. I asked Michael if he would run to the "Black Bastard."

His face turned white and his eyes grew very large. "What did you just say?"

"The Black Bastard. You know, down on Lamar Street, where they rent movies."

"Oh, *Blockbuster!*" he said. Well, sometimes I get confused and things just come out wrong (it's really not Tourette's Syndrome, I promise!). Some things I say are actually very benign, like when I say "duck" and it sounds like "dog"! But for some reason (I'll let you guess why) I always seem to get into trouble when I say the word "focus."

One lazy summer day, drifting in my pool, Michael and I began to discuss human nature, how each person is made up of so many different personalities. We decided to name ours. Michael said, "There is the part of me that is the artist. That one I want to call 'Leonardo'. The gay part of me is definitely 'Patsy'!" He was referring to the character "Patsy" on the BBC comedy hit show *Absolutely Fabulous*, a character Michael loved to emulate.

"And the 'border-town-slut' side of you has got to be 'Vaselina'!"

"That's perfect!" He started to giggle.

I said, "And my inner little girl has to be 'Lilli'!...Ooh, and the bitch part of me is 'Sylvia'!"

"What about your 'inner blonde'?"

"Definitely 'Barbie'!"

We laughed for hours at this idea, and named quite a few personalities. To this day we will find ourselves saying, "Shut up, Patsy!" when Michael gets a little too worked up, or "How does Lilli feel today?" when I am being a little too cutesy, and we know exactly what the other one is talking about. It's almost a secret code to keep each other in line. When we take off on one of our all-day shopping extravaganzas, we are not Michael and María, but Eduardo the wealthy Count and Meg the slam-shopper!

After conquering my fear of living alone, I decided to continue and see what other phobias I could check off the list. One of my great fears has always been going under the knife. When my mother had breast cancer many years ago in Argentina, they had really butchered her. I was terrified by any kind of surgery. But that old vision of me floating in the pool in my bikini did not match the reality of my body. In fact, even taking a shower was not a comfortable experience for me. Even though Alvaro and I hooked up every once in a while after our divorce, it had been some time since that had happened, and it was now apparent to me that he and I were history. I was comfortable being alone, I even loved it at times, and I was reluctant to start to think about dating again. Why not, right?

Why not? Because I felt fat! So I decided that it was time to face fear number two.

I made an appointment with a doctor at a plastic surgery clinic. Before I knew it I was being wheeled out of an operating room, bandaged from head to hips, flying high on anesthesia and painkillers. Michael babysat me the first four days after surgery, but I have to admit that during this time Alvaro was a real friend. He came over every evening and spent the night, never once pinching, pushing or punching me in the arm or anywhere else.

So fear number two bit the dust with a little bit of anesthesia! Not bad — but by now you know me, and although the surgery completely altered my silhouette for the better, I began to obsess about the parts of my body that had remained untouched by the doctor's suction tubes. Also, I was not thoroughly pleased with my first surgeon's end product; there was some unevenness, some lumps and some dips that I didn't like. So I found another surgeon, Dr. Gorman, to fix these flaws and to do a little more work as well. He proved to be an excellent surgeon, and when I would ask for something he didn't think was necessary (which was often) he would tell me no.

• • •

··· 35 ···

When Michael suggested we go to his brother Terry's wedding in Las Vegas on February 16, 2001, I said, "Let's go!" I was still a party girl, after all.

I had returned to Vegas several times over the years, but this time I was returning with a vastly different perspective. We were dining lavishly at restaurants I once had to sneak out of without paying. Michael and I did some early-morning shopping the day of the wedding. I bought some things to wear to the ceremony: jewelry, new shoes, beauty products and a faux mink coat. It was less than three weeks after my liposuction and I was still in quite a bit of pain.

After Michael and I had finished our shopping, we wandered around an area just off the strip where I had once spent so much time with Flaca years before. We came across the Uptown Motel, one of the last places Flaca and I had stayed together back in the old days. I stood there, lost in my memories, holding shopping bags filled with stuff I'd just bought on a whim – stuff that had cost more money than Flaca and I used to spend in a month. I was deeply moved by the contrast. The Strip had changed a lot: there were new hotels towering above the older ones I remembered from those early days of fear and poverty. But this old section looked just as it had all those years ago and it caused me to reflect on all the changes I had made in my life since first leaving Argentina as a teenager.

It is at moments like this when I am confronted with the harsh reality of my former life, and I see how far I have come since those days. I stood in front of that motel for a long time, just looking and remembering. Then it was time to head to the Paris Hotel to join the wedding party and all the friends who had flown in from various parts of the country. We hailed a taxi and we sped away from my past.

···

A year and a half later, lipo-surgery number four (!) had to be postponed by fear number three: cancer. And not just cancer, but breast cancer.

During a regularly scheduled exam, my doctor found lumps. The recent trip to visit Flaca had only added fuel to the fire of the fears that my mother's early botched cancer surgery had instilled, and fear number three was upgraded to fear number one.

A few months earlier, Flaca had suffered another setback of sorts. A donkey had actually bitten the hell out of her right and only surviving breast! It was terribly bruised and excruciatingly painful. When I called to tell her about my tumor, she told Axel that María had the same sickness his mommy had. His face became very serious, and he asked Flaca, "Did a donkey bite her tit, too?"

That night I went home in a panic-filled terror, and as I was sitting on the bed, imagining all the possible scenarios, I happened to glance over at Sissy. She was on her little cushion on the floor, just staring at the wall and breathing slowly as if she were in pain. My own fears for myself were pushed back as I examined her more closely: she didn't look good at all. I called Fernando to see if he could get away from the restaurant to drive Sissy and me to the animal emergency room, but the restaurant was packed. So I took her myself. The vet said that she would need to stay overnight for observation, but there was little hope for her. I told the vet to do whatever it took to save her.

At about a quarter to one in the morning the vet called to say that the news was grim, she wasn't responding to treatment, and that she had a long list of ailments and problems—that if they could keep her alive, she would need daily injections of medication and her life would not be active or happy.

After great consideration and thought, I agreed to let the doctor ease her out of her misery. Sissy was then seventeen years old and she'd had the best life any dog in her condition could have had. Still, I went outside and sat on my back steps and cried all night and all the next day, hardly moving from the spot. Sissy was cremated and is now in a sweet little wooden chest next to Puppy Hot, where I hope they are keeping each other company and are continuing to follow me on this crazy road of life.

A few days later I received Sissy's ashes, and along with the little wooden chest of my little baby was a beautiful poem (attributed to Edwin Arnold) that I found very comforting. It read:

"Farewell, Master, yet not farewell,

Where I go, ye, too, shall dwell,

I am gone, before your face,

A moment's time, a little space.

When ye come where I have stepped

Ye will wonder why ye wept."

The next day my doctor scheduled a needle biopsy, which was more terrifying than any of my previous lipos. I was scared. I was afraid I would lose everything: my looks, my new hair extensions, my house, my business, and my life. You know, you sometimes think funny things when you are confronted with total devastation. I found myself pulling out my hair extensions and placing them on my pillow and thinking about chemotherapy. And crying. A lot.

The doctor had promised that his office would call in twenty-four hours. It was a full two days later that the doctor's office called to say that the results were in. Of course, they wouldn't tell me over the phone if the news was good or bad. When I got to the office, a nurse led me to a little room and a few minutes later the doctor came in with a folder of papers. She sat down across from me and opened the folder.

The results were negative for cancer! I almost cried with relief and gratitude. I followed the doctor out to the waiting room to give my insurance card and to write a check for the deductable. As I was doing that, the doctor, behind the desk, was calling the clinic where I had had my test done. I was just walking out the door, I was so excited, and I was already planning to resume plans for lipo number four, when something clicked in my head. I stopped, dead in my tracks, turned and ran back into the waiting room.

"Which clinic were you just talking to?" I asked the doctor with dread.

"Oh, such and such clinic," she replied matter-of-factly. "Why?"

"Because I went to the *other* clinic to have these tests," I said.

"What? How can that be...?" She quickly retrieved my folder and opened it. Her face went white. "María, there has been a terrible mistake," she stammered. "This *is* your file, but the dates are wrong. This is from three years ago!"

"Oh, my God! And I was about to walk out that door, thinking I was okay, that I had my life back! What the hell are you telling me?" I was in a panic.

So I had to go back home, and wait another twenty-four hours for her office to order and receive the correct test results. I only had three little strings of extensions left on the back of my head the next afternoon when I returned to the doctor's office to face the music. Would it be a Sousa march or a funeral dirge?

I have never been a fan of marches, but I could have done "Stars and Stripes Forever" all the way home! The lump was not malignant. Of course, I still had to go under the knife one more time to remove the benign tumor, and as I was wheeled into the operating room my last conscious thought before going under the surgeon's scalpel was that I was in good hands because the nurse, Linda, and the anesthesiologist were both good customers of Taco Xpress! I will be on Tamoxifen for the next five years, but overall, the news was fantastic. And one more time Flaca came to my rescue emotionally. She called twice a day because she knew only too well how depression and terror feels.

Plastic surgery number four proceeded a couple of weeks later. Call me *loca*, but I also selected an acid peel, Botox injections, and, for dessert, collagen injections in my upper lip. The next weekend I drove myself, surgical girdle and all, to my friend Debra Carter's hair salon to have my extensions redone. Spring was coming on, the pool would soon be a sparkling aquamarine set in emeralds in my backyard, I still had two boobs, and with a world full of men to catch, I needed the hair to do it!

• • •

··· 36 ···

The restaurant continued to amaze me, both with its success and popularity, and because of my wonderful employees. Most of them had been with me for years at this point.

For my forty-first birthday, I threw myself a party in the backyard of my house with about fifty of my closest friends and ex-husbands. It was a blast (and I was blasted, too), but the really wonderful part came later in the night, after the restaurant had closed, when I saw all of my employees begin to file into the backyard. These were not rich people, you understand, but they had brought presents and balloons, a huge ice cream cake…and they were followed by a seven-member mariachi group which they had pitched in and hired to serenade me! I couldn't hold back the tears; the gesture was so beautiful! I was thinking at that moment that should I ever retire or want a change in my life, I just might leave the restaurant to my dear employees.

In May of 2002, I got a phone call from Beto's mom. She had never accepted the likelihood of Beto's death. She called me to ask if I had heard from him, and I told her, "No, Ma'am, not a word." It had been eleven years since Beto disappeared. She told me that she was sure Beto felt responsible for his brother Chacho's death, and that she thought that is why he never called her again. She asked me to make sure that if he ever called, I was to tell him she still loves and misses him. She invited me to come and visit her in Tampico. I told her I would try.

Thoughts of Beto plunged me back into sadness. I thought about his little girl, Sara, whose birth he never got to witness, and how sad it was that he would never have the opportunity to see her grow. I thought about the terror he must have felt as he lost his brother, and the horror he must have experienced—especially if he was tortured at all—before he was killed. To numb myself from the pain of these thoughts, I reached for my bottle of scotch. I had started drinking at fourteen; now I was forty-two, and still drinking. Good news, bad news. I never drank less; it was always more. More, more, more.

(left to right) Monoyo, Alejandra, my mother, me and Margarita

··· 37 ···

I had stopped going to Argentina many years ago. In fact, the last time was when I was still married to Dale and they had discovered my little nephew's brain tumor. Still, it hurt to feel no connection to my homeland, no relationship with my mother, other than one of constant bickering and repeated insults. I did call her once in 1997, but otherwise we had completely lost contact. But after my cancer scare, I began to think about the pain we had caused each other, and over many months of reflection I was beginning to come to an understanding of what she must have gone through.

My first bout with cancer came when I was thirty-six years old, the same age she had been when she had undergone her disfiguring mastectomy, and I thought I finally knew what she must have endured when I was a tiny girl. Also, my years of poverty and hard work gave me another insight into what hell her life must have been like after my father's death. I, too, have had to work three jobs at once just to survive, and I didn't even have children to support.

There were still many attributes of my mother that drove me crazy, but I was beginning to accept that we were just very different people. I realized that time was no longer on my side; if I wanted to ever come to terms with this most painful aspect of my life, I needed to do it now. My mother wasn't a young woman anymore, and I didn't want her to die thinking that I had no good feelings for her at all.

So I invited her to Austin for a visit.

As the day approached for her arrival, I was eaten up with apprehension. We had quite a history and I really feared that this trip was going to be a huge mistake. What if things got even worse? How would I live with myself? But now it was too late. I had offered, she had hesitantly accepted, and she was already in the air. Was there any way I could leave town real fast? My fear grew to overwhelming proportions as I drove to the airport.

I saw her getting off the plane and I was shocked to see that her posture was stooped, her face wrinkled and worn. She was shorter, too, and looked like another person entirely. It scared me and broke my heart for her, for myself, and for our awful past. Her greeting was cordial but I could see that she was putting on a front, obviously as defensive as I was and prepared to fight or flee, if need be. There had been so much pain between the two of us.

As we drove I didn't argue or comment when she started to babble, pointing out everything her eyes took in on the way to the house. "Oh, the lines in the road are yellow here. Look at your car, it's black outside and gray inside. Do you like that? How far is your house from the airport? How old is that airport?" I bit my tongue and tried to ignore her pointless conversation.

After a while, though, she started to open up a little more. She told me that she had been afraid to come, afraid that nothing would have changed, that we would fight again. She told me that she had almost backed out until she went to visit a ninety year-old friend who advised her to come, to try to make up, to not judge my life or the way I lived. The old lady told her that she was through raising me, like it or not, and to just come and spend time with me. I started to listen to what my mother was saying. So even though I had to weed through a lot of senseless information, I saw that maybe she did have something to say. She was trying. I took the next step.

And so began reconciliation between mother and daughter.

My mother stayed fifteen days. She was enchanted with the restaurant. She saw how many people liked the place, and me. She met my new friends and they treated her beautifully. By the end of her visit she was sitting at the restaurant and writing little stories and poems about it to give to me. For the first time ever she seemed proud to call me her daughter. Our conversations grew more and more meaningful over those two weeks, and when it was time for her to leave we kissed and hugged each other.

She came to visit again two years later, and many times after that. With every trip we kept making progress. We spoke on the phone frequently. It no longer mattered so much anymore that she would run off at the mouth about inconsequential things. When I read between the lines I could see that she was always just a person who was dealing with life the best way she knew how, and it had been a life full of pain.

Despite our past, now she was telling me that I was beautiful. Now she was telling me how proud she was of me. She was telling me that I was smart. I told her that I loved her. And, after all those years, I knew that I meant it.

• • •

When I came to accept my mother for the person she was, she met me half way and accepted me as I was. And that went a long way in helping me accept myself, and the things that I have done.

With the devastating collapse of the economy in Argentina, I thank God for my success in the United States, because I am now in a position to help my mother get by in a country where the bank accounts are frozen, the people are starving and the future is uncertain. After the hell my mother endured at my hands when I was a girl, it caused me great happiness to be in a position to help her in her old age, when she needs so much. I know I can never erase the mistakes that I made, but as she reached the later part of her life, I found a little peace in being able to make it a little easier for her.

My Chimichurri sauce at Whole Foods!

Appearing on an Austin Capital Metro bus: Me and Taco Xpress!

Taco Xpress! 2003

··· 38 ···

On May 12th, 2003, Michael came over early, around ten-thirty in the morning. I was already up and moving around like a whirlwind – NOT! He knocked on the door and yelled to me, knowing that I could hear him from my bedroom.

"María, are you awake yet?" Michael usually sounded pretty upbeat, even at this hour.

"What you want, fucker?" I yelled hoarsely in the direction of the front porch.

"I left my smokes on the dining room table when I left — are they still there?"

"Your guess is good as mine. Just a minute…"

I crawled out of bed, nearly stepping on the dogs, and stumbled to the front door. I undid the latches and turned the knob for Michael to come in.

"Oh, shit, María! Sorry I woke you up, but I've been up two hours already without a cig. Go back to bed!"

"What? I've been up for hours, too. Don't I look beautiful?" I didn't need to check the mirror to know that statement wouldn't be too accurate.

"Did I drink all the beer last night?" Michael had found his cigarettes and was blowing out a cloud of yummy first-cig-of-the-day smoke in my direction. We both coughed and headed for the kitchen to check for any leftovers from the previous night's party, and I don't mean food.

Guaca let out a head splitting squawk that stopped us both in our tracks. "Shit, Guaca!" It was obvious that we wouldn't find a drop of beer, whiskey, wine or any other similar libation here. Bottles lay overturned on the counter, ashtrays spilled over onto the table, playing cards were strewn about everywhere, and the stale smell of smoke was repulsive. "Guess I forgot to clean up after everybody left," I mumbled.

Just then a voice from under a blanket on the sofa begged us to shut up.

"Apparently," Michael offered, "not everyone left! Who *is* that?"

"Hell if I know!" I walked over to the sofa and lifted up the blanket. "Oh, it's you!"

We had been partying with some guys in an East Coast band that we met at Taco Xpress the night before, and apparently at least one of them was still here. "Baby, where are your friends?" I asked him, afraid of the answer.

"They're gone." With a moan he grabbed back at the blanket and covered his head again. So *that* mystery was solved. Where they went, who they went with, and whether they were ever coming back were questions whose answers would have to wait till later. Some time later. Maybe later today, maybe not.

Michael helped me straighten the kitchen and eventually I started to feel a little more human. I filled the sink with hot water and Pine Sol and started to mop the floors. More than anything, I have to have a house that smells clean. A little later in the afternoon the other guys showed back up at the house to retrieve their comrade and to thank me for the party and the party favors and to exchange numbers. They threatened, very nicely, to give us a call the next time they came to Austin. I was fairly sure that they would — it had been fun.

We watched their bus pull out of the driveway, waved good-bye, and then looked at each other. I said to Michael, "So, what do you want to do now, Vaselina? You want to catch a movie? We could grab a bite and then catch a matinee?" What I really wanted to do was to order another gram of coke and sit in the house all day with the curtains pulled tightly together, but I didn't know if Michael would be up for that this early.

"Well, we could get more coke..." he started. There were several reasons Michael and I were such good friends. Being on the same page most of the time was just one of many.

Like the movie *Groundhog Day*, I awoke the morning after that to another trashed house. This time it was empty of other people, but the memories lingered on the counter, the table, the floor, in the air. It might have been Monday or Thursday or Sunday, for all I knew, but the previous night had been yet another "Saturday Night at *Casa Loca*." This time I just wandered through the house, taking in the damage, the dirt and the futility of getting the mop out again....

Why do it? Why?

That one word, with all its meaning, came oozing down upon me like molten lava. Why fucking do *anything*? Why do I keep doing the same thing over and over? Why even get out of bed? Why even go on living, if this is it? A deep depression came over me; black clouds and tormenting devils and the whole apocalyptic picture blinded me to anything else.

And *still*, all I really wanted was more coke and another bottle of scotch.

Then a moment of clarity came to my mind. I was still drunk, still totally fucked up, but I was suddenly terrorized for my life. "I can't continue like this," I thought. After all, I wasn't a teenager anymore, but I was still partying like I was one. I opened the Yellow Pages with the determination to check myself into rehab. But after making the call I was in shock. Apparently you can't even get recovered if you're not a fucking millionaire.

"Goddammit," I said out loud. Here I finally decide to get sober — and the price of rehab was scary! No facility was cheaper than $18,000 a month. It could be even get as high as $30,000!

What I really wanted, really needed at that moment was for the person on the other end of the line, this stranger, to solve this dilemma for me, because I couldn't do it. Little did he know that one of his ideas actually worked for me. "Well, have you tried Alcoholics Anonymous?" he asked.

I told him what I really needed was "Alcoholics Unanimous"! My head was spinning, I was pretty much hallucinating, the top of my head was numb, my voice sounded worse than a croaking frog, my lungs hurt like hell from smoking one cigarette after the other, my nose was bleeding, my vision was blurry, and all of my thoughts were negative, paranoid, fearful, terrorized. But even through that thick black fog I knew that I had a lot to do if I was going to overcome this.

Like any addict or alcoholic, in my heart I always knew I had something that was way out of control. And I was very embarrassed to admit it. Come on, who wants to say "I'm an alcoholic and a drug addict and I go to Alcoholics Anonymous"?

But I grabbed the little piece of paper with the address that this stranger/angel/savior (whatever you want to call him) gave me, and without even a shower—I don't think I even had the strength to take one—I drove myself to an AA meeting.

I marched into this little building and, very shyly sat on the first chair in the corner as soon as I opened the door. I don't know if I sat close to the door because I was embarrassed to walk in front of all those people, or if I just wanted to get the fuck out of there as fast as I could if I needed to. Probably both.

The place was kind of old, not fancy at all, but it filled me with peace. It had the most beautiful signs all around the walls that said, *"Let Go and Let God," "Live and Let Live,"* and the most beautiful prayer that I had ever heard, called the Serenity Prayer:

God, grant me the serenity

To accept the things I cannot change

The courage to change the things I can

And the wisdom to know the difference

And another one was:

"Think, think, think."

Just reading these signs gave me hope. When I was fourteen years old, I already felt that I had a big black hole in the center of my body, but throughout the years that hole kept on getting bigger and bigger and bigger. And my only way of knowing how to deal with that black hole was *not* to deal with it.

So I had created a way of living that was getting worse by the minute, and I knew the consequences of that way of life were barreling toward me like an avalanche of snow, like an erupting volcano. Actually, snow is pure and white and pretty, and how I was really feeling was more like that dangerous, black volcano. Nobody can survive molten lava. You will die for sure. And I was doing just that. My biggest enemy was myself.

I didn't know what to expect in the meeting. One by one, those who wanted to share did so. There were sometimes lapses of silence. And I found it so amazingly peaceful and reassuring to find that, damn! There were actually other people like me, and they were doing something about it. I saw hope for the first time.

At the end of the meeting everybody got up and got in a circle and started to hold hands. I stayed seated on my chair, put my head down, and hunched my shoulders. I didn't know what to do. Just then this beautiful guy next to me extended his hand. He gestured for me to join him. I had no clue what they were all doing, but I got up and I took his hand, and then this other woman next to me grabbed my other hand, so now I belonged to their circle. And we prayed. The meeting was over.

I tried to make myself as inconspicuous as possible, but when the meeting ended someone said, "Hey you're María, right?" And I thought, "Oh shit." I knew this guy from Taco Xpress. And I realized my secret was out, that everyone was going to know that I'm a drunk and a drug user. I felt so little. And then I said to myself, "You know what? That's fine. I want everyone to know who I am. Who am I to be perfect and fault-free? I have this addiction and I am going to try to conquer it."

Maybe it's one of the reasons I'm writing this book – as therapy for me. I don't want to lie anymore. Not to myself, not to my friends. I had spent all my life from 14 to 42 doing just that. And who was I kidding anyway? Everybody knew when I was fucked up! If sober and clear-minded I'm considered "out there," then drunk I was totally out of control. I realized it was better that everybody knew the truth, and most importantly, that *I* knew, that the secret was out — and that I accepted my secret myself.

I learned in the meeting that the Twelve Steps of AA were supposed to help me one at a time — *if* I gave the program the time and my honesty. But as I sat there in that meeting I knew in my heart that the most important step of those twelve for me was the one in front of the front door of that building. So I can truly say now that I'm glad I picked up my leg and let it down. Step One.

It reminds me of the little anecdote—you might be familiar with it already—that has to do with helping yourself. This is the way I heard it:

A man was living in a little house. One day a flood came, and the man prayed for God to save him. Early on, a neighbor knocked on his door and urged him to evacuate, but the man refused, saying, "God is going to save me." As the waters rose he climbed onto the roof of his house, praying as he did so. A man in a rowboat offered him a lift, but he refused, saying, "God is going to save me." He kept praying, and finally a rescue helicopter arrived with a ladder. Once more he refused it, saying, "God is going to save me." Finally the man was swept away by the flood and died. As he stood in Heaven he asked God why He didn't save him. And God said, "But I sent you help three times, and each time you refused it."

Maybe you've heard different versions of this story, but the moral is pretty clear to me. As they say: God helps those who help themselves.

After I had been attending AA meetings for some time, I met a guy named Freddy. He was gorgeous, and his past was much like mine...one glass after the other, or should I say, one bottle after the other. But I really came to love him with all my heart.

One night before going to bed, I was reading my daily reflections book from AA. and I asked, "Can I read this out loud to you?" At that moment he was drunker than a skunk, and he said, slurring his words, "Maybe one day you will get through to me." I knew he meant it from the bottom of his heart. But like me, he was going to have an uphill road to travel. Still, the potential was there, and to my surprise, the day actually came.

As I watched him begin to embrace sobriety, I was filled with hope and I thought, "Whoa, maybe we have a chance." It's an arduous task, becoming sober, but as I watched his journey, I was able to see myself in him — and I sort of put him under my wing of protection. I would drive for him when he was too drunk. I would help him keep his house tidy and I would give him all the things that had helped me put my life in order.

It seemed to work. Our life together became full of really fun moments. We went on trips. We shared memories and we ate candies, chocolate, and potato chips like crazy. And we did it all without booze! So we replaced one addiction with another?

Once again, I was in love.

It is said that in the first year of sobriety one shouldn't make big decisions. But you know me, and in the midst of falling in love again, I didn't help him obey this very important command. After all, *my* first year was already behind me, and I was impatient. Our first mistake was to buy a ranch together. Anyone who has ever bought even a tiny property knows how aggravating it can be, and in the first year of sobriety everything can seem so much more intense.

Things didn't work out. Too many changes, too fast, too soon. We started to fight, first about big issues, then about smaller ones, then out of habit. Neither of us were inclined to hold grudges, so we quickly made up. And broke up, made up.

We split up about a month after sealing the deal on the ranch and destroying the deal on our relationship. In the end, he bought the ranch from me. I had wanted a ranch since childhood when our family ranch was lost — once again a dream was gone.

But when one path turns out to be a dead end, I don't sit there and wait for someone to come and build a new road. I told myself, "Oh well, I don't have a ranch. I wanted one. But I also wanted a beach house. And a lake house. And a mountain house." And I thought—in my own words—"Fuck! I just need to sell more tacos and do it myself."

I bought an RV that can move from ranch to beach to mountains as quickly as I can change my mind. And it was okay. It still is. Now, I get to go everywhere on my own. I have all those houses in one. I painted murals with happy jungles on the exterior, happy clean bright colors on the inside, and off I went!

Freddy's path crossed mine at a time when, no matter what happened between us, we were meant to be together for those precious moments. As far as I'm concerned, he will always be my buddy, he will always make me laugh. He bought me a horse named Dan for Christmas one year. He bought himself a horse, too, named Duck. They adored each other and it was obvious that if they were to be split up they would miss each other terribly. I don't do to animals what I wouldn't like done to myself. I left my horse behind, so that they could be Duck and Dan, together, even if it was no longer possible to be Freddy and María together.

• • •

At this moment at forty-two, I was finding peace in solitude, strength in my own accomplishments, and independence. This was due, in part, to my new financial security, but also to maturity and experience. The surgeries I had did more than reshape my physical body—they were also helping to re-sculpt a psyche that had known too many years of depression and insecurity. I was continuing that work in AA as I examined my mental and psychological self, to adjust the image in the mirror accordingly. Really for the first time, I was starting to like my own reflection.

Freddie and Maria.

··· 39 ···

In the Fall of 2003 I got a call from Flaca. "María, you're not gonna believe this shit. They think I have lung cancer."

"What? No!" Not again. *How much more can one woman endure*, I thought. "How did you find this out?"

"I haven't been able to breathe, so I went to the clinic and they took x-rays. They showed me the pictures – my lungs are all clouded up like a ghost."

"Don't worry about it, Flaca, it's probably nothing. You'll be okay."

But she wasn't.

She called me a week later when her test results came back. I arrived the next morning at the most depressing hospital anyone could imagine and I was extremely shocked to see that Flaca, always very thin, had lost a tremendous amount of weight. My heart ached all the more to see the conditions she was forced to endure. While the staff was kind and conscientious, the hospital was understaffed and under-equipped—and Flaca was "under-rich." This was a facility for the poorest of the poor, with homemade blankets on the beds, not clean, crisp white sheets and pillowcases.

Flaca was scared and in terrible pain because they had had to drain the fluids from her lungs by punching a hole through her back. But she could not afford the anesthesia, so they had done this without the use of any painkiller. I held her tiny hand as I sat next to her bed and listened to her as she recounted the list of horrors that she had been undergoing, her breath labored and shallow, her voice barely audible. I learned that there were two doctors on staff, and that the results of this last round of tests were due the next day. She asked if I would speak to the doctor on duty. I assured her that I would. We spent the rest of the day together, my Flaca finally dozing off for short periods of time towards evening.

I spent the night in Flaca's room and the next morning I went off to find the doctor on duty. He was a young man, very kind, and he told me that the prognosis was the worst: her cancer had spread rapidly and there was next to nothing that could be done. He said that he didn't think she had more than six months left to live.

My mind went blank. I couldn't believe it. What is this, a curse? My father, Dean, Beto, Flaca — the people who I loved kept leaving my life. You never know when someone is going to die. But how do you tell someone that it's coming?

I told the doctor, "What do I tell her? How do I tell her? She is already so depressed, I don't know if she will even want to go on if she knows how serious her condition is."

"Then do not tell her. This is what I recommend to you, although it is completely up to you to make the decision. You know her far better than I, and you can better make this judgment call. What I do believe is that attitude means a great deal in how long a person in your friend's condition can continue to fight and to hang on to life. I will go along with whatever decision you think is wise."

I knew immediately that he was right, and I did not hesitate to agree with him. "But what do we tell her about the test results?" I asked.

"Very well, we will say that... that the tests revealed a..."

"A treatable cancer..."

"Yes, a very treatable cancer. She needs rest and quiet. And, although at this point it doesn't really matter, try to limit her smoking. There is no point in her adding nicotine withdrawal to her anxiety level at this late stage, but try to keep her cigarettes to a minimum."

As I made my way down the corridor to her room, I tried to stop the tears that were flowing freely down my cheeks. Six months? Six months? How long was that? It had been twenty-five years since *El Quince* and the cabins, some twenty years since Mexicali and Las Vegas. And those days seemed no more than a few months ago, so vividly detailed were they in my memory. Six months? And I had my restaurant, my animals, and my other life in Austin. I couldn't abandon all that – my employees depended on me, my animals needed me. I had three more days in Mexico before I was scheduled to return. But how do I return now?

I paused outside her door and tried to compose myself.

Then I heard voices and my Flaca crying. The voices were not cruel, but they were speaking matter-of-factly about a situation that was anything but matter-of-fact. I tore into the room, my face growing hot with anger.

"What is this? What are you saying? Who the hell are you?" I was nearly shouting.

Flaca looked devastated, terrified, panic-stricken. She was pulling at her tubes, trying to undo them. I raced to her bed and took her struggling hands in mine. I turned to face the woman in the room. "Who the hell are you? What are you doing here?"

"I'm with the social services — the doctor has sent me here to discuss the patient's condition with her in order to facilitate any last plans or preparations —"

"*Get out!*" I shouted. "You are upsetting her! You are in the wrong room!"

"I don't understand; this is the correct room, isn't it?" She began to search through her paper work, but before she could find the room number and ruin everything, I pushed her into the hallway and shut the door behind us.

"How dare you, are you insane?" she began, affronted.

"How dare *you*?" I fired back. "I just came from the doctor. We have decided not to tell her how serious her condition is, and you have ruined everything. You have just killed my friend."

"But I have just come from the doctor, and he sent me to this room, see here?"

She was a little unsure, but held her ground. I snatched the papers from her hand and scanned them. I found that they were authorized by a doctor whose name was unfamiliar to me.

"This is not her doctor," I said, pointing to the signature.

"Yes, of course he is. He is the doctor in charge of this hospital at night. He is in charge of all the patients here."

"But this is not the doctor I just came from, he was Doctor ..." Then I remembered that Flaca had *two* doctors. "Oh, this is terrible," I said, and the woman seemed now to understand, too.

"You just came from the day doctor, no?"

"Yes, not more than two minutes ago. We decided —"

The woman nodded her head, "I'm sorry, I had no way to know. The other doctor scheduled me to come first thing this morning."

"Don't you people know that there are two doctors in charge here? Don't you need both approvals before you —"

"We are so understaffed here, if we had to get two approvals each time, nothing would get done. I'm sorry. Shall I go back in and tell her something?"

"No, please, just go. I'll tell her there was a mix up."

"Will she believe you?"

I felt defeated. "I don't know."

I returned to Flaca's room and sat next to her bed. Her trembling subsided as I described to her the stupid woman's mistake about the wrong room, the wrong person.

"Really?" Flaca begged it to be true.

"Of, course, Flaca. I told you not to trust these people."

"I knew it," she said, "It couldn't have been true. So what did my doctor say? What is my situation?"

"Well, there is a small cancer, but it is treatable. He is going to prescribe some medication and you have to take care of yourself: no partying, no coke, and you need to cut back on the cigarettes. Just until you get better."

"I can do that! I promise! Oh, I was so scared, I thought it was all over. I thought I was dying!"

"No, baby, no. But you have to do as the doctor says and be a good girl. Just for a while."

For the first time since I arrived, she smiled. "When can I leave? Today?"

"Well..." I wasn't quite prepared for this one.

"I feel so much better already, María. And I'm starving. Let's go get a bite to eat somewhere."

I couldn't say no. I thought I would be compromising her whole attitude if I told her she had to stay one more minute after what had just happened. I looked at her and she seemed to grow stronger, more hopeful, right before my eyes. "Okay, let me just check with the doctor. I'll be right back. Be thinking about what you want to eat."

"Thank God you came, María."

"Well, I'll be right back." I went to the doctor and asked him for permission to check Flaca out of the hospital. I described to him the miscommunication that had just occurred with the woman from social services. He apologized but said that Flaca should still stay another day or so for observation, and for him to have time to prescribe some painkillers.

"All right, I'll tell her," I said sincerely.

Back in Flaca's room, I found her trying to stand next to her bed.

"Am I signed out?"

"Sort of," I lied.

"Then let's get the hell out of this miserable hellhole. There's a little place around the corner that makes really good soups. I was thinking I should start with some soup."

She had already pulled out the IV from her arms. I helped her dress herself and we escaped out a side door, where she paused and felt the wind in her thinning hair and the sun on her face. She smiled again, and hobbled ahead of me, leading the way. I thought, 'What the hell, what does she have to lose? We'll just call later for a prescription.' I wanted, more than anything, to make her happy. At least for now.

Back at her little house Flaca was almost her old self, minus some forty pounds. The place was a disaster — clothes strewn about everywhere, dirty dishes. I sent Yuri and Axel into the little village and I began to clean while Flaca took the nap I had insisted on. An hour later the guys returned as I was putting away the last of the dishes. Axel carried an armful of fresh flowers and I took down several glasses and made small arrangements to distribute around the room so that everywhere she looked there would be something beautiful and alive. Finished, I sat down next to Yuri and lit a cigarette. Worry creased his sad face as he watched little Axel climb onto the futon and caress his sleeping mother's head out of habit and out of love.

"This is too much for my son to go through, María. He's still so young. I'm worried for him." Yuri lit a cigarette and exhaled a cloud.

"I know it's a lot, Yuri, but does anyone else hold her, caress her, massage her sore body? Does any one else show her any affection?"

He looked away to the window and into the dirt of the front yard, but he didn't answer. Moments later, as he stubbed out his cigarette, he turned back to me, almost in tears. "She won't let me."

Selecting Yuri to be the father of her son was merely practical; they had been friends for so long. But Flaca was not in love with Yuri. I saw now that Yuri was in love with Flaca, and was paralyzed to do anything to show it.

"I'm sorry, Yuri, I didn't mean..."

"Flaca is what she is. I know that. Still..."

I stood and looked around the room. It was hard not to see the concern, the love, the need to protect his mother from the world, that made Axel seem to have the soul of a very mature man as he gazed at his mother's sleeping form. All of us in the room knew Flaca to be fiercely independent. It made you want to protect her from herself, even, at times where no one and nothing *could* protect her. It was the source of her attractiveness, and the reason no relationship ever endured too long, except that of mother and son.

I saw now why Flaca insisted against all reason that she wanted a child. I understood now, and my heart broke all over: for her, to know now that she had created a person to love her no matter what; for Axel, to have to be that person at so young an age; for Yuri, to be forever connected to her through Axel, yet forever spurned by a woman that he loved; and for myself—for not simply having been the person she needed to have in her life.

Flaca awoke to a clean little home, filled with flowers and surrounded by those people who loved her. "How do you feel, Mommy?"

"A little weak," was all she could get out, and she must have been terribly exhausted, both emotionally and physically.

"What can we get you?" I asked, handing her a small cup of water.

"The place looks beautiful, María. Thank you. It reminds me of the old days, remember?"

"You really should have a maid, Flaca. You are too weak to manage this place alone."

"A maid? Are you trying to make me laugh? And besides, who needs a maid with you around?"

"That's just it. I have to go back tomorrow. To work, you know, and my little doggies, and Guaca."

Axel sat up concerned. "Don't go, María."

"I have to, Axel. I have responsibilities."

"Oh. I wish you didn't have any 'sponsibisnesses.'"

"Me, too," I said regretfully.

The Aztec people have a ceremony called a *Tamascal*. Similar to a North American Indian sweat lodge, it is a ritual to cleanse and purify and to prepare the soul to move on to the next world. It took me by surprise when Flaca told us that she thought it might make her feel better to have one.

"Flaca, what are you talking about, honey?" I was scared that she knew the truth.

"Oh, I don't know, María. I just think it would be a cool thing to do while you're still here."

Well, whatever my Flaca wants...

So I went into the village and sought out a person to perform this ancient ritual. By late afternoon a little wood-frame hut—covered with brush and blankets and whatever else we could find—was constructed in the backyard and stones were being heated red-hot in a fire pit. We draped Flaca, toga-like, in a clean, white sheet and carefully led her out to the hut when it was time for the ceremony.

Full of mysticism and strangeness, the *Tamascal* is an experience like no other. Because of the heat and steam from the hot rocks and because of her fragile health, Flaca vomited throughout most of the ceremony and emerged, at the end, as weak as I have ever seen her, although she claimed to feel better. Later that night Flaca called me aside from the others and said she had to discuss something very important with me. "What is it?" I asked.

"It's about Axel. I have been thinking about this a lot, María, so I hope you will listen to me."

"Of course, Flaca, what is it?"

"You have such love in you, María —"

"What are you getting at?" I was feeling concerned and a little uncomfortable.

"If I die —"

"— You are not going to die. It's bad, but you are going to get through this."

"You said you would listen. So listen. *If* I die, I want you to raise Axel."

"Oh, Flaca, I don't know..."

"Axel adores you. As seldom as we see each other, he speaks of you all the time. I've seen you with him. You love him, too."

"I do, you're right. But he has a father — Yuri."

"I am his mother and it's my decision. Yes, Yuri is helping me right now while I am sick, but then what? Yuri has work, he has a separate life, he has …"

"Flaca, he will adjust. He will change his obligations. He loves Axel. Hell, he loves *you*!"

"Stop it! Look, will you do it or not? Axel is *my* child, my child alone. You are in a position to help him. You know what my childhood was like: the good schools, the opportunities, the doors that open only to people in our class, wrong as that may be. I want Axel to have it all, as I did. Yuri wouldn't know how to begin, even if there were any way. But you would. You can do it. And that's what I want—if it is ever necessary…." She began to cough violently and she collapsed back onto the futon bed, but her eyes never left mine.

"I'll think about it. I promise. I do love Axel. Let me think about it."

"Fine, María. But please—this is my wish for my son—and for you."

Up until the end, she begged me to adopt Axel, and to prove that she meant it she never signed the papers recognizing Yuri as the biological father.

Through hugs, tears and kisses, I left Flaca, Yuri and Axel the next day and returned to Austin with promises to come back again soon. Two days later Yuri called to say that Flaca was back in the hospital. He told me that tumors had blocked her intestines and they had performed a colostomy, and that she now had a plastic baggie on her side with a tube that drained her intestines. She was absolutely desolate, growing visibly thinner daily, and, he said, she was growing impossible to be around.

"What can I do, María?" he asked me. "She is half crazy most of the time. Axel should not have to see this. He should be in school, he's almost six. But she won't let me take him. She says she needs him around. What am I to do?"

When Flaca returned home the next day, I called her. She said she couldn't bear for Axel to be away from her; he was the only one who loved her. I reminded her of our conversation about what she wanted for Axel's

• • •

life and told her he *should* be starting school. "But I'll be all alone," was her response.

We spoke every day on the phone and in a short time I arranged for a girl from her village to come by every day to clean her house, cook her meals, and to bathe her. For a month I sent a weekly check to pay her, but at the end of the month the girl called me terribly upset. She asked why I had stopped sending her money, and she told me that she found drug paraphernalia while she was cleaning. She said Flaca was too moody and she, the girl, was about to have a nervous breakdown.

I got Flaca on the phone, but before I could lay into her about spending my money on coke instead of paying the girl, she cried out that she was dying and for me to call an ambulance. She dropped the phone and I didn't know if she had died or not. Panic-stricken, I called for an ambulance.

Well, the girl quit and Flaca was alone again except for Axel and for a few concerned friends in the village, her dealer among them, who would occasionally pop by to see if she was still alive.

I had a huge internal battle with myself about how best to help her. Money I sent seemed to go right into the dealer's pocket, so that wasn't helping her. But if I did nothing, that wasn't helping her, either. I loved Flaca, but she sure was pissing me off. I called Yuri and asked if I should come back.

"Why?" he asked.

Then he thoughtfully added, "You don't want to see her, María. Believe me, if you have any chance of remembering her as she was the last time you saw her, do that. And she has lost another twenty pounds. She looks like a skeleton wrapped in a dirty napkin. She was almost arrested the last time we went into town."

"Why was she almost arrested?"

"I don't know how, but somehow she went into town to the bank to pick up a money transfer you had sent her for medication."

"You took her?"

"No, I guess she walked, or crawled, I don't know."

"That's more than three miles!"

"Well, she got there somehow, just as they were closing. They actually locked the door in her face. Well, you know Flaca ..."

"God, what did she do?"

"She started kicking the glass of the doors. Hard! They called the police! She was screaming that she was dying and she needed the money for her medication! The girls inside were terrified. The police finally calmed her down and took her home. She didn't get the money until the next day. Boy, was she pissed!"

Flaca continued to deteriorate over the next month. The incident with the bank occurred in early December, and all of us who loved her were subjected to more abuses. To add to the drama, Flaca's mother Jovita, former millionaire socialite, former drug runner, and the prancing gorilla of Mexicali, had just passed away. She'd also had cancer.

On the morning of January 8, 2004, Flaca awoke in a good mood. She pulled Axel close to her and kissed him, smiling and playing with his hair. "Go put on your best clothes, Axel. Today you are going to go to school!"

"Really, Mommy? Really? I'm going to go to school like a big boy?"

"Of course! You *are* a big boy, and I do love you!"

Yuri came to take Axel into the village for his first day of school and as they were leaving, Flaca said, "Thank you, Yuri. Thank you for everything." She smiled at him for the first time in many months. Half an hour later Yuri returned to the house. Flaca had passed out of this life and left behind all pain and regret.

I think of her now as she was when I first saw her in *El Quince*: seventeen years old, completely broke, and having the time of her life. I said then that poverty suited her better than wealth ever did. Now, just maybe, she has moved on to an existence that suits her better still. That is my prayer for her: hitchhiking and hanging-out in Heaven, being brilliant and unique, there on the 'other side' as she was here, and once again young and beautiful and free of pain. In the end, that is what I hope for us all.

• • •

I think about Flaca every day—how can I not? Flaca was born on March 22, 1962, the very day, the very year, and possibly the exact moment my father had a heart attack and died when I was not yet two years old, eons ago on that dirt road outside Buenos Aires. And so it was on her birthday, March 22, 2004, that I sat outside on my wide wooden deck with Pixie, with Mamacita and with Patchouli and Guaca, and I prayed to my father to take care of Flaca, to show her around and to keep her safe there, wherever that is. And then I prayed to Flaca to find us a little cabin over there somewhere where we can laugh and talk about the old days when I finally join her.

Flaca, her baby Axel, and her brother Alex

··· 40 ···

The same night I learned of Flaca's death, Fernando and I were having a meeting in my dining room. Suddenly, I heard a terrible commotion outside in my backyard. I had the back door open for my dogs so they could freely move in and out. Fernando and I ran outside, and witnessed the following horror: The neighbor's dog had leapt the fence dividing our yards and made a dash for little Pixie—my little Chihuahua angel—and picked him up in his ferocious mouth and tore at him mercilessly, puncturing most of his internal organs.

Fernando and I rushed my puppy to the emergency clinic. He held on into the night, but a call at one o'clock in the morning informed me that he could not be saved: the damage had been too terrible. Stunned – more than stunned – I allowed Pixie to be helped to the other side, and as I cried into the early morning hours, I prayed again to Flaca to take care of my little angel Pixie.

I was at my wit's end. Any more tragedy, I thought, I do not think I can bear to withstand—my soul was worn thin. In the past, it was at times like this that I would have reached for a bottle or something, anything, to numb myself from the pain. But I had been "clean and sober," as they say, for over a year, and it was the daily meetings at AA that gave me the strength to keep going. I was also trying to cycle down from my head medication, my "happy pills" that I took for my manic depression, or quit them altogether. So instead of my old pattern, I got myself to a meeting.

I was reflective. I knew there was still great beauty ahead of me in this life, but at this moment it was so difficult to imagine where and how to find it. Other days, of course, it was blindingly there, right in front of me—sometimes in the smallest of things—a flower, a new friend, a kind word from a stranger, sometimes just the way the sky looked early in the morning. I knew deep in my heart that all the people, all the things I have ever loved are truly with me always, that the memories I have collected along the road of life are my sustenance into the future.

And the future is beautiful.

Inside my RV - my beach house/lake house/mountain house!

Miss 4th of July for calendar.

··· 41 ···

In its own unique way the restaurant, originally created to look as if it had been born of the South Austin earth itself, was a great source of pride and a sense of completeness for my soul. So it was quite a shock when I arrived one morning to see a giant "Property for Sale" sign next to the parking lot!

"What?" I said out loud, although the word that tore through my mind was considerably more graphic. I ran up to the sign, almost demanding that it answer my questions, appease my initial sense of shock, calm the dread that had begun to creep up my spine. Even though I was freaking out, I managed to get the restaurant open and once everything was running smoothly, I went to an AA meeting. It was a good meeting and I began to calm down and to think more clearly.

I had always been a month-to-month tenant here, ever since the first days of Curiosity. My relationship with the landlords had always been wonderful, but there had been rumors from time to time that they were thinking about selling. Up until I saw that sign I had never been too worried.

I didn't have a back-up plan. So I called Gene, the owner. "Baby, how's it goin'?" I started.

"Oh, fine, María, how are you?"

"Fine, Honey. Listen, I want to ask you a question. I was wondering if… that is, I was hoping…uh, Gene, how about giving me a lease for the restaurant?"

There was a pause long enough to die from and then, "Sure, why not? What are you thinking? A year? Year and a half?"

"Baby, how about ten? If you sell the property then, who knows, I could be out on the streets. This way the new buyers won't kick me out."

Gene laughed good-naturedly, and then a few days later I had it. A ten-year lease! I felt more secure now and the dread completely passed.

For months the restaurant continued normally. Every once in a while, men in suits would wander through the restaurant. We would find them out back behind the walk-in cooler or scribbling notes as they tripped through the maze of tables and chairs on the patio. Then they would disappear and for weeks we could almost forget that the restaurant, Noel's boot store next to me, and the trailer park behind us were all for sale. I didn't really think about it very much. Until...

Gene came one day with a new group of "suits" with brief cases and notepads, secretaries and bankers. He was in negotiations, he told me, for the sale of the property. The men represented a huge corporation interested in demolishing everything and putting in high-rise condos. "Here?" I asked in disbelief. "In South Austin? Condos? *High rise*? Aren't you gentlemen on the wrong side of the river?"

South Austin was always the funky, cool, laid-back part of town, with the hippies and old rednecks, and immigrants and artists — my clientele, basically. The notion of a high-rise condo development right here made me think that these guys had just missed the turnip truck altogether.

Addressing my cleavage, they smiled broadly as they extended their generous offer to buy me out of my lease with twenty thousand dollars and a truck to move my stuff out. Their smiles faded slowly as my words crept out from underneath my heavier-than-usual Argentinean accent. *"Than' jou, but I don' thin' so!* I like it here. My employees like it here. My customers like it here. Where could I go with twenty thousand dollars? A couple weeks on South Padre Island?"

The head "suit" assumed an air as if he were addressing a child. "But surely, this little taco shack, as, uh, *quaint* as it is, doesn't begin to bring in —"

"We sell more than a million tacos a year, Sir. And then there are the liquor sales on top of that, and the costs associated with changing location – assuming I can find another location that offers what this one does – then the advertising costs to notify my clients in this area that we are moving and to attract clients in a new area. Changing all my banking information, postal information, deliveries, decorating a new space to maintain this 'quaint', as you called it, atmosphere — I'm sorry, sir, but I just wouldn't be able to accept twenty thousand dollars and a truck to move my stuff out. But thanks, anyway... can I buy you some lunch?"

Eyes bulged, mouths flapped open, but no more words came out. Gene was looking down at the floor and my heart did go out to him. I knew that I had just possibly screwed up a very lucrative business deal for him, but what they offered me wasn't justifiable. Gene knew it, I could tell, and he never said an unkind thing to me – ever – and I felt bad about my new position as an albatross around his neck.

Still, I had more than twenty employees who depended on me, a loyal following and besides that, I knew how much work was involved in starting a new business. How many times had I already tried and failed? Moving was a huge risk and would be more effort than I wanted to think about. So as they left, I jumped into my car and barely made it to a five o'clock meeting.

A few weeks passed and I got a call. The same "suits" were asking to negotiate. I hired a real estate attorney. She and I were fashionably late to the meeting at their corporate headquarters downtown.

"Sorry to keep you gentlemen waiting," my attorney tossed out as we took our seats. At the beginning of the meeting the "suits" were energetic, and they did not make the same mistake that they did before, assuming me to be some naïve taco vendor.

Too bad *my* attorney did.

When my attorney confidently countered their new offer of seventy-five thousand with one hundred and fifty thousand dollars, she looked at me like she had just accomplished the unimaginable on my behalf. I looked at her and asked to speak to her out in the hall. Still smiling, she followed me out. "What did you think of that?" she beamed as she went on. "They may not go for it, but you should always start high. We can settle around a hun ..."

"Thank you," I interrupted her, "but I won't be needing your assistance anymore. Send me a bill for your time. I've got to get back in there and fix this."

I walked quickly back into the room and the gentlemen remained standing after I had taken my seat, expecting the attorney to be following me. They looked uncomfortably towards the closed door for a moment, and I let them. Then I informed them that I would be handling my own negotiations from this point forward. I opened my briefcase and took out my notepad and a pen. "Shall we start over, gentlemen?"

• • •

After months of negotiations and pleading, offers and counteroffers, the suits opted for another property north of the river on which to build their high-rise condominiums, and things in my life returned to normal. (*Pap, pap, pap!*)

Well, normal for me, anyway. My focus was very much on maintaining my sobriety. Michael and some of my other friends were in and out of my life during this period, as most of them continued to party regularly. More and more I filled my time with new friends from AA, with the restaurant and my family.

Really!

My mother and sisters came up from Argentina several times over the next few years and with each visit we grew closer. My mother would start to drive me crazy all over again and I would run to the AA house in search of understanding and peace. I formed close friendships with several of the men and women from my group. Their help and support allowed me to wake up each day and vow to stay sober; it is a constant temptation that must always be acknowledged and resisted.

Through all these many months the "For Sale" sign in my parking lot seemed to be a continuous threat, but rather than run to a bar, I would make that always comforting phone call to Doctor Botox, or Doctor Collagen, or one of their associates. It was a distraction that provided fairly instant results and was less destructive than other options. No one is without their vices, you see – you just have to choose and edit them throughout your life in order to maintain. Anyway....

Eventually the inevitable happened again. More "suits" began overrunning the restaurant and its surrounding property. My anxiety level skyrocketed. I called Gene and asked who they were. They were the men from Walgreens, he said.

"Walgreens? The drug store? They have a Walgreens two blocks down the street—why do they want to put another one here?"

"They're renting down at that strip mall. They want to build a larger one with a drive-through window."

"Did you tell them I've got a lease, Gene?"

"Had to, of course. They're talking about leaving you there and building behind you."

"Really? But then if they buy the land, they'll be my landlords! And they'll boot me out when the lease is up —"

"María, your lease gives you plenty of time to figure that one out. I've got to sell that trailer park. I can't take it any more."

"Well, I guess it's ironic that they want to take that "illegal drug store," the trailer park, and put in a legal one."

He chuckled as he hung up the phone.

Once the news was out on the street that Walgreens wanted to put in a mega-store right behind Taco Xpress, people began to attend neighborhood meetings in unprecedented numbers. A low grumble turned into a roar when Walgreens presented its plan to the city and showed that, because of my restaurant's physical situation and the fact that I would not be moving, Walgreens was planning to make the major entrance and exit to their establishment to the side on Bluebonnet Street, a quiet neighborhood street with homes and children on bicycles and skateboards.

The people in the trailer park banded with the neighborhood association, and the news media was immediately on this hot story. It was a "David and Goliath" saga of South Austin's fight to maintain its unique personality. Pot-smokers and tree huggers joined alongside neighborhood soccer moms with a sprinkling of a variety of derelicts, street people, magicians, musicians, drag queens and illegal aliens, who marched with signs and were shown conversing with attorneys and city officials in the most astonishing way! The Walgreens' plan was presented before the city zoning and planning committee and the people opposing the proposal spoke eloquently and long into the night with vigor and determination.

Their persistence paid off—the proposal was defeated. But that was only the first round in a very long battle that was still to come.

The Walgreens representatives came to me, personally, not long after.

"What if we move you, ourselves, on our dime?" they proposed.

I rolled my eyes and told them that I had already been through all this with the other guys and my answer was still the same.

"What if we build you a new building and you own it?" they countered.

"What if you guys just go away?" But I didn't quite have the same force of conviction behind my voice this time. I realized that this was a pretty generous offer. "It would never work for me unless I also owned the land *under* the restaurant."

They said that wouldn't be possible; that would be too much money, and it would never get approval from the higher-ups.

"Well, that's the only scenario I might even consider. Looks like you guys need to find yourselves another location. Sorry." We shook hands and they left, and my guilt over having thwarted Gene's deal once again loomed high enough over me to bring me some more sleepless nights. But what was I supposed to do? Nobody was looking out for me; that was *my* job. And if I let them, each and every one of them—except Gene, always an angel to me—would have just scooped me away like cat turd!

I assumed "that was that" and I went back to business as usual. But not for long.

Meanwhile the people of the trailer park returned to their old habits, the people of the neighborhood went back to their lives, and I went off to another AA meeting. But what if I *did* own a little chunk of that land? What if I *did* own the restaurant outright? Well, it would cost too much money to be anything but laughable. There was no way I could swing that. There was no way...

...There was no way I could go to sleep now! I tossed and turned and played imaginary number games in my head all night. And the next night. And the night after that.

There were five acres for sale. Walgreens really only wanted two. That left three acres of ugly drug-ridden trailer park for Gene to have to maintain and deal with. I knew that I couldn't even afford one acre of this so-called "prime" real estate. Gene didn't want to subdivide it; he wanted it all off of his hands. Walgreens was apparently willing to coexist with Taco Xpress, but they wouldn't want to be abutted next to that hideous trailer park. What to do? What to do? I might never get to sleep. Ever!

I had pretty much just given up, and that wasn't like me. Not any more. Every way I twisted the situation in my head, I came up with nothing but a huge headache. The time left on my lease was disappearing with each tick of the clock, and I knew that as time went by it would be cheaper and cheaper for some huge corporation to buy me out. A ten-year lease was one thing, seven years was not too bad, but if I waited another couple of years my bargaining power would decrease to very low levels and the corporate dragons could chew me up and spit me out.

I could either stay where I was and wait for the axe to fall, or I would have to try something. And that "something" would have to work, and work well, or I would risk losing it all. My mind ached and my heart skipped beats regularly as I contemplated my future. Terror had moved in and I couldn't escape its ugly, threatening presence. Faith in God was one thing I was taught in Alcoholics Anonymous. Faith in God was one thing, but it was His intervention that I needed now!

Miracles do not always present themselves as large bodies of water parting in the middle or dead people getting up from their graves and dancing a jig. Sometimes they are more subtle, but nonetheless, they happen. I had survived so much already in my life and that fact alone was miraculous. I prayed for a solution to this problem, I prayed that my dear employees would not lose their source of income and their security, I prayed that all the hard work I had put into this place, this quaint little restaurant, would not simply and quietly end. It represented so much more than a building or a service establishment for cranking out tacos to hungry people.

My employees were my devoted friends; the customers were friends, too, and people I cared about. I knew many of them so well that we were like family, and I was concerned when they didn't make their regular appearance. I knew when they were sick or in distress. I saw them grow and marry and have children over the course of so many years. I was there, too, when more than a few of them died, like old Charlie who lived in the trailer park and left his sweet little dog all alone. These were real people to me and they gave my life meaning and purpose. When I started out with the little trailer so many years ago, the one that Michael painted, I had no idea that it would come to mean almost everything to me. So I prayed to God that some way to save all of this would manifest.

The next day I pulled up to the restaurant, and I was surprised to see the guys from Walgreens out in the parking lot. Gene was there, too, and some other men I didn't know. Gene waved me over as I got out of the car. I shook his hand and I greeted the guys from Walgreens. I smiled hopefully.

The other gentlemen, I found out, were a developer and his associates. He was interested in the back two acres. He wanted to put up a three-level mixed-use building, commercial spaces on the ground floor and condos above it.

"Oh, really? But what about the access? The neighborhood already fought putting an entrance on Bluebonnet Street and they won. How can you get around that?" It wasn't making any sense to me at all. One of the Walgreens guys spoke up next.

"What if we return to our last proposition — that we build you a new restaurant, move you to the side acre over there, and then..."

"But I already told you, I couldn't consider that unless I owned the land as well, and I just don't have that kind of money."

"How about if you buy one acre? Can you afford that?"

"Oh! I don't—I don't know! Maybe if I...if I...I'm not sure. Can I have some time to think about it?" My mind was reeling! Could I do it? Would the bank make me a loan? Was this God's answer to my prayers?

Gene chimed in, "Maybe I could reduce the price for you, María. I want to make sure you're safe..." *(Didn't I tell you he was an angel?)*

I couldn't believe that this was happening after three long years of negotiations. I had to buy that land — just had to! In my mind I was mulling over every scenario imaginable. What jewelry could I sell? What if I robbed a bank? What if I ask two hundred and fifty thousand customers for one dollar and I pay them back by discounting their tacos? I can always go back to driving an old beat-up truck, couldn't I? After all these lipos I don't look so bad — where can I find a rich husband?"

Just then, Dale's big red pickup truck pulled in off Lamar Street and rolled up next to us. "You working today, María, or just flirting with these men? Can an ex-husband get a taco around here?" Dale flashed that broad smile of his as the sunlight struck the chrome of his side mirror, and for just a moment he looked just as he had all those years ago when I spoke only two words of English and I asked him to marry me. This was the same Dale, the Dale that flew us in his little plane to the coast every weekend, the Dale that was always there for me – if I wanted him to be.

"Dale, you can have one of my tacos anytime you want it!" The other men laughed as I introduced him to the guys and they all shook hands. And for the first time in days, I laughed, too. As Dale and I walked into Taco Xpress together, I thanked God.

Of course, Dale agreed to lend me the money to buy the acre that I would own completely, and with that the deal was agreed upon by all parties involved. It wasn't over yet, not even nearly, but it was started. The old Taco Xpress would be demolished to make room for a new Walgreens, with a main entrance on South Lamar Street, and I would finally own my restaurant outright. My employees would be able to stay with me and take care of their families.

And I would finally be able to sleep.

Inside my RV

··· 42 ···

The sad day came when the bulldozers showed up to knock down my little baby. That little building was, for me, a chameleon. It went from a gift store to a convenience store to a restaurant, and now it was going to be dust. I've always characterized myself as someone who never plans things too much. I usually act on impulse. After all, that's what landed me in this location the day I saw the "For Rent" sign. But I had not planned, nor had I been emotionally prepared, to lose my little building and all its memories forever.

I remember very vividly Dale's comment when I told him I was going to open a restaurant. Even though he was my ex at the time, I still valued his opinions. He said, "Girl, you need to stop and think. It wasn't enough for you to open two businesses in three years and realize they were failures due to your lack of information? And now you're going to open what? And you're going to have a little restaurant with only five tables? And no offense, Honey, but you cook like shit. You were a funny wife to have but cooking really isn't your forte! And María, think twice: you have Matt's El Rancho next to you and Kerby Lane across the street..."

Well, six months and a couple of articles in the newspaper later, he showed up for a breakfast taco. He hugged me and said, "Girlfriend, I think we divorced too soon!" We both laughed and I said, "Well, you made yourself a millionaire, and now it's my turn! I only have to sell a million tacos, don't I?"

With all of these memories swirling around in my head, I looked at the bulldozer. I thought, "Shit, what am I going to do with such a huge loan, a brand new restaurant, and I really mean a *brand new* restaurant—when my success was due in large part to the ambiance of my little old building — and my fresh, huge, cheap tacos?" I felt *panic*. How was I going to achieve this?

They started the bulldozers. At five-thirty in the morning they began pouring the foundation for the new Taco Xpress. I haven't been up that early since my days of never even going to bed! It was cold, so I put on a big jacket, planted my feet and with my little camera started to take pictures of my new beginnings.

In order for me to be able to keep my restaurant running during the new construction, the bulldozers started to dig around my old Taco Xpress, and pretty soon I looked like a little cast-away, just the building, my patio, and a few parking spaces. To the right was the monstrosity of Walgreens, and on the other side was our new scary house that was going to need a lot of work.

Maybe I should say, a lot of *love*.

Six grueling months later, in the middle of the summer with no A/C (!), I was working twelve to sixteen hours a day, decorating, designing, painting, trashing, and gathering junk to try to imitate the look I once had and that people loved. And you know, I think I've done it successfully if I go by the comments I've gotten.

Still, what do humans do? We all are cut with the same scissors! The most commonly-heard comment was, "María! I love what you've done with the new building, looks great! It's got the same vibe! Where did you get this or that? Ah...but I still miss the old one." Deep in my heart I was thinking, "If one more human being repeats that phrase I'm gonna push them into the middle of Lamar and let them get run over!" (Just kidding about the part about letting them get run over. But I really did want to push them away!)

Through many tacos cooked in the new location, and the same smiling faces of my loyal customers, some fantastic music by talented local musicians, I knew that all the components needed for success, happiness and well-being were all there.

You and me.

One more thing! Just as they finally bulldozed my little chameleon building together with its memories, the news media and many of our regulars showed up. I hugged Fernando and I cried. So did he. Something important to me was dying, but at the same time, it was great to know that it was important to so many other people too. Like a well-loved part of my heart, we have pictures of our baby all over our new house, and I thanked God for every one.

EPILOGUE

I lie in the pool, floating and dreaming of what I wish for the golden years. I dream of retiring to a huge house with windows facing the ocean, with many rooms for all my friends who are single, widowed or just too old and ugly to catch someone. I dream of a good Samaritan (with a good salary) who would wheel us out to the beach and park us next to a bar where we can play poker and reminisce about the old days. I dream of having a chauffeur to drive us around (like Driving Ms. Daisy) and maybe a butler to serve our drinks (in case AA is too far and I decide 'What the hell,' I will die soon anyway, may as well ease the pain) as the light from the fireplace sparkles and shines off the drool from our wrinkled, withered lips.

My original intention in writing down the stories of my life was simple: to have a record by which to remember these lessons should my mind begin to leave me, for whatever reason. It has since come to be more than that, in that I have been forced to analyze and reflect on not only the events themselves, but on their significance and the many implications relative to who I am deep inside. This has been difficult, to say the least, for there are a great many episodes in my life that cause me shame. Still, it is my life, immutable in its detail, unforgivable in part, but overall a life just like anyone else's: a journey into one's self and a reflection on the people and events that are forever strewn into one's path.

That, to me, is now what my life is about: growth and understanding, overcoming the obstacles in my way and helping the people that I love. I believe that we each are a composite of our own genetic profile, imprinted at birth, but also molded by our life experiences, constantly being reshaped by those people with whom we come into contact, whether we love them or dislike them, whether they adore us or beat us up. I found that every minute of my life is an opportunity to become either a better person or a bigger victim; it is usually as simple as how I choose to respond to the myriad situations I encounter on a daily basis.

Life is like a road. It can be a peaceful stroll, a competitive race, an uphill climb or a dead end, but it is traveled in an attempt to reach a destination. For whatever benefit that you, the reader, may gain from my story, I wish you well. As for myself, I have traveled my own road, and I accept — no, I treasure — each and every step.

• • •

Maria with Rachael Ray, from the Food Network: Best Eats in Town on $40 a Day.

ACKNOWLEDGEMENTS

Thank you, thank you, thank you and thank you to: (alphabetically speaking so no hearts are broken because everyone of you is deeply appreciated): Elise Ballard, Karen Bernardo, Mary Bruton, Alejandra Corbalán, Tiger Davis, Cristina Fernández, Viviana Fernández, Patricia Fiske, Melissa Gable, Samantha Martin, Michael Peschka, Mariano Reynoso, Cyndy Smilie, Dee Ann Smith. Thanks to Susan Bright and Plain View Press. And of course and absolutely, to my FAVORITE beings — ALL animals on this planet.

www.ingramcontent.com/pod-product-compliance
Lightning Source LLC
Chambersburg PA
CBHW070054110526
44587CB00013BB/1538